逆势上扬

[加] 柯马克 著
本书翻译组 译

上海远东出版社

图书在版编目(CIP)数据

逆势而上/(加)柯马克著;本书翻译组译. —上海:上海远东出版社,2023
ISBN 978 - 7 - 5476 - 1883 - 7

Ⅰ.①逆…　Ⅱ.①柯…②本…　Ⅲ.①中国经济—经济发展—文集
Ⅳ.①F124 - 53

中国版本图书馆 CIP 数据核字(2022)第 250020 号

责任编辑　曹　茜
封面设计　王　崟　李　廉

逆势而上
[加]柯马克　著
本书翻译组　译

出　　版　上海远东出版社
　　　　　(201101　上海市闵行区号景路 159 弄 C 座)
发　　行　上海人民出版社发行中心
印　　刷　上海新华印刷有限公司
开　　本　710×1000　1/16
印　　张　22.25
字　　数　431,000
版　　次　2023 年 3 月第 1 版
印　　次　2024 年 3 月第 2 次印刷
ISBN 978 - 7 - 5476 - 1883 - 7/F · 707
定　　价　88.00 元

本书翻译组

黄　晓　董佳煜　徐　翔
陈　琛　张　蕾　任婷婷

本书工作组

陈　娟　于　舰　朱立明
申江波　张玉硕　于　明

长期主义者的理性观察

2022 年，全球经历了众多挑战，从新冠肺炎疫情到地缘冲突，从通货膨胀到股市下跌，在史无前例的多重压力之下，人们的情绪似乎都无法保持理性平和的状态。在这种时候，我们尤其需要冷静专业的声音。

第一财经研究院高级学术顾问、一财全球评论版主编柯马克（Mark Kruger）是一名拥有超过 30 年经验的中国专家。他自 20 世纪 80 年代来到中国学习，曾任加拿大驻华使馆公使衔参赞、加拿大财政部驻华代表等多个重要职位，并长期在加拿大中央银行和国际货币基金组织任职。

作为一位长期在中国生活并熟悉中国的经济学家，柯马克见证了中国经济高速发展的全过程，也近距离观察了中国如何应对经济高速发展带来的各种问题。自 2020 年加入第一财经以来，他持续通过扎实的数据分析向海外受众讲述中国经济发展模式及其背后的发展逻辑。本书收录了他自 2020 年起为第一财经定期撰写的多篇关于中国经济的评论文章，是一位长期主义者的理性观察。

这个世界太需要回归理性和常识。尊重市场规律，坚持实事求是，提倡科学精神，这是我们基本的底线。在新的一年，全球经济依然面临衰退、疫情和战争的巨大挑战，我们期待这个世界早日回归如常。而自由的思想，理性的态度，专业的精神是铸就我们信心的方法。当一个人有了信心和期待，他就一定会更忍耐、更坚定、更乐观，也一定会感染到身边更多的人。让我们一起相信专业的力量、思想的力量、信心的力量，一起相信未来。

杨宇东

第一财经传媒有限公司总编辑、

《第一财经日报》总编辑

Introduction

I have wrote the essays in this collection for Yicai Global since 2020. I intended them to explain developments in the Chinese economy to a foreign (non-Chinese) audience. While Chinese economic news and statistics have become increasingly accessible over time, many foreign media outlets often fail to provide sufficient context for the most recent data point, leaving their readers ill-informed. My goal was to write data-driven, pertinent and concise pieces that draw on China's recent economic history and the experiences of other countries.

China's economy has evolved very rapidly. Indeed, the country I encountered in 1985, when I moved from Calgary to Tianjin to study Mandarin would be unrecognizable today. China was still plagued by pervasive shortages. As a result, we needed ration tickets to buy household necessities like rice, flour and cloth. There were no privately-owned cars and we got around on bicycles and incredibly crowded busses. Unlike Tianjin, Beijing had a subway system, but its two lines didn't actually connect. There were very few private restaurants and the state-owned establishments had filthy table cloths and wait staff that perhaps would, or perhaps would not, take notice of you. Shopping was a hit or miss experience and we were often told the goods we wanted were not in stock, sold out or that we should come back tomorrow. At that time, China still used two currencies. The renminbi was used for most domestic transactions. However, since foreign exchange was in short supply, imported goods and export-quality Chinese goods could only be acquired with Foreign Exchange Certificates.

Today, China has more than $3 trillion in foreign exchange reserves, about twice Canada's GDP. I can shop for a mind-boggling array of goods on my phone while riding Shanghai's subway — the world's most extensive — and have my purchases delivered to my front door. When I get hungry, I can dine on any cuisine I desire in restaurants where the food is delicious and the service is polite and attentive.

My training at the Bank of Canada taught me how important is to put context around numbers. Telling you that the debt of China's non-financial sector was RMB 274 trillion at the end of 2020 is practically meaningless. That number has to be scaled by GDP and then compared to the debt-to-GDP ratios of other countries before it begins to mean something. If we want to consider the sustainability of China's debt, we would have to look at its currency composition, its maturity profile and the nationality of the creditors in addition to its size relative to GDP.

The essays in this book are divided into four parts.

Those in Part Ⅰ look at the growth path implied by the Central Committee's desire to have per capita GDP double by 2030. They stress the importance of innovation and productivity. They discuss China's successes in satellite technology, digital currency, high-speed rail and 5G communications. They then turn to the risks posed by stagnating productivity, the debt burden, demographic decline and the housing market.

In Part Ⅱ, the essays explain the frameworks central banks use to analyse economic developments. They also offer examples of how alternative data sources can enhance our understanding of the business cycle.

In Part Ⅲ, the essays discuss China's relationship with the rest of the world. While acknowledging the tensions, they stress the high costs of decoupling and the extent to which the foreign business community is in China for the long haul.

In Part Ⅳ, the essays describe how the pandemic affected China's economy and the role of government policy in limiting the fallout from COVID‑19.

These essays try to be evidence-based and the points they make are supported with extensive reference to economic data. This book is designed to inform the interested layperson as well as the economic expert. I hope that by providing a clearer context for China's economic news, these essays can contribute to a deeper understanding of the country's challenges and its policy choices.

It has been a privilege to write for Yicai Global. I would like to thank Yang Yanqing, Chen Juan and Xia Ruirui for their support and encouragement.

前　　言

本书中的文章是我自 2020 年起为一财全球所撰写。我想通过这些文章,向外国(非中国)读者阐释中国经济的发展。虽然随着时间的推移,中国的经济新闻和统计数据变得越来越容易获得,但是许多外国媒体往往不能为最新的数据点提供足够的背景,这使得它们的读者一知半解。我的目标是,借鉴中国近期的经济史和其他国家的经验,写出以数据为导向、中肯而简洁的文章。

中国的经济发展非常迅速。事实上,我在 1985 年从卡尔加里搬到天津学习汉语普通话时邂逅的这个国家,今天已经依稀难辨了。当时的中国还受困于普遍存在的短缺中。因此,我们需要配给票来购买大米、面粉和布料等生活必需品。当时没有私家车,我们出行靠的是自行车和拥挤不堪的公交车。与天津不同的是,北京有一个地铁系统,但它的两条线路实际上并不连通。私营餐馆很少,国有餐馆的桌布很脏,服务员可能会理睬你,也可能不会。购物或成功或遗憾,我们经常被告知我们想要的商品没有存货,卖完了,或者我们应该明天再来。那时候,中国仍然使用两种货币。大多数国内交易使用人民币。然而,由于外汇紧缺,进口商品和出口品质的中国商品只能用外汇券购买。

今天,中国拥有超过 3 万亿美元的外汇储备,大约是加拿大 GDP 的两倍。我可以在乘坐全世界最长的地铁——上海地铁时,在手机上选购数量多到令人难以置信的商品,而且有人会将我购买的东西送上门。饿了的时候,我可以在餐馆里吃到任何想要的美食,餐馆的食物很美味,服务礼貌而周到。

我在加拿大银行的培训告诉我,把数字的来龙去脉说清楚是多么重要。只告诉你中国非金融部门的债务在 2020 年底是 274 万亿人民币,实际上是没有意义的。这个数字必须以 GDP 来衡量,然后与其他国家的债务与 GDP 的比率相比较,才开始有意义。如果我们要考虑中国债务的可持续性,除了其相对于GDP 的规模外,我们还必须研究其货币构成、到期情况和债权人的国籍。

本书中的文章分为四个部分。

第一部分探讨了中央委员会希望到 2030 年人均 GDP 翻番的愿望所暗示的增长路径。这部分文章强调了创新和生产力的重要性,讨论了中国在卫星技术、数字货币、高速铁路和 5G 通信方面的成功,而后转向生产力停滞、债务负担、人口下降和房地产市场带来的风险。

在第二部分中,文章解释了中央银行用来分析经济发展的框架。并提供了一些例子,说明替代数据来源如何能够加强我们对商业周期的理解。

在第三部分中,文章讨论了中国与世界其他国家的关系。在承认紧张关系的同时,强调了脱钩的高成本以及外国商界在中国的长期发展程度。

第四部分的文章描述了疫情如何影响中国的经济,以及政府政策在限制新冠影响方面发挥的作用。

这些文章试图以事实为依据,其中提出的观点得到了大量经济数据的支持。本书旨在为感兴趣的非专业人士以及经济学专家提供信息。我希望这些文章通过为中国的经济新闻提供一个更清晰的背景,可以帮助读者更深入地了解中国面临的挑战及其政策选择。

很荣幸能为一财全球撰稿。谨此感谢杨燕青、陈娟和夏睿睿的支持和鼓励。

CONTENTS

Part I   Growth and Risk Over the Medium Term / 1

How Fast Will China Grow Over the Next 15 Years? / 3

China's Path to High-Income Status: Lessons From Recent
   Success Stories / 11

Can China Be the Next South Korea? / 23

Beidou: China's First Outer Space Infrastructure Project / 33

PBOC's Virtual Renminbi Is Becoming a Reality / 38

China's High-Speed Rail: A Case Study in Independent Innovation / 46

5G and the Competition to Win the 21st Century / 52

Is China's Investment Really That Unproductive? / 58

How Sustainable Is China's Debt? / 66

China Needs More Defaults and More Meaningful Credit Ratings / 77

Is China Facing a Demographic Crisis? / 84

How Can China Promote a Sustainable Increase in Household
   Consumption? / 94

Mooncake Madness / 102

American Families Only Half as Rich as Those in Chinese Cities / 107

How Should We Think About Rising Home Prices? / 113

Property Developers' Debt: Taking Aim at the Grey Rhino / 122

Why Not Eliminate Corporate Income Taxes? / 130

How Can China Achieve Carbon Neutrality by 2060? / 140

Part II Data and Analytic Techniques / 149

China's Economy: The View From the IMF / 151

Are Central Banks Behind the Curve on Inflation? / 159

Big Mac Prices — No Bull / 170

Is the US Chip Export Ban Consistent With Its WTO Commitments? / 180

Can Robots Help Mitigate China's Demographic Decline? / 188

The Demise of China's Private Sector: Greatly Exaggerated / 201

Part III China and the Rest of the World / 213

US Companies: In China for the Long Haul / 215

Will Japanese Firms Desert China? / 224

Shall the Twain Never Meet? / 232

The High Cost of US-China Decoupling / 244

China's Balance of Payments Show the Dual Circulation Strategy
  at Work / 250

How Long Will Foreign Investors' Love Affair With Chinese Bonds
  Last? / 261

Can China and the US Cooperate and Reform the WTO? / 271

Are the Worst in US-China Relations Behind Us? / 279

China and American Foreign Policy for the Middle Class / 289

Part IV The Pandemic and the Chinese Government's Response / 295

Advice From VoxEu: Act Fast and Do Whatever It Takes / 297

How Will China Manage Massive Layoffs? / 303

Is China Decapitalizing Its Banks? / 309

Are the Chinese Banks Really Supporting the Recovery? / 317

COVID－19 Is Accelerating China-US Convergence / 326

Trust in Chinese Government Defies Global Trend / 332

目　　录

第一部分　中期经济增长和风险 / 2

未来 15 年中国经济预期增速是多少? / 7

中国通向高收入国家之路 / 17

中国会成为下一个韩国吗? / 28

北斗:中国首个外太空基础设施建设工程 / 35

中国人民银行虚拟人民币正在成为现实 / 42

中国高铁:自主创新的案例研究 / 49

5G 与赢得 21 世纪的竞争 / 55

中国的投资真的没有收益吗? / 62

中国债务的可持续性如何? / 72

中国债券市场需要更多"违约"和更有意义的信用等级评定 / 81

中国是否面临人口危机? / 89

如何促进中国家庭消费的可持续增长? / 98

月饼狂热 / 105

美国家庭只有中国城市家庭一半富有 / 110

我们应该如何看待房价不断上涨? / 118

房地产开发商债务:瞄准"灰犀牛" / 126

何不取消企业所得税? / 135

中国如何在 2060 年前实现碳中和? / 144

第二部分　数据及分析技巧 / 150

中国经济:国际货币基金组织如是观 / 155

中央银行在通胀问题上落后了吗？ / 165

巨无霸价格：牛年不吹牛 / 175

美国芯片出口禁令符合其世界贸易组织承诺吗？ / 184

机器人能否帮助缓解中国人口下降的趋势？ / 194

中国私营部门的败落：被过分夸大了 / 207

第三部分　中国与世界 / 214

美国公司：在中国作长远打算 / 220

日本企业会离开中国吗？ / 228

无问西东，相向而行 / 238

中美"脱钩"的高昂代价 / 247

中国的国际收支表明"双循环"战略正在奏效 / 256

外国投资者和中国债券的"恋情"会持续多久？ / 266

中美可以合作并改革世界贸易组织吗？ / 275

中美关系触底了吗？ / 284

中国与美国对中产阶级的外交政策 / 292

第四部分　新冠肺炎疫情和中国政府的应对之策 / 296

来自 VoxEu 的建议：不惜一切代价迅速行动 / 300

中国将如何应对大规模裁员？ / 306

中国欲削减银行资本？ / 313

银行真在支持中国经济复苏吗？ / 322

新冠肺炎疫情加速缩小中美经济规模的差距 / 329

全球信任度下滑之际，中国政府信任度逆势上升 / 336

Part I

Growth and Risk Over the Medium Term

While China does not have an official medium-term growth target, many analysts interpret the Central Committee's desire to see China's per capital GDP reach that of "moderately developed countries" by 2030 was implying a doubling of GDP. This is an ambitious targe given the size of the Chinese economy and its currently level of development. While the target represents a significant slowing of growth from what was recorded in the previous 15 years, many risks need to be carefully managed in order to achieve it.

We look at the implied growth path both from the perspectives of China's economic policy and the experiences of countries that recently attained developed-country status. With investment rates high, the debt burden large and demographics a drag on growth, a premium needs to be put on raising productivity. We highlight some of China's recent successes in satellites, digital currency, high speed rail and 5G communications.

Debt, demographics and stresses in the housing sector all pose risks, as does the possibility that productivity will stagnate. We try to assess the magnitude of these risks by comparing China's situation with those of other countries.

第一部分

中期经济增长和风险

虽然中国并没有官方的中期经济增长目标，但是许多分析人士认为，政府希望中国的人均国内生产总值（以下简称 GDP）到 2030 年达到"中等发达国家"水平，这意味着 GDP 将翻一番。鉴于中国的经济规模和目前的发展水平，这是一个雄心勃勃的目标。虽然该目标增速显著低于过去 15 年的水平，但要实现这一目标仍需谨慎管理各种风险。

我们从中国的经济政策和最近才晋升为发达国家的经济体的经验两个角度来看中国的发展路线。在高投资率、高负债以及人口结构拖累增长的背景下，尤其需要提高生产率。我们注意到中国最近在卫星、数字货币、高铁和 5G 通信方面的成就。

除了生产率停滞的可能性，负债、人口结构以及房地产行业的压力也会产生风险。我们尝试通过对比中国和其他国家的情况来估测风险的大小。

How Fast Will China Grow Over the Next 15 Years?

November 6, 2020

In late October, the Party's Central Committee held its fifth plenary session. At this meeting, the Central Committee set out a number of objectives for the country to achieve by 2035. From a macroeconomic perspective, the Central Committee's goal that "per capita GDP will reach the level of moderately developed countries", was particularly interesting, as it gives us a hint as to the Central Committee's expectation for growth over the next 15 years. The key is what the Central Committee means by "moderately developed countries". A convenient framework to use here is the World Bank's country classification system, which divides countries into four income groups. The World Bank regularly updates its income thresholds and the July 2020 version is shown in Table 1.

Table 1   World Bank Income Classification Thresholds (July 2020 update)

Income Group	Gross National Income per Capita in Current US $
Low income	Less than $1,036
Lower-middle income	$1,036 – 4,045
Upper-middle income	$4,046 – 12,535
High income	More than $12,535

Source: World Bank, Yicai

The World Bank calculates that China's per capita income was $10,410 in 2019. This would put China at the higher end of the Upper-Middle Income group. Thus, one way to interpret the Central Committee's objective is that China will rise toward the middle of the High Income group by 2035. The World Bank includes 58 countries in the High Income classification. It's a broad range, from Romania with a per capita income of $12,630 to Switzerland at $85,500. The median per capita income for this group was $30,390, which corresponds exactly to the reading for Spain. China's per capita income would have to grow at an average annual rate of

3

7. 4 percent, in real terms, over the next 15 years to achieve Spain's 2019 level. This would represent a significant acceleration from current trend growth, which is closer to 6 percent.

Table 2 presents seven scenarios, based on selected growth rates, for the level of per capita income China could achieve in 2035 and the country that was at that level in 2019. At the high end, if China were to maintain 6 percent growth over the next 15 years, per capita incomes would grow by 150 percent, to reach Slovenia's $25,000. At the low end, 3 percent growth would translate into a 60 percent increase in per capita incomes to the $16,140 achieved by Hungary.

Table 2　Scenarios for per Capita Income Growth (2020 US $)

Real per Capita Income Growth	China's per Capita Income in 2035	Corresponding Country in 2019
6. 0%	25,000	Slovenia
5. 5%	23,220	Estonia
5. 0%	21,500	Czech Republic
4. 5%	20,200	Greece
4. 0%	18,700	Lithuania
3. 5%	17,400	Latvia
3. 0%	16,140	Hungary

Source: World Bank, Yicai

In addition to growing in real terms, per capita incomes in China are likely to rise as a result of relatively rapid productivity growth. It is normally the case that the more rapid a country's productivity growth is, the faster the increase of its domestic prices. This empirical regularity is called the "Balassa-Samuelson Effect" after the two economists that independently recognized it in the early 1960s.

Figure 1 presents an estimate of the Balassa-Samuelson effect for China. It graphs the Bank for International Settlements' real effective exchange rate for China — a measure of relative domestic price levels — against the ratio of Chinese per capita incomes to those in the US. It shows that as China catches up to the US — the ratio of Chinese per capita incomes to those in the US grows — the real effective exchange rate appreciates.

Given the relationship presented in Figure 1, we can adjust Table 2's scenarios for the Balassa-Samuelson Effect. We assume that US per capita income growth over the next 15 years is 1. 4 percent. Given the speed of catch up with the US implied by the selected growth rates, we can calculate the increase in the real exchange rate and adjust the 2035 estimates of per capita income.

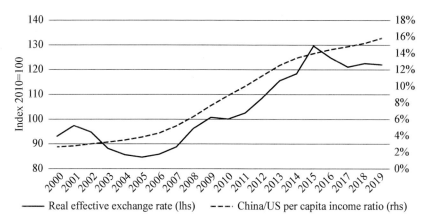

Figure 1   Balassa-Samuelson Effect: China

Source: BIS, Wind, Yicai

Table 3 shows that at 6 percent growth, Chinese per capita incomes could grow by an additional 1. 9 percent per year, as the real exchange rate appreciates. Under these assumptions, Chinese per capita incomes could reach \$33,367 in 2035, or the same level as South Korea in 2019.

Table 3   Adjusted Scenarios for per Capita Income Growth (2020 US \$)

Real per Capita Income Growth	Annual Balassa-Samuelson Effect	China's Adjusted per Capita Income in 2035	Corresponding Country in 2019
6. 0%	1. 9%	33,367	South Korea
5. 5%	1. 7%	29,839	Spain
5. 0%	1. 4%	26,597	Slovenia
4. 5%	1. 2%	24,256	Estonia
4. 0%	1. 0%	21,672	Czech Republic
3. 5%	0. 8%	19,534	Slovakia
3. 0%	0. 6%	17,552	Latvia

Source: World Bank, Yicai

In this analysis we have been comparing estimates of China's future income to actual incomes of moderately developed countries in 2019. However, it is unlikely that those countries' incomes will stand still for 15 years. Indeed, the median of the high-income countries grew by 2. 8 percent per year over the last 15 years and those of the countries presented in Table 2 grew at an average annual rate of 5. 7 percent over the same period. So, China could be chasing a moving target!

Perhaps a simpler way to think of the Central Committee's objective is a doubling of per capita incomes over the next 15 years, from roughly $10,000 to roughly $20,000. This would correspond to an average annual growth rate of 4.7 percent and would bring China's per capita income to that of Greece's in 2019.

It is worth noting that 14 Chinese cities have already achieved per capita incomes in excess of $20,000 (Figure 2). Incomes in Shenzhen last year were close to those of Spain, those of Shanghai like those of Saudi Arabia and those of Xiamen similar to those of Greece. With 140 million people living in these cities already enjoying a moderately-developed-country standard of living, Chinese policymakers have a number of success stories to draw on in achieving their 2035 goals.

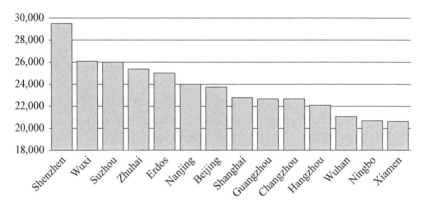

Figure 2   Urban per Capita Income in US $

Source: NBS, Guangcha, Yicai

未来 15 年中国经济预期增速是多少？

2020 年 11 月 6 日^①

在 2020 年 10 月末召开的中国共产党第十九届五中全会上，2035 年远景目标被审议通过。从宏观经济角度看，"人均 GDP 达到中等发达国家水平"的目标特别有意义，因为这向我们暗示了对未来 15 年经济增长的预期。问题的关键是理解"中等发达国家"的含义。这里我们使用世界银行的国家分类系统，将国家分为四个收入组。世界银行定期更新其收入起点，表 1 为 2020 年 7 月公布的版本。

表 1　世界银行收入分类门槛（2020 年 7 月版）

收入组	2019 年美元现值人均国民总收入 采用图表集法
低收入	低于 1,036 美元
中等偏下收入	1,036 美元—4,045 美元
中等偏上收入	4,046 美元—12,535 美元
高收入	高于 12,535 美元

数据来源：世界银行、第一财经

根据世界银行的计算，2019 年中国的人均国民总收入（以下简称"人均收入"）为 10,410 美元，处于中等偏上收入组的较高位置。因此，从这个角度解读中共中央的目标是，到 2035 年，中国将跻身高收入组别的中间层。世界银行将 58 个国家归入高收入组，其涵盖的收入范围很广，从人均收入为 12,630 美元的罗马尼亚到人均收入为 85,500 美元的瑞士都属于该组别。这一组的人均收入中位数为 30,390 美元，西班牙恰好位于这个水平。未来 15 年，中国的人均收入

---

① 本书文章标题下的日期皆为该文首次在第一财经发布的时间，文中出现的时间、人物职位等皆截至其发布时间。——编者注

必须以年均 7.4% 的速度增长(扣除物价因素)才能达到西班牙 2019 年的水平,这一增速显著高于目前接近 6% 的趋势增速。表 2 呈现了中国在 2035 年可能实现的人均收入水平的七种情景,以及 2019 年达到该水平的国家。如果中国在未来 15 年保持 6% 的增长,则人均收入将增长 150%,达到斯洛文尼亚的 2.5 万美元;如果增长率只有 3%,意味着人均收入增长 60%,达到匈牙利的 16,140美元。

表 2　人均收入增长的不同情景(2020 年,单位:美元)

实际人均收入增长	中国在 2035 年时的人均收入	2019 年达到该水准的国家
6.0%	25,000	斯洛文尼亚
5.5%	23,220	爱沙尼亚
5.0%	21,500	捷克
4.5%	20,200	希腊
4.0%	18,700	立陶宛
3.5%	17,400	拉脱维亚
3.0%	16,140	匈牙利

数据来源:世界银行、第一财经

　　除了经济的实际增长速度以外,中国的人均收入可能由于相对较快的生产率提升速度而提高。通常情况下,一个国家的生产率增长越快,国内市场的物价上涨速度也会越快。这样的实证规律叫作巴拉萨-萨缪尔森效应(Balassa-Samuelson Effect),以两位各自在 20 世纪 60 年代早期发现此规律的经济学家命名。

　　图 1 是对中国的巴拉萨-萨缪尔森效应的估计。该图对照了国际清算银行提供的中国的实际有效汇率(衡量国内相对价格水平)和中美人均收入的比值,结果是随着中美人均收入相对差距的缩小,人民币实际有效汇率也在上升。

　　我们参照巴拉萨-萨缪尔森效应来调整表 2 中的情境。假设美国未来 15 年的人均收入增长率为 1.4%,我们就可以针对不同的情景计算实际汇率增长并调整对于 2035 年人均收入的预估。也就是表 3 的结果。随着实际汇率的升值,中国的人均收入如果以 6% 的速度增长,每年还可能再额外增长 1.9%。在这些假设下,中国人均收入到 2035 年可能达到 33,367 美元,或者与 2019 年的韩国处于相同水平。

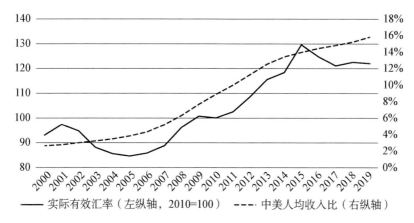

图 1　巴拉萨-萨缪尔森效应：中国

数据来源：国际清算银行、万得资讯、第一财经

表 3　人均收入增长的调整情景（2020 年，单位：美元）

实际人均收入增长	年度巴拉萨-萨缪尔森效应	调整后中国 2035 年的人均收入	2019 年达到该水准的国家
6.0%	1.9%	33,367	韩国
5.5%	1.7%	29,839	西班牙
5.0%	1.4%	26,597	斯洛文尼亚
4.5%	1.2%	24,256	爱沙尼亚
4.0%	1.0%	21,672	捷克
3.5%	0.8%	19,534	斯洛伐克
3.0%	0.6%	17,552	拉脱维亚

数据来源：世界银行、第一财经

在上述分析中，我们一直在把对中国未来收入的估计与 2019 年中等发达国家的实际收入进行比较，但这些国家的人均收入也不太可能 15 年都不变。实际上，高收入国家人均收入在过去 15 年年均增速的中位数是 2.8%，表 2 中列出的这些国家年均增速中位数更达到了 5.7%。所以，中国正在追赶的是一个不断变化的目标！

也许可以从更简单的角度来理解这个问题：中共中央的目标是 15 年后实现人均收入翻一番，从大约 1 万美元提高到大约 2 万美元。这相当于 4.7% 的年增长数据，结果是 2035 年中国人均收入达到希腊 2019 年的水平。

值得关注的是,中国有 14 个城市已经实现了人均收入超 2 万美元(图 2)。深圳、上海、厦门 2019 年的人均收入分别相当于西班牙、沙特阿拉伯和希腊。生活在这些城市中的 1.4 亿人口已经达到了中等发达国家的生活水平。因此,中国的政策制定者在实现 2035 年目标时已经有了很多可以借鉴的成功案例。

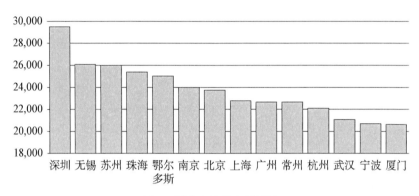

图 2 城市人均收入(美元)

数据来源:中国国家统计局、观察网、第一财经

China's Path to High-Income Status: Lessons From Recent Success Stories

November 16, 2020

Last week, we looked at scenarios for how fast China needs to grow to become a "moderately developed country" in the next 15 years. This week, we examine the experiences of a set of countries that was successful in achieving high-income status over the last 15 years. In order to distill lessons for China, we compare these countries against a second set, which remained stuck in the "middle-income trap".

We begin in 2000 with 16 countries which had similar levels of per capita income. Nineteen years later, 10 of these countries successfully crossed the World Bank's high-income classification threshold, which is indicated by the dotted line in Figure 1. Drawing on economic theory, we want to find out why some countries were successful while others were not.

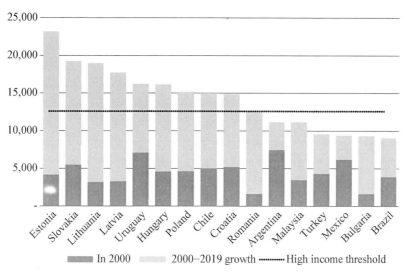

Figure 1   Per Capita Income Current US $

Source: World Bank, Yicai

We will be looking at a series of correlations. We need to be aware that correlation does not imply causation and that causation can run in both directions. For example, we will find that high-income status is correlated with educational attainment. It is quite likely that an educated work force is needed to attain high-income status. But it can also be the case that rich countries have more money to spend on schooling and this is what the correlation is picking up.

To address this problem, we assess the two sets of countries by taking snapshots of their fundamentals in 2009. The premise here is that the fundamentals in 2009 are more likely to be causal of outcomes in 2019 than vice versa.

Economists have long relied on insights from the Solow model to explain differences in wealth between countries. In this model, high per capita incomes result from the extensive use of physical inputs — capital and labour — and elevated productivity — the efficiency with which these inputs are used.

Figure 2 shows measures of how extensively capital and labour were used by the two sets of countries in 2009. The median unsuccessful country benefitted from a somewhat larger labour input by employing a greater share of its population. The median successful one provided its workers with significantly more tools, as measured by the capital-to-GDP ratio. The median capital stock in the successful countries was about one-fourth larger, as a percent of GDP.

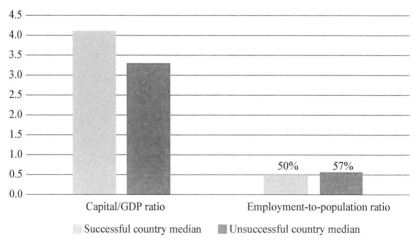

Figure 2   Labour and Capital Inputs (2009)

Source: World Bank, Penn World Tables, Yicai

Economists have stressed that labour's quality can be improved through education. Robert Barro made an important modification to the Solow model in showing the important role that "human capital" accumulation plays in the process of economic growth.

Figure 3 shows that the median successful country tended to invest more in education than its unsuccessful counterpart. In particular, the median successful country enrollment rate for tertiary education was close to double that of the unsuccessful country median. Thus, successful countries were able to compensate for their relatively low employment rates by investing in the education of their workers. The importance of human capital is good news for those countries that are undergoing demographic changes and are facing shrinking labour forces.

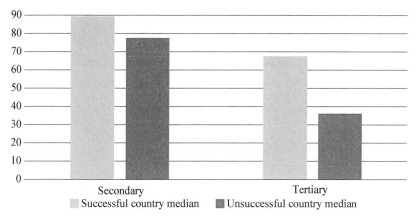

Figure 3   Education Enrollment Rates (2009)

Source: World Bank, Yicai

From the physical inputs of capital and labour, we now turn to productivity. There are two aspects to productivity. The first is improved technology, which is reflected in new products or better ways of doing things. Technological improvement often arises from investment in research and development.

Figure 4 presents two R&D indicators: spending as a percent of GDP and researchers per 1,000 people. Surprisingly, unsuccessful countries spent 0.13 percent of GDP more on R&D than the successful ones. In contrast, the unsuccessful countries engaged only half as many researchers as their successful counterparts.

These indicators imply that technological improvement is, in essence, a human undertaking. The experience of the successful countries suggests that technological improvements are more likely to occur if R&D resources are spread widely.

The second aspect of productivity is the set of incentives that lead participants in the economy to be as efficient as possible. These incentives arise through the establishment of effective institutions.

One such institution is openness to international trade. An open trading regime keeps import-competing firms on their toes and allows exporters to source inputs

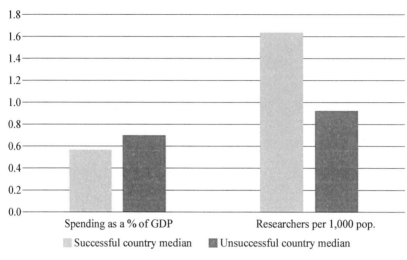

Figure 4 R&D Indicators (2009)

Source: World Bank, Yicai

efficiently. Moreover, exporting firms that compete in the global marketplace have every incentive to produce first-class goods and services. Figure 5 shows that successful countries were more open to trade than unsuccessful ones. Their trade-to-GDP ratio was about 30 percentage points higher.

A second institution which acts to align incentives is a well-regulated domestic market. To operate efficiently, markets need clear rules that are consistently enforced. Intelligent regulation helps ensure that markets do not run amok. As Figure 5 shows, regulatory quality was higher in the successful countries, which likely improved the efficiency of their market outcomes.

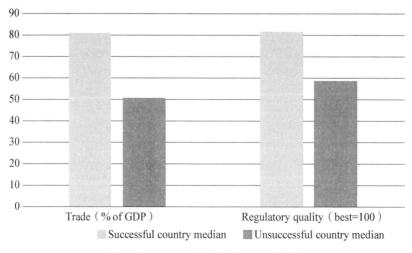

Figure 5 Competition Indicators (2009)

Source: World Bank, Yicai

Governments are institutions which can provide the physical, legal and social frameworks to support high incomes. Harvard's Ricardo Hausmann notes that "… a biomedical plant is more valuable if there is good infrastructure, a trusted drug authorization system, and health insurance. These inputs are deeply affected by government actions, embodied in millions of pages of legislation and thousands of government agencies."

The effective provision of these frameworks requires stable sources of funding. Figure 6 shows that successful countries were better able to mobilize national revenue, which could be used for investing in public goods, health and education. Moreover, governments in successful countries were rated as more effective than those of the unsuccessful group, suggesting that the spending financed by this revenue was less likely to be wasteful.

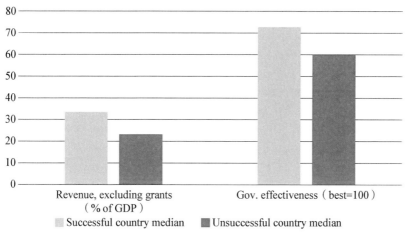

Figure 6   Government Indicators (2009)

Source: World Bank, Yicai

Let's take stock of the lessons suggested by the experiences of the successful countries. First, the accumulation of both physical and human capital is important. Second, R&D resources should be spread among an extensive group of researchers. Third, institutions matter. Domestic markets should be open to trade. They should operate within a high-quality regulatory system. Governments need access to sufficient funding to provide physical, legal and social frameworks and they should be highly effective to make sure these resources are well-targeted.

While China may be a decade and a half away from high-income status, it is not too early to see how it stacks up against those countries that avoided the middle income trap. Table 1 presents the most recent reading of the indicators discussed above for China and the two sets of countries. China does extremely well in mobilizing labour and physical capital. However, it is lagging somewhat on human capital. China is devoting significantly more financial and human resources to R&D. It lags on openness to trade and regulatory quality. While its government effectiveness rating is close to the successful country median, its government revenue-to-GDP ratio is close to the median of the unsuccessful group.

The extent to which the lessons of the ten successful countries can apply to China is limited. The Chinese economy is much larger and much less service-based than those of the countries we have been considering (Table 1). To some extent, China will have to make its own way to high-income status. In a recent speech, President Xi said that it is "entirely possible" that China could double its per capita GDP and cross the high-income threshold by 2035. China's per capita income is still a third below the successful country median. However, as Table 1 shows, it already exceeds the successful countries in a number of areas and appears to be off to a very good start to reaching high-income status.

Table 1   Development Indicators

Indicators (2019 or Latest)	Successful Country Median	China	Unsuccessful Country Median
Per capita income 2019 (US$ Atlas method)	16,185	10,410	9,520
Capital/GDP	3.9	5.0	3.3
Employment-to-population ratio (%)	57	67	55
Secondary school enrolment (%)	91	88	84
Tertiary school enrollment (%)	69	54	45
R&D spending as a % of GDP	0.87	2.19	0.75
R&D researchers per 1,000 population	2.5	4.4	1.5
Trade as a % of GDP	113	36	70
Regulatory quality (100 = best)	83	43	57
Government revenue as a % of GDP	35	25	24
Government effectiveness (100 = best)	75	72	52
Memo item			
Service share of employment (%)	67	47	63

Source: World Bank, Yicai

中国通向高收入国家之路

2020 年 11 月 16 日

我们曾研究了在未来 15 年中国需要以多快的速度发展才能成为一个"中等发达国家"。现在,我们分析那些在过去 15 年中成功跨过高收入门槛的国家的经验,并将其与那些深陷"中等收入陷阱"国家进行对比,从而帮助中国迈入通向成为高收入国家的道路。

我们将 2000 年作为研究的起点,样本包括当时 16 个人均收入水平相似的国家。19 年后,这些国家中有 10 个成功越过了世界银行的高收入分类门槛(如图 1 中的虚线所示)。借助经济理论,我们想弄清为什么有些国家成功而有些国家却没有。

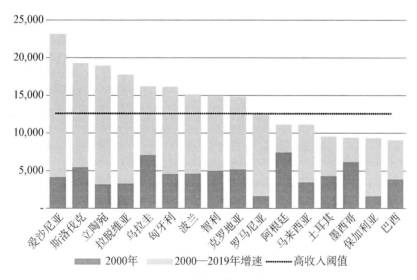

图 1　人均收入(单位:美元)

数据来源:世界银行、第一财经

我们会关注于一系列的相关性,但我们需要认识到,相关性并不一定意味着因果关系,而且很多因果关系也可以是双向的。例如,我们会发现高收入与受教育程度是相关的,原因可能是一个国家需要受过教育的劳动力才能实现高收入,但也有可能是那些成功变富的国家才开始有更多的钱花在教育上,而后者导致了教育水平与收入水平的正相关。

为了解决这一问题,我们对这两组国家 2009 年的基本情况进行了评估,我们认为 2009 年的基本面是造成 2019 年结果的原因,而不是相反。

长期以来,经济学家一直依赖索洛模型来解释国家之间的财富差异。这一模型中,高人均收入来自对有形投入(资本和劳动力)的广泛使用以及生产率的提高(对这些投入的使用效率)。

图 2 显示了这两组国家在 2009 年如何广泛使用资本和劳动力。未达到高收入门槛的国家(以下简称"不成功国家")劳动人口占比中位数更高,相反,成功达到高收入门槛的国家(以下简称"成功国家")资本占 GDP 比重中位数更高,比不成功国家高出约四分之一。

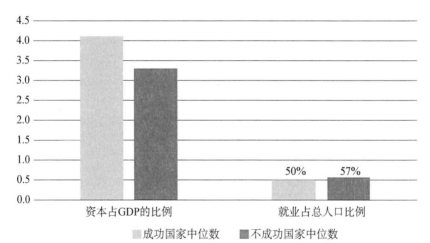

图 2　劳动力及资本投入(2009 年)

数据来源:世界银行、佩恩表、第一财经

经济学家强调,通过教育可以提高劳动力质量。罗伯特·巴罗(Robert J. Barro)对索洛模型进行了重要修改,以体现"人力资本"积累在经济增长过程中的重要作用。

图 3 显示,从中位数上看,成功国家比不成功国家更倾向于在教育上进行更多投资。特别是成功国家的高等教育入学率中位数接近不成功国家的两倍。因此,成功国家能够通过对工人教育的投资来弥补其相对较低的就业率。对于那些正在经历人口变化并且面临劳动力萎缩的国家来说,人力资本质量尤为重要。

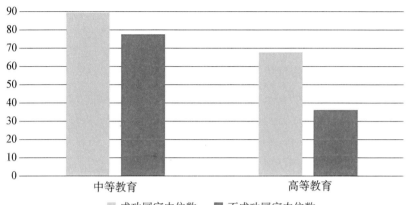

图 3　入学率（2009 年）

数据来源：世界银行、第一财经

看完了资本和劳动力这种有形投入，我们再来看一下劳动生产率。劳动生产率的提高来自两个方面。首先是技术进步，这反映在新产品或更好的做事方式中，技术的进步通常来自对研发的投资。图 4 显示了两项与研发相关的指标，即（相关）支出占 GDP 的百分比以及每千人中的研究人员人数。令人惊讶的是，不成功国家的研发投入 GDP 占比比成功国家高 13%，但不成功国家聘用的研究人员仅为成功国家的一半。

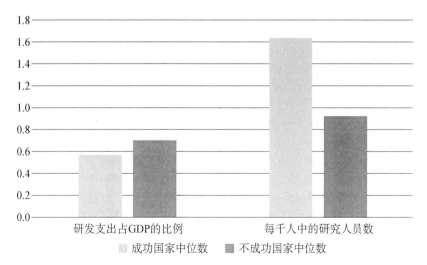

图 4　研发相关指标（2009 年）

数据来源：世界银行、第一财经

这些指标表明：从根本上说，技术进步是一项"人的事业"。成功国家的经验告诉我们，研发资源分布越广泛，科技进步越有可能发生。

劳动生产率提升的第二个来源是一套可以使经济参与者尽可能提高效率的完善激励措施，这些措施是通过建立有效机制而产生的。

其中之一便是开放的国际贸易制度。开放的贸易制度能保持市场的竞争性，并允许出口商们有效地获取投入。此外，在全球市场上，有竞争力的出口商会有足够的动力生产一流的商品和提供一流的服务。图 5 显示，成功国家相较于不成功国家在贸易上更为开放，它们贸易的 GDP 占比会高出约 30 个百分点。

第二个机制就是对国内市场良好的监管。需要明确及稳定的规则来确保市场的有效运行。聪明的监管能避免市场陷入混乱，如图 5 所示，成功国家的监管质量较高，而高质量的监管很可能会提高市场效率。

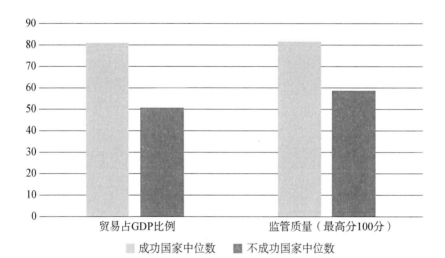

图 5　竞争指标（2009 年）

数据来源：世界银行、第一财经

政府可以提供实物、法律和社会框架来支撑高收入目标的实现。哈佛大学的里卡多·豪斯曼（Ricardo Hausmann）指出："……如果拥有良好的基础设施、可靠的药品授权系统和健康保险，那么生物医学工厂将更具价值。所有的一切很大程度上取决于政府的行动，包括大量的法律法规条文和数以千计的政府机构。"

这些框架的有效制定需要稳定的资金来源。图 6 显示，成功国家能够更好地调动本国的收入用于投资公共产品、卫生和教育，且成功国家的政府比不成功国家的政府更有效率，说明由政府投资被浪费的概率更低。

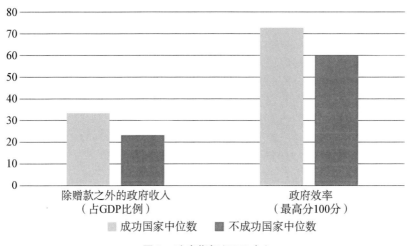

图 6　政府指标(2009 年)

数据来源:世界银行、第一财经

分析成功国家的经验可以看出:首先,实物和人力资本的积累都很重要。其次,研发资源应更广泛地分配给研究人员。最后,制度非常关键。各国应该开放贸易,并纳入高质量的监管体系。各国政府需要获得足够的资金来提供实物、法律和社会框架,还需要确保这些资源得到合理利用。

要想达到高收入国家水平,中国大概还需要 15 年的时间。那么从现在来看,中国与那些成功避免中等收入陷阱的国家相比有哪些不同? 表 1 列出了最近几年中国以及两组国家在上文提到的各个指标的具体数值。中国在劳动力市场参与度和实物资本方面表现非常好,但是在人力资本上有些落后。中国在研发方面投入了大量财力和人力资源,但在贸易开放性和监管质量方面比较落后。尽管中国政府效率评级接近成功国家的中位数,但其政府收入占 GDP 的比重却接近不成功国家的中位数。

十个成功国家的经验对中国的适用范围有限。与这些国家(表 1)相比,中国的经济规模更大,对服务业的依赖更小。从某种程度上来讲,中国将按照自己的方式成为高收入国家。习近平主席在最近的讲话中指出,到 2035 年实现人均GDP 翻一番,中国迈入高收入国家门槛,是"完全有可能"的。中国的人均收入仍比成功国家的中位数低三分之一,但如表 1 所示,中国的一些地区已经超过了成功国家,这为成为高收入国家开了一个很好的头。

表 1　中国与两组国家的发展指标对比

指标（2019 年或最新）	成功国家中位数	中国	不成功国家中位数
2019 年人均收入（单位：美元）	16,185	10,410	9,520
资本/GDP	3.9	5.0	3.3
就业人口比例（%）	57	67	55
中学入学率（%）	91	88	84
高等教育入学率（%）	69	54	45
研发支出占 GDP 的百分比	0.87	2.19	0.75
每千人中的研究人员数	2.5	4.4	1.5
贸易占 GDP 的百分比	113	36	70
监管质量（最高分 100 分）	83	43	57
政府收入占 GDP 的百分比	35	25	24
政府效力（最高分 100 分）	75	72	52
备注			
服务业就业比例（%）	67	47	63

数据来源：世界银行、第一财经

Can China Be the Next South Korea?

March 30, 2021

As part of this month's Two Sessions, China released the final version of its 14th Five-Year Plan. These planning documents outline the government's medium-term strategic thinking. They are required reading for those who want to know where the leadership wants to take the country. I think the 14th Five-Year Plan is particularly important because it represents a turning point in China's economic development.

For close to 40 years, one of China's key development objectives was the creation of a moderately prosperous society. It was a policy first enunciated by Deng Xiaoping in the late 1970s. Deng borrowed the term from the Confucian classic the *Book of Rites*, which is believed to have been compiled in the Han dynasty, more than 2,000 years ago.

In its original context, the *moderately prosperous society* is presented as a somewhat second-rate state of affairs. It is unfavourably contrasted with the utopian *great community*. However, Deng's choice was intentional. In creating his development plan, he wanted to set a low bar so as not to feed unrealistic expectations.

Deng's vision was a qualitative one. Chinese society would, over time, evolve from scarcity to relative comfort. Deng's successor, Jiang Zemin, went a step further, operationally defining the *moderately prosperous society* as a quadrupling of GDP between 2000 and 2020. That target implied average real GDP growth of just over 7 percent per year for two decades. In the event, growth was significantly higher during Jiang's tenure and that of his successor Hu Jintao. After Xi Jinping took office, growth continued to exceed 7 percent and, by 2015, GDP was essentially four times higher than in 2000 (Figure 1).

In 2013, Xi Jinping associated the establishment of a *moderately prosperous society* with a doubling of GDP between 2010 and the celebration of the Party's 100th anniversary in 2021. He recently stated that he expects that doubling to be achieved later this year. Indeed, given the government's 6 percent plus growth

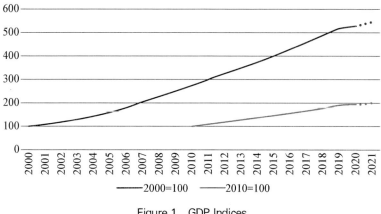

Figure 1　GDP Indices

Source: Wind, Yicai

target, we should reach moderate prosperity sometime this summer (Figure 1).

China's *moderately prosperous society* will be characterized by a reasonable standard of material well-being. In 2000, its per capita GDP (PPP basis) ranked in the bottom third of all countries. By 2020 it ranked in the top 40 percent. While China does exhibit a high degree of income inequality, the work done to eliminate poverty last year shows the efforts made to ensure that the fruits of growth were shared with the least fortunate.

With the *moderately prosperous society* established, the 14th Five-Year Plan ushers in a new stage in China's economic development: building a modern socialist country. With a basic level of material comfort achieved, a greater stress will be put on environmental remediation and green growth. Aggregate demand will increasingly rely on a robust domestic market. And innovation will become a driving force for development.

It is easy to see why the 14th Five-Year Plan emphasizes innovation. China's working age population is shrinking. Its investment rate is already very high and the rapid increase in debt in recent years limits how much more capital accumulation can contribute to growth. This leaves increasing productivity as the most rational way to develop.

So, how innovative is China?

While innovation is hard to measure, Bloomberg has, for some time, published an index that tries to cut into this question. The index is a weighted average of seven elements. China ranked 16th out of 60 countries in the 2021 edition of Bloomberg's index: just ahead of Ireland and behind Norway. It's a pretty good result, considering China is not nearly as rich as its European "neighbours". The individual elements of Bloomberg's index suggest the areas in which China might want to work, in order to increase its ability to innovate. Figure 2 shows China's ranking on each of the seven components, along with its overall rank. China does well on patent filings, creating high-tech companies and spending on research and development. Its weak spots are productivity and researcher concentration.

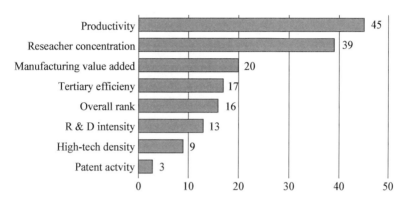

Figure 2　Bloomberg 2021 Innovation Index: China's Ranking

Source: Bloomberg, Yicai

China ranked 45th on productivity, which considers the level and change of output per employed person. China's poor performance here echoes the recent comments made by Miao Wei, the former Minister of Industry and Information Technology. Miao said that China is at least 30 years away from achieving its goal of becoming a strong manufacturing power.

If we compare China's manufacturing sector with that of the US, we do, indeed, find a large productivity gap. Table 1 shows that the value added of China's manufacturing sector was 1.6 times as large as the US's in 2019. However, that output was produced by more than three times as many workers. So, the productivity of China's manufacturing sector — in terms of value added per worker — was only half as high as the US's.

Table 1　Manufacturing Sector Indicators (2019)

	US	China	China/US
Value Added ($billion)	2,346	3,828	1.6
Workers (million)	12.5	38.3	3.1
Value Added per Worker ($)	187,969	99,897	0.53

Source: Wind, Yicai

China spends a lot on research and development but it is less successful on the human resources side. Bloomberg ranked it 39th in the employment of researchers (as a share of the workforce). Based on the experience of other countries, China should be engaging five times more researchers than it currently does, given its research and development expenditures (Figure 3).

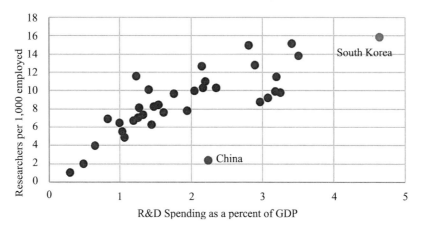

Figure 3　Research and Development Indicators (2019 or Latest)

Source: OECD, Yicai

Figure 3 also shows that South Korea is an outlier both in terms of how much its spends on research and development and the number of researchers it engages. It will come as no surprise, then, that Bloomberg ranked South Korea as the world's most innovative country. South Korea's achievement — like China's — is noteworthy because its innovation ranking is much higher than one would expect given its per capita income (Figure 4).

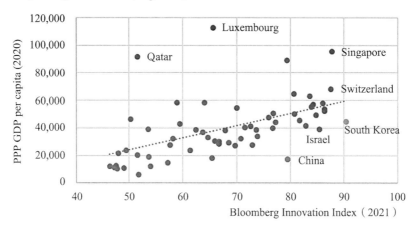

Figure 4　Per Capita Income and Innovation

Source: Bloomberg, IMF, Yicai

How do we explain South Korea's success in innovation and what lessons might it hold for China?

There are three aspects of the South Korean model that stand out. First, South Korean firms are large, they have significant resources and can quickly scale up new products. This is especially true of South Korean conglomerates — the chaebols. Perhaps because of their scale and dominant market positions, firms play a much larger role in funding research and development in South Korea than businesses in other countries. While the government supports investment in research and development through tax credits, it also makes sure domestic firms are subject to the discipline of competition. Second, there is close collabouration between government and business. The government facilitates innovation by engaging in targeted programs. In the mid-1990s, it invested to build up the country's broadband infrastructure. More recently, it announced a Digital New Deal, which will create smart hospitals and digital management systems for traffic, water resources and disaster response. Working with the chaebols, the government has developed a number of innovation centres in an effort to create industrial clusters. Third, South Korea puts a high premium on creating and attracting human capital. Close to 70 percent of South Koreans between the ages of 24 - 34 have tertiary education. This is well above the Organization for Economic Cooperation and Development (OECD) average of 45 percent and the highest among all countries surveyed by the OECD. South Korea has also been successful in re-attracting South Korean academics who studied abroad.

South Korea's firms have emerged as world leaders in memory chips, cell phones, and liquid crystal displays. Moreover, its innovative cultural industry is having a world-wide impact. K-pop is a global phenomenon. South Korean TV dramas are all the rage here in China. My wife was crazy about *My Love from the Star*. And movies like *Parasite* have received critical acclaim internationally.

A friend of mine, who served as a diplomat in Seoul, describes South Korea's experience with innovation as comprising three phases: imitation, continuous improvement and ground breaking invention. And South Koreans describe themselves as moving from "fast-followers" to "pace-setters".

China is squarely in the continuous improvement phase. A lot can be achieved here. Indeed, the South Korean experience suggests that successful innovation, at this level, offers considerable scope to avoid the middle-income trap.

中国会成为下一个韩国吗？

2021 年 3 月 30 日

　　在前不久召开的"两会"上，中国发布了"十四五"规划的最终版本，概述了政府的中期战略思想。只有阅读这份文件，才能知道中国未来的发展方向。我认为"十四五"规划非常重要，因为它代表了中国经济发展的一个转折点。

　　近 40 年来，中国的主要发展目标之一是创建"小康社会"，这是邓小平在 20 世纪 70 年代末首次提出的。邓小平从儒家经典《礼记》中借用了这个词，该书被认为是在两千多年前的汉代编纂而成的。在原文的语境中，"小康社会"被视为一种次于"大同社会"的状态。不过，邓小平的选择是经过深思熟虑的，在制定发展计划时，他希望设定一个较低的标准，以免提出不切实际的期望。

　　邓小平的愿景是定性的，随着时间的推移，中国将从物质匮乏的社会变为相对充足的社会。江泽民在任总书记时更进了一步，将"小康社会"定义为 2000 年至 2020 年中国 GDP 翻两番，这意味着在这 20 年里实际 GDP 的年均增长率只需要 7% 以上就能实现目标。实际的情况是，在江泽民和胡锦涛的总书记任内经济增长率明显超出这个水平。在习近平总书记上任后，经济增长率继续超过 7%，到 2015 年，GDP 基本上是 2000 年的 4 倍（图 1）。

　　2013 年，习近平总书记把建成"小康社会"与在 2021 年庆祝建党 100 周年之际 GDP 自 2010 年翻番的目标联系在了一起。他最近表示，GDP 翻番预计将在今年晚些时候实现。事实上，考虑到政府 6% 以上的增长目标，我们应该可以在今年夏天某个时候实现"小康"（图 1）。

　　中国"小康社会"的特点是物质生活水平提高。2000 年，中国的人均 GDP（按购买力平价计算）排在全球所有国家的后三分之一，到了 2020 年，中国的这一数据排名前 40%。虽然中国确实表现出高度的收入不平等，但去年为消除贫困所做的工作，展现了中国为确保与最不富裕的人群共享经济增长成果做出的努力。随着全面建成"小康社会"目标的实现，"十四五"规划引领中国经济发展进入新阶段，即

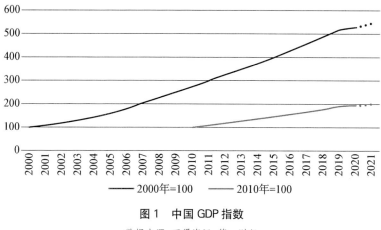

图 1　中国 GDP 指数

数据来源：万得资讯、第一财经

全面建设社会主义现代化国家。随着物质逐步充足，环境整治和绿色增长将面临更大压力，总需求将越来越依赖于强劲的国内市场，创新将成为发展的动力。

为什么"十四五"规划强调创新？这一点并不难理解。中国的劳动年龄人口正在减少，投资率已经非常高，而近年来债务的迅速增加限制了资本积累对经济增长的贡献，这使得提高生产率成为最合理的发展方式。

那么，中国的创新情况如何呢？尽管创新很难衡量，但彭博社一段时间以来发布了一项指数（该指数是 7 个要素的加权平均数），试图切入这个问题。在彭博社 2021 年的指数中，中国在 60 个国家中排名第 16 位，领先于爱尔兰，落后于挪威。考虑到中国没有其欧洲"邻国"富裕，这已经是一个相当不错的结果。彭博社指数中的个别因素则表明中国可能需要在哪些领域开展工作，以提高创新能力。图 2 显示了中国在 7 个组成要素中的相应排名以及总体排名，其中，在专利申请、创立高科技公司和研发支出方面做得很好。中国的不足之处在于生产率和研究人员密度。

在反映就业人员人均产出水平和变化的生产率方面，中国排名第 45 位。中国在生产率上表现不佳，印证了工业和信息化部前部长苗圩最近的评论。苗圩表示，中国距离实现制造业强国的目标至少还需要 30 年的时间。

如果将中国的制造业与美国进行比较，会发现两国确实存在巨大的生产率差距。表 1 显示 2019 年中国制造业增加值是美国的 1.6 倍。然而，这一产出是由三倍多的工人生产的。因此，中国制造业的生产率（按人均增加值计算）仅为美国的一半。

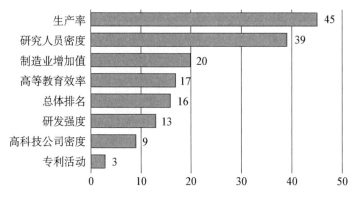

图2　2021年彭博创新指数：中国排名

数据来源：彭博社、第一财经

表1　中美两国制造业指标比较（2019年）

	美国	中国	中国/美国
增加值（十亿美元）	2,346	3,828	1.6
工人数量（百万人）	12.5	38.3	3.1
人均增加值（美元）	187,969	99,897	0.53

数据来源：万得资讯、第一财经

　　中国在研发方面投入了大量资金，但在人力资源方面却不太成功。彭博社将中国的研究人员就业（占劳动力的比例）方面排名第39位。根据其他国家的经验，按中国的研发支出，中国应该雇佣比目前多五倍的研究人员（图3）。

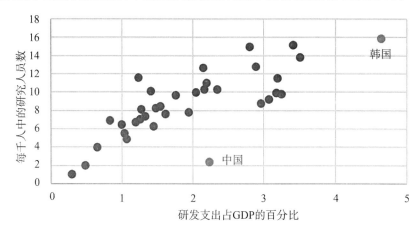

图3　中国的研发指标（2019年或最近）

数据来源：经济合作与发展组织、第一财经

　　图 3 还显示,韩国在研发投入和研究人员就业方面都是一个例外,彭博社因此将韩国列为世界上最具创新力的国家也就不足为奇了。韩国的成就(与中国一样)是值得关注的,因为其创新排名远高于人们基于其人均收入的预期(图 4)。

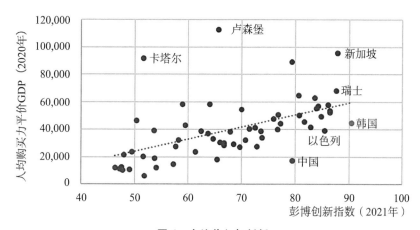

图 4　人均收入与创新

数据来源:彭博社、国际货币基金组织、第一财经

　　如何解释韩国在创新方面的成功? 对中国有什么启示?

　　韩国模式有三个突出的方面。首先,韩国企业规模很大,它们有丰富的资源,可以迅速扩大新产品的规模,尤其是韩国的财阀。也许是因为它们的规模和市场支配地位,韩国企业在资助研发方面比其他国家的企业发挥了更大的作用。虽然政府通过税收抵免支持研发投资,但它也确保国内企业受到竞争纪律的约束。其次,政府和企业之间有密切的合作。政府通过参与有针对性的项目来促进创新。20 世纪 90 年代中期,韩国政府投资建设了该国的宽带基础设施。最近,它宣布了一项"数字新政",将为交通、水资源和灾害应对建立智能医院和数字管理系统。政府通过与财阀合作,已经建立了许多创新中心,努力打造产业集群。第三,韩国非常重视创造和吸引人力资本。在 24 至 34 岁的韩国人中,近70% 的人接受过高等教育,远高于经济合作与发展组织(OECD,以下简称"经合组织")45% 的平均水平,也是经合组织调查的所有国家中最高的。另外,韩国也成功吸引在国外学习的韩国学者回国工作。韩国企业已经成为存储芯片、手机和液晶显示器领域的世界领导者。此外,其创新文化产业正在全世界产生影响,韩国流行音乐是一种全球性的现象,韩剧在中国风靡一时,电视剧《来自星星的你》和类似《寄生虫》这样的电影在国际上受到好评。

　　我的一位曾在首尔担任外交官的好友把韩国的创新经历描述为三个阶段：模仿、持续改进和突破性发明。韩国人则称自己正在从"快速追随者"转变为"领跑者"。中国正处于持续改进的阶段，这个阶段可以实现很多目标。事实上，韩国的经验表明，在这个阶段的成功创新，可以为避免陷入"中等收入陷阱"提供相当大的空间。

Beidou: China's First Outer Space Infrastructure Project

August 13, 2020

On July 31, President Xi Jinping announced that China had completed the construction of the third phase of the Beidou Navigation Satellite System. This gives China a constellation of 55 operational positioning and navigational satellites. As the working lives of the second-generation satellites expire, the basic constellation will consist of 30 third-generation satellites, the last of which was launched on June 23.

These satellites are like outer space lighthouses. They send radio signals to the earth, which are encoded with the time at which the signal was sent and the satellite's location. If the receivers in your car or cell phone can pick up the signals from four satellites, then they can accurately triangulate your position.

China began work on positioning and navigation satellites in 1994. It launched its first satellite in 2000 and began to provide services domestically. In 2007, more satellites were launched to expand the coverage to the Asia-Pacific region. This regional system has been fully operational since 2012. In November 2017, China began the third phase, which is designed to give the Beidou system global coverage. This involved the launch of 30 satellites and the building of 40 ground stations in the past two and a half years. With last month's launch, the constellation was completed six months ahead of schedule, no mean feat given the challenges presented by the fight against COVID – 19!

Global navigation satellite systems are not new. They were originally designed for military purposes, such as the precision guiding of weapons to targets. The US began the construction of its Global Positioning System (GPS) in 1978 and the Soviet Union followed with its Global Navigation Satellite System (GLONASS) in 1982. The European Union also has a global system (Galileo), while the satellites in India and Japan provide regional coverage.

Like lighthouses, global navigation satellite systems appear to be pretty close to perfect public goods. The signals they send are freely available to anyone with a receiver and the quality of the signal does not diminish even as the number of receivers greatly increases. Moreover, receivers do not compromise their security when they use satellite signals, since the communication is only one way.

Given the public good nature of the existing systems, why did China invest in one of its own?

There are essentially three reasons.

First, a country's satellite constellation can be tailored to provide more precise positioning to its domestic or regional users. While the Beidou system has global coverage, its location services are more accurate in the Asia-Pacific region: 10 cm, compared with 30 cm for the US's GPS.

Second, as the number of services that rely on satellites increase, the economic cost of a system failure rises. Satellites are used for positioning in a host of transportation services. However, since their signals are based on very precise clocks, they are also used to time financial transactions and to synchronize information across power grids. Global navigation satellite systems do fail from time to time. The worst instance was Galileo's outage over July 10 – 17, 2019. Other systems have also experienced minor technical glitches. Thus, multiple satellite constellations make sense given the high cost of systemic failure.

Third, a country can block access to its satellite signals in times of conflict. Indeed, to ensure that its potential adversaries do not use GPS, the US military is dedicated to the development and deployment of "regional denial capabilities". China has too much at stake — and will likely have much more at stake in the future — to risk being excluded from the US's GPS system. Security concerns and the risks of being denied access to core technologies have also likely influenced China's decision to ensure that its third generation satellites, including their 500 key components, were made domestically.

Unlike other countries' global navigation satellite systems, Beidou offers a messaging capability that allows for two-way communication in areas that are beyond the reach of cell phones, for example sailors lost at sea. With the rollout of the third generation of satellites, Beidou's short message communication service has been upgraded. It now allows for regional text messages of 14,000 bits (1,000 Chinese characters) and global messages of 560 bits (40 Chinese characters).

China's development has long benefitted from the government's timely provision of key infrastructure. In the past, this meant ensuring that there were sufficient power and transportation resources to avoid costly bottlenecks. Now, China has completed its first outer space infrastructure project. China's satellite navigation sector, currently employs over 500,000 workers to produce hardware such as chips, card boards, antennas and electronic maps, as well as a wide range of software products. Beidou's global rollout is sure to support the production of high value-added satellite-related goods and services for years to come.

北斗：中国首个外太空基础设施建设工程

2020 年 8 月 13 日

7月31日，中国国家主席习近平宣布中国完成了北斗卫星导航系统第三阶段的建设，至此完成了55颗定位导航卫星的星座[1]建设。由于二代卫星工作寿命已经终结，所以星座将包含30颗三代卫星，其中最后一颗于6月23日成功发射。

这些卫星就像位于外太空的灯塔，向地球发射无线电信号，信号包含发射时间和卫星的位置信息。如果你车里的接收器或者手机能够接收到这些信号，那卫星就可以定位你的位置。

中国的定位导航卫星研发工作始于1994年，于2000年发射第一颗卫星并开始在国内提供服务。2007年，中国发射了更多卫星，将服务范围扩大到亚太地区。该区域系统自2012年开始全面运转。2017年11月，中国开始北斗卫星导航系统第三阶段建设，将其服务范围扩展至全球。第三阶段在过去两年半的时间里共发射了30颗卫星并建设了40个地面卫星接收站。随着上个月发射工作结束，北斗星座比原计划提前6个月完成，在面临新冠肺炎疫情挑战的情况下，这是一项非常了不起的成就。

全球卫星导航系统其实并不算新技术，它们最初应用于军事，比如武器对目标的精准制导。美国的全球定位系统（GPS）于1978年开始建设，前苏联的全球卫星导航系统（GLONASS）开始于1982年。欧盟也有自己的全球定位系统（Galileo），印度和日本的定位系统仅能提供区域服务，不能提供全球服务。

和灯塔一样，全球卫星导航系统基本上属于公共财产，只要有无线电信号接收器就可以免费接收，而且信号的质量也不会随着接收人数的增加而降低。而

---

[1] 中国卫星导航系统管理办公室测试评估研究中心（http://www.csno-tarc.cn/en/system/constellation）。

且接收卫星信号并不会给接收人带来安全隐患,因为这样的信号交流是单向的。

既然目前各种卫星导航系统都是公用的,中国为什么还要研发自己的导航系统呢?

主要有以下三个方面的原因。①

第一,一个国家的卫星星座可以更精准地为本国或本地区的用户提供定位服务。北斗系统信号可以覆盖全球,定位服务在亚太地区更加精准②,可以达到10 米,而美国的 GPS 系统只有 30 米。

第二,随着依赖卫星的服务数量增多,卫星系统失败的经济成本也在上升。在交通运输服务中,卫星用来定位,但由于卫星信号基于非常精准的时钟,因此也会用于金融交易计时和电网信息同步。全球卫星定位系统有时也会发生故障③,最严重的一次是 2019 年 7 月 10 日至 17 日发生的伽利略卫星导航系统故障。其他的卫星系统也曾经历过一些小的技术故障。由此看来,考虑到系统故障的高昂成本,研发多个卫星星座是有意义的。

第三,与其他国家发生冲突的时候,可以阻断其他国家接收本国卫星信号。美国军方为了阻止其潜在对手使用 GPS 而努力研发部署"区域屏蔽功能"。美国 GPS 屏蔽中国的风险很大,将来可能会更大。安全问题以及被核心技术屏蔽的风险是中国决定在国内制造第三代卫星的原因,包括 500 个重要组件④。

北斗系统跟其他国家的全球卫星定位系统不一样,它的信息传递能力可以在没有手机信号的地区实现双向交流,比如在海上失踪的水手。第三代北斗系统升级⑤了短信息交流服务,可以实现区域内 14,000 比特(1,000 个汉字)和全球范围内 560 比特(40 个汉字)的信息传递。

中国的发展长期得益于中国政府即时提供的关键基础设施。过去是保证足够的动力和运输资源来避免昂贵的瓶颈制约。现在中国已经完成了首个外太空

---

① 中国自主研发的全球定位系统开始全面运转(https://www.forbes.com/sites/ramseyfaragher/2020/08/01/chinas-homegrown-gps-is-now-fully-operational/? sh = 1369510d10f2)。

② 中国将完成北斗系统,在全球卫星导航领域与美国 GPS 系统竞争(https://www.reuters.com/article/us-space-exploration-china-satellite/china-set-to-complete-beidou-network-rivalling-gps-in-global-navigation-idUSKBN23J0I9)。

③ 从伽利略卫星导航系统信号故障中总结的经验教训(https://insidegnss.com/lessons-to-be-learned-from-galileo-signal-outage/)。

④ 北斗三号全球卫星导航系统建成开通新闻发布会召开(http://en.beidou.gov.cn/WHATSNEWS/202008/t20200803_21013.html)。

⑤ 北斗三号全球卫星导航系统建成开通新闻发布会召开(http://en.beidou.gov.cn/WHATSNEWS/202008/t20200803_21013.html)。

基建工程,卫星定位领域就业人数超 50 万,生产和制作包括芯片、纸板、天线和电子地图在内的各种硬件以及各种软件产品。[①] 北斗系统在全球范围内推出,将在未来几年内支持与卫星相关的高附加值产品和服务。

① 中国通过北斗全球服务实现了关键的自主技术(https://www.globaltimes.cn/content/1196264.shtml)。

PBOC's Virtual Renminbi Is Becoming a Reality

September 14, 2020

After more than five years of intensive design work, the People's Bank of China (PBOC) has started to pilot its digital currency. In southern Shenzhen, eastern Suzhou, mid-western Chengdu, and northern Xiong'an, public servants and employees of state-owned institutions are receiving a small amount of their remuneration in the digital renminbi, which can be spent at a host of retail stores and restaurants.

The PBOC is hardly unique among central banks in working to develop a digital currency, but it is one of the most advanced. According to a survey carried out by the Bank for International Settlements (BIS) late last year, while 80 percent of central banks are engaged in some sort of digital currency research and development, only 10 percent have progressed to pilot projects. Moreover, 70 percent of the banks say that they are unlikely to issue digital currencies, even in the medium term.

The PBOC is being motivated, in part, by rapid domestic financial innovation, which has led to the declining use of cash. Data from the BIS shows that the ratio of banknotes and coins in circulation to GDP is rising in the United States and the euro area. However, it is falling sharply in China, where consumers are abandoning cash for mobile payments made via their cell phones (Figure 1). China's mobile payment infrastructure has become particularly well developed. The two dominant platforms — Alibaba's Alipay and Tencent's WeChat Pay — had 890 million users in 2018.

As a Chinese resident, having downloaded the two companies' apps and linked them to my debit card or credit card, I use my phone to shop anywhere, from upscale malls to street vendors. All I need to do is scan the ubiquitous Alipay or WeChat Pay QR codes and enter the purchase price. Almost immediately, a mechanized voice informs the vendor that a purchase of a particular amount has been made. I really never have to carry cash. Indeed, I see far fewer automated teller machines in Chinese cities than in their North American and European

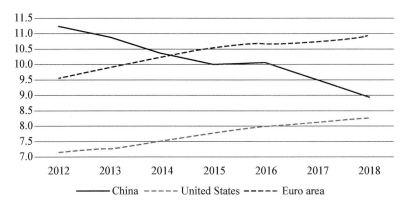

Figure 1   Banknotes and Coins in Circulation (as a % of GDP)

Source: BIS, Yicai

counterparts, because there is really no need for people like me to refill our wallets with bills.

The rise of mobile payments has meant greater convenience for consumers, but it has been an even bigger boon for Chinese merchants, especially the smaller ones. Consider Mrs Ma, who makes delicious Shandong-style savoury pancakes (a typical breakfast snack) at her street-side stall by my local subway station. Mobile payments allow her to continue serving the queue of commuters without having to take off her cooking gloves and count change. Indeed, most of her customers have already scanned her QR code before they arrive at Mrs Ma's griddle to tell her whether they want hot sauce, spring onions or lettuce on their pancakes. Mrs Ma no longer has to spend time managing her cash. She need not worry about the risks of theft or loss, as her sales have been instantly credited to her Alipay and WeChat Pay accounts.

Given how well the existing system of mobile payments works for China's consumers and vendors, why is the PBOC keen to issue its own digital currency?

First, a digital renminbi could stem the loss of seigniorage that arises from the decline in the use of cash. Second, it could mitigate the competitive and operational risks involved with having two private companies process a large and growing share of China's retail payments. Third, it could enhance financial inclusion. Anyone who lacks access to the Alipay and WeChat Pay platforms — for example, the elderly, residents of rural areas and visitors from overseas — can run into problems paying with cash or credit cards. Indeed, in 2018, the PBOC had to crack down on retailers who refused to accept cash.

The PBOC's work on the digital renminbi is also likely motivated by the advent of cryptocurrencies and Libra. It sees the digital renminbi as an issue of national currency sovereignty and wants to assume a leading role in digital currency development rather than play catch-up to innovation taking place elsewhere.

The digital renminbi is centrally managed and based on "loosely-coupled account links". It is not a decentralized token system like bitcoin. Nor is it mainly based on blockchain, as blockchain technology cannot keep pace with China's tremendous volume of mobile payments.

The digital renminbi is designed to leverage the existing mobile payments infrastructure and is not being set up as a parallel system. Individuals need not open new accounts; they simply download the digital wallet app to their cell phones and link it to their bank cards. Their financial institutions, who will have bought the digital currency from the PBOC at 1∶1, provide them with the digital renminbi by debiting their bank accounts.

The PBOC is being careful to ensure that the digital renminbi has a minimal impact on monetary policy and financial stability. Financial institutions will have to provide 100 percent backing to use the digital currency. This backing ensures that no additional money is created, and that the digital renminbi remains the liability of the central bank. The PBOC has stressed that the digital renminbi is essentially a digital banknote and it will not pay interest. An interest-bearing digital renminbi would have the potential to lead to disintermediation, as consumers could move out of interest-bearing bank deposits for the more convenient mobile currency. Such disintermediation could force the banks to raise interest rates to retain depositors. However, keeping funding costs low and stable is an important consideration in China, where small banks typically have challenges in raising deposits.

Given how well China's mobile payment system is already working, will there really be a demand for the digital renminbi?

The digital renminbi offers three advantages compared to the existing mobile payment system: lower cost, greater anonymity and reduced reliance on the internet.

Merchants like Mrs Ma are charged volume-based fees for her customers' use of the Alipay and WeChat Pay systems. Moreover, while she can freely use the balances of her Alipay and WeChat Pay accounts to purchase goods and services, Mrs Ma would be charged an additional fee should she wish to take them outside of their systems, for example, to deposit these balances in her bank. In contrast, no fees are associated with the use of the digital renminbi, just as with any other form of cash.

Currently, consumers must provide personal information in order to access the Alipay and WeChat Pay payment systems, but the digital renminbi will provide for "controllable anonymity". Small-value transactions will be, essentially, anonymous. However, the PBOC is looking to strike a balance between the public's desire for privacy and the need to prevent money laundering, terrorism financing and tax evasion. This will be done by limiting the size of the digital wallets and setting limits on the value of transactions that can be made in the absence of providing personal identification.

The Alipay and WeChat Pay systems typically rely on internet connections — either Wi-Fi or cellular — to connect a credit card to the vendor's account. While the digital renminbi app allows for the full range of payment options currently available through Alipay and WeChat Pay, it also permits a Bluetooth-enabled transfer of funds that will not depend on internet connectivity. Alipay and WeChat Pay permit users to load money from their bank accounts on to their phones and pay via Bluetooth, in case internet connectivity is lost. As there is a cost to re-depositing these funds, transaction balances on phones are typically kept low. In contrast, users of the digital renminbi would not incur such transaction fees and one could imagine that they would carry larger balances.

The digital currency could accelerate the internationalization of the renminbi. In addition to addressing the domestic concerns noted above, there is potential for it to be the platform of choice for small, cross-border payments. Remittances are incredibly expensive; for example, a recent report by the World Bank estimates that it currently costs US $13.58 to remit US $200. With the digital renminbi, the cost of remittances would essentially fall to zero.

PBOC Governor Yi Gang has emphasized that the digital renminbi has not yet been officially issued and that there is no timetable for its full rollout. However, he recently suggested that further piloting could take place at the 2022 Beijing Winter Olympics. This will give foreign visitors a chance to see just how easy it is to pay with China's digital currency.

The preceding was first published by the Centre for International Governance Innovation, copyright 2020.

中国人民银行虚拟人民币正在成为现实

2020 年 9 月 14 日

经过 5 年多的紧张设计,中国人民银行(下称"人民银行")启动了虚拟货币试点。在南部城市深圳、东部的苏州、中西部的成都以及北部的雄安,公务员和国有机构员工薪酬中的一小部分以虚拟货币的形式发放,可以在很多商店和餐馆使用。

人民银行并不是唯一研发虚拟货币的央行,但却是进展最快的。国际清算银行 2019 年末的一项调查显示,80% 的央行在研发虚拟货币,但只有 10% 进入了试点阶段。另外,70% 的银行中期内没有发行虚拟货币的计划。

人民银行发行虚拟货币,一方面是因为国内金融创新迅速,使用现金的人越来越少。国际清算银行的数据显示,在美国和欧元区,流通中的纸币和硬币占GDP 的比例呈上升趋势,但在中国却大幅下降,中国的消费者放弃现金,使用手机进行移动支付(见图 1)。中国的移动支付基础设施已经相当发达,阿里巴巴

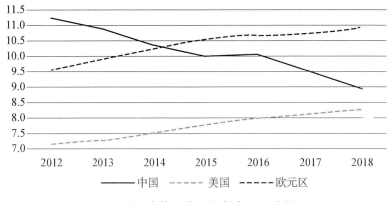

图 1　流通中的纸币和硬币(占 GDP 比例)

数据来源:国际清算银行、第一财经

的支付宝和腾讯的微信支付这两大平台在 2018 年共拥有 8.9 亿用户①。

生活在中国,我只要下载这两个应用软件(App)并绑定储蓄卡或信用卡,就可以随时使用手机支付了。从大型超市到街边小店,只需用手机扫描一下支付宝或微信的二维码,然后填上付款金额支付,马上就能听到机器的声音通知商家我支付的金额。我从不带现金出门,中国城市里的自动取款机也比美国和欧洲少,因为像我一样,人们确实不需要携带现金。

移动支付的兴起为消费者提供了极大的便利,对商家,尤其是小型商家来说更是非常大的福音。比如,在我家附近的地铁站口,有位摆摊卖山东煎饼(一种非常好吃的早餐小吃)的马太太,有了移动支付,她就不必在给排队的顾客做煎饼的时候停下来,然后摘掉手套给顾客找零钱了。在拿煎饼(要不要酱、葱、生菜)之前,大多数顾客就已经扫好了二维码,马太太也不用分心照看钱,不用担心被偷或丢,因为她的支付宝或微信支付的账户能马上收到顾客付的煎饼钱。

现在的移动支付系统已经给中国消费者和商户带来了如此大的便利,人民银行为什么还要发行虚拟货币呢?

首先,数字人民币可以避免因现金使用减少而造成的铸币权损失。其次,可以降低因两家私营公司占中国零售支付市场份额越来越大带来的竞争和运营风险。最后,可以增强金融包容性。无法使用支付宝和微信支付的人群,比如老年人、农村地区居民以及外国游客,可能会遇到商家不接受现金或信用卡支付的问题。所以,2018 年人民银行出手严厉打击拒收现金的商家。②

人民银行推出数字人民币的另一个原因是受到加密货币和脸书币(Libra)的驱动,人民银行认为数字人民币属于国家货币主权,应当在数字货币的发展过程中起到主导作用,而不是作为后来者去追赶其他地方的创新行为。

数字人民币属于集中管理,具有与银行账户松耦合的特性。比特币属于分散管理的代币制度。数字人民币也不是基于区块链的,因为区块链跟不上中国移动支付的巨大体量。

数字人民币旨在利用现有的移动支付基础设施,而不是与其并行的独立系统。用户不需要开立新的账户,只需在手机上下载数字钱包 App 并绑定银行

---

① 中国政府支持的数字货币(https://www.sixthtone.com/news/1005716/chinas-government-backed-digital-currency%2C-explained)。

② 在中国,现金已经不再为"王"了(https://asia.nikkei.com/Business/Business-trends/In-China-cash-is-no-longer-king)。

卡。金融机构将从人民银行1∶1兑换数字人民币,记入用户的借方账户。

人民银行正采取谨慎措施将数字人民币对货币政策和金融稳定的影响降到最低。金融机构将全力支持数字人民币的使用,以保证不会制造额外的钱,从而确保数字人民币依然是央行的负债。人民银行强调,数字人民币本质上是数字货币,不会产生利息。如果数字人民币有利息,就可能导致"脱媒现象",即消费者会跳过有利息的银行存款,转而选择更加便利的数字货币。如果出现了"脱媒现象",银行就会被迫提高存款利率来留住客户。但是,在中国保持低廉、稳定的融资成本是一个非常重要的考虑因素,中国的小型银行通常在吸引存款方面面临挑战。

中国的移动支付已经如此成熟完善,对数字人民币真的有需求吗?

相对于现在的移动支付系统,数字人民币有三大优势,即成本更低、匿名性更强、网络依赖性更小。

消费者用支付宝和微信支付,像马太太这样的商贩需要支付一定比例的费用。另外,她可以自由使用支付宝和微信支付账户余额购买商品或服务,但是如果想把余额提现,比如,转存到她的银行账户,就要缴纳一定的费用。相比之下,使用数字人民币就不会产生任何费用,就像现金一样。

目前,消费者需要提供个人信息才能使用支付宝和微信支付,而数字人民币可以实现"可控制匿名性"。小额交易基本上都可以匿名进行。人民银行正在寻求大众对隐私的保护和防止洗钱、恐怖主义融资、逃税之间的平衡,比如限制数字钱包额度和无需提供个人身份信息的情况下可以进行交易的额度。

通过支付宝和微信支付向商家支付都需要网络,无线网或数据流量都可以。数字人民币支持支付宝和微信支付中支持的所有付款方式,还支持蓝牙转账,不需要网络连接。支付宝和微信支付用户可以在没有网络连接的情况下,将自己银行账户里的钱放到手机上,再通过蓝牙支付。因为将手机上的钱转回银行卡是要收费的,所以一般手机上的余额都不多。相比之下,数字人民币没有交易费用,用户可以保留较多的余额。

数字货币可以加速人民币国际化。除了以上提到的国内使用的情况,数字人民币也可以成为小额、跨境支付的可选渠道。国际汇款费用相当高,根据世界银行最近的一份报告,如果汇200美元,需要支付13.58美元的费用。如果有了数字人民币,汇款手续费基本上可以降到零。

人民银行行长易纲强调数字人民币尚未正式发布,而且也没有发布时间表。

但是,他最近表示将在 2022 年东京奥运会上试点数字人民币①,届时外国游客就可以看到使用数字人民币进行支付的便利性。

本文由加拿大国际治理创新中心于 2020 年首次发布

---

① 中国人民银行行长易纲在"两会"期间就金融保市场主体等问题接受《金融时报》《中国金融》记者采访
（http://www.pbc.gov.cn/en/3688110/3688175/4031198/index.html）。

China's High-Speed Rail: A Case Study in Independent Innovation

February 4, 2021

A couple of weeks ago, President Xi, took a high-speed train from Beijing to Zhangjiakou, one of the venues for Beijing's 2022 Winter Olympics. The train, which travels at an average speed of 222 km/hr, cut the trip between the two cities from three hours to only 47 minutes. President Xi took the opportunity to applaud China's achievements in high-speed rail, calling them successful examples of China's independent innovation.

Given that innovation of this type is at the centre of its new growth model, it is worth examining China's experience with high-speed rail in a bit of detail.

China's first high-speed service — from Beijing to Tianjin — started in 2008. By the end of last year, 37,800 km of high-speed rail track have been laid, accounting for just over a quarter of the entire network.

I often choose to take the high-speed train when I travel from Shanghai to Beijing. The 9 AM train takes four and a half hours to reach Beijing's South railway station. Its average speed along the 1,318 km distance — including stops at Nanjing and Jinan — is just over 290 km/hr. At that speed, I can make a late afternoon meeting or an evening event.

My second-class ticket costs around CNY 600. This is about half the price of the 9 AM flight, which takes two hours and 20 minutes. The airlines do offer more competitive pricing later in the day, with the 225 PM flight only costing CNY 560.

Because of the train's high speed, it must travel on special tracks, which are designed to be as straight as possible. This makes for a smooth and comfortable ride. The cars are equipped with free Wi-Fi and I can order food to be delivered. This is convenient as the train stops in Jinan at noon.

Train ridership was off last year due to the pandemic. In 2019, close to 2.4 billion trips were made on China's high-speed trains, up from only 700 million five years earlier.

In its early days, China's high-speed trains relied heavily on German, French and Japanese prototypes and parts. Over time, domestic inputs have substituted for foreign ones and today an estimated 90 percent of high-speed rail's supply chain is made in China. Domestic innovations include cars on the Beijing-Harbin line that can withstand very cold temperatures.

China's high-speed rail project has also led to advances in engineering. For example, the Dali-Ruili Railway Bridge and Gaoligong Mountain Rail Tunnel, are the world's longest span bridge and Asia's longest tunnel. And the Badaling Great Wall Station, on the Beijing-Zhangjiakou line, is China's largest underground.

While Chinese firms have benefitted from the learning-by-doing afforded by the construction of high-speed rail, foreigners have not been shut out. For example, Bombardier Sifang Transportation — a Sino-Canadian joint venture — has supplied hundreds of high-speed rail cars to China State Railway Group and has contracts to maintain the cars following their manufacture.

Last August, the China State Railway Group released its plan for developing the rail system over the next 15 years. The national network will comprise 200,000 km of track (up from 146,300 as at the end of last year), of which 70,000 km will be high-speed rail (Figure 1). The goal is to provide a rail link to all cities with populations of 200,000 and a high-speed link for those of 500,000.

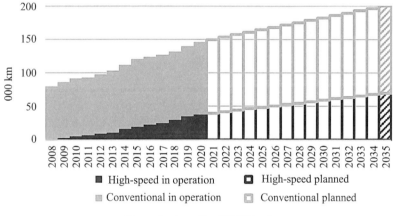

Figure 1   Length of Rail Track

Source: Wind, Xinhua, Yicai

While the planned expansion of the rail network should bring a host of benefits, it is not without risk.

A recent report by the World Bank noted that some of China's heavily used lines — like the one that connects Shanghai and Beijing — generate enough revenue to pay for their operations, maintenance and debt service. However, many lines with low traffic can barely cover their operating and maintenance costs. Moreover, they will be unable to contribute to their debt service costs for many years unless their fares are increased significantly.

If many existing lines are struggling to make ends meet, how will the new lines, which will likely extend to less populated areas fare?

A study just released by MacroPolo, the in-house think tank of the Paulson Institute, provides an assessment of China's high-speed network as at the end of 2019. It finds that high-speed rail conferred a net benefit of $378 billion (2.4 percent of GDP) to the economy. It's annual return on investment is estimated at 6.5 percent.

MacroPolo attributes high-speed rail's largest benefit, more than 40 percent of the total, to time savings. For distances of 800 km or less, high-speed rail travel is quicker than going by plane. This is because airports are often far from city centres and security checks are time-consuming. This benefit should continue to be important as the network spreads to smaller cities.

Those who are critical of China's high-speed rail expansion concentrate on loss-making lines and rising debt. These are attributed to ticket prices which are too low to cover the full cost of rail service.

However, transportation is an industry in which market prices do a poor job of balancing true costs and benefits. While traffic jams are the most visible transportation externality, greenhouse gas emissions are even more important. Since no mode of transportation currently prices in its full carbon costs, it is difficult to be sure if ticket prices really are "too low".

A study by the International Union of Railways concluded that high-speed rail's carbon footprint can be up to 14 times smaller than car travel and 15 times smaller than travel by plane. These estimates are measured over the full life cycles of planning, construction and operation of the different transport modes.

Given that China is heading toward carbon neutrality by 2060, perhaps a wider rollout of a low-carbon rail system makes sense. In this context, low ticket prices, loss-making rail lines and rising debt are simply the interventions needed to make rail competitive with high-emissions forms of transportation.

High-speed rail, then, is not only a case study in independent innovation, but also a key part of China's low-carbon future.

中国高铁：自主创新的案例研究

2021 年 2 月 4 日

几周前,习近平主席乘坐高铁从北京前往 2022 年北京冬奥会的举办场地之一河北省张家口市。习主席乘坐的列车的平均时速达到每小时 222 千米,将两个城市之间的旅行时间从 3 个小时缩短到 47 分钟。习主席借此机会表达了对中国高铁建设的赞美,称其为中国自主创新的成功范例。[1]

自主创新是中国新增长模式的核心,所以我们有必要详细看一下中国的高铁建设。

作为中国第一条高速铁路,京津高铁(北京至天津)于 2008 年建成。截至 2020 年底,中国已完成 3.78 万千米的高铁轨道建设,占整个铁路网的四分之一以上。

当我从上海去北京时,我经常选择乘坐高铁。上午 9 点从上海出发的列车,用了 4 个半小时到达北京南站,全程 1,318 千米(包括在南京和济南的中途停留),平均时速超过 290 千米。照这个速度,我可以赶到北京参加一场下午晚些时候的会议或晚上的活动。

我买了一张二等座的票,价格约 600 元,差不多是早上 9 点航班(时长 2 小时 20 分钟)机票的一半。晚些时候的机票会便宜一点,下午 2 点半左右的航班票价只要 560 元。

因为高铁的速度快,所以列车轨道必须是特制的,在设计上越直越好,这样列车在行驶过程中才能保持平稳舒适。高铁车厢覆盖无线网络(Wi-Fi)信号,可以免费使用,我还可以叫外卖,非常方便,因为列车中午刚好停在济南站。

由于新冠肺炎疫情,2020 年火车客流量下降。2019 年,中国高铁客流量接

---

[1] 习近平:高铁是我国自主创新的一个成功范例(http://www.xinhuanet.com/english/2021-01/20/c_139683283.htm)。

近 24 亿人次,而 5 年前仅为 7 亿人次。

在中国高铁建设初期,它依赖于德国、法国和日本的技术原型和零部件。随着时间的推移,国内技术、零部件逐渐取代进口,截至目前,大概 90% 的高铁供应链都是国产。中国的创新,比如京哈(北京至哈尔滨)铁路线上的高铁车厢,可以抵御严寒。[1]

中国的高铁建设也带动了很多工程的发展。[2] 例如,大理至瑞丽铁路怒江特大桥和高黎贡山隧道分别是世界上最大跨度的铁路拱桥和亚洲最长的铁路山岭隧道。京张(北京至张家口)铁路八达岭长城站是中国最大的地下高铁站。

从中国高铁建设的"边做边学"模式中受益的不仅仅是中国公司,外国公司也没有被拒之门外。例如,中加合资公司青岛四方庞巴迪铁路运输设备有限公司向中国国家铁路集团有限公司(以下简称"国铁集团")供货数百节高铁车厢并提供后续维修服务。

2020 年 8 月,国铁集团发布了未来 15 年高铁建设规划。[3] 届时,全国铁路网将达 20 万千米(2020 年底为 14.63 万千米),其中高铁 7 万千米(见图 1)。该规划将在 20 万人口以上城市实现铁路覆盖,50 万人口以上城市高铁通达。

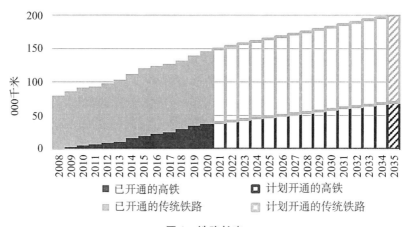

图 1　铁路长度

数据来源:万得资讯、新华社、第一财经

---

① 中国推出"子弹头"高铁,可以在严寒环境中运行(https://edition.cnn.com/travel/article/china-bullet-train-cold-weather-fuxing/index.html)。

② 中国高铁是如何快速超越其他国家的(https://www.engineering.com/story/how-chinas-high-speed-rail-zooms-past-other-countries)。

③ 中国 50 万人口的城市将在 15 年内拥有高铁(https://www.chinadaily.com.cn/a/202008/13/WS5f34ddfaa3108348172601d0.html)。

虽然扩大铁路网可以带来很多好处，但也不是没有风险。

据世界银行最近的一份报告，中国一些繁忙的铁路线，如上海至北京的铁路，已经产生了足够的收入来支付铁路的运营、维修费用和债务。但业务量低的铁路线仅能勉强支付运营、维修费用，除非大幅提高票价，否则未来几年无法支付偿债费用。[①]

很多现有的铁路线都在努力维持收支平衡，那么在人口较少的地区建设的新线路又如何呢？

保尔森基金会（Paulson Institute）内部智库 MacroPolo 研究院[②]刚刚发布的一项研究对截至 2019 年底中国的高铁网络进行了评估，发现高铁为中国经济创造了 3,780 亿美元的净收益（占 GDP 的 2.4%），年投资回报率预计为 6.5%。[③]

MacroPolo 研究院认为高铁最大的一个好处（占所有优势的 40% 以上）就是节省时间。800 千米及以下的路程，坐高铁比坐飞机快，因为机场通常离市区较远，而且安检也比较费时间。随着高铁扩展到小城市，这一优势依然非常重要。

对中国高铁扩张的批评主要是由于那些亏损的线路和不断上升的债务。这主要是因为票价太低，无法覆盖铁路服务的所有费用。

然而，运输行业在市场价格平衡和收支平衡方面确实表现不佳。交通拥堵是最明显的交通外部性，温室气体排放则更为重要。由于目前没有任何交通方式是根据其全部碳成本定价的，因此很难界定票价是不是真的"太低"。

国际铁路联盟的一项研究认为，高铁的碳足迹比汽车低 14 倍，比飞机低 15 倍。[④] 这些是按照不同交通方式的规划、建设和运营的整个生命周期进行估算的。

中国正在朝着"2060 年前实现碳中和"[⑤]的目标迈进，或许会更广泛地推出低碳铁路系统。在这种情况下，低票价、亏损的铁路线和不断增加的债务只是为了让铁路与高排放运输方式竞争而采取的干预措施。

届时，高铁便不仅仅是自主创新的案例，更是中国低碳未来的重要组成部分。

---

① 中国高铁建设发展报告（https://documents1.worldbank.org/curated/en/933411559841476316/pdf/Chinas-High-Speed-Rail-Development.pdf）。

② MacroPolo 研究院（https://macropolo.org/about/）。

③ 中国高铁发展的成本与收益（https://macropolo.org/digital-projects/high-speed-rail/methodology/）。

④ 高铁：从快速交通到可持续交通（https://uic.org/IMG/pdf/uic_high_speed_2018_ph08_web.pdf）。

⑤ 中国如何在 2060 年前实现碳中和（https://www.yicaiglobal.com/opinion/mark.kruger/how-can-china-achieve-carbon-neutrality-by-2060-2）？

5G and the Competition to Win the 21st Century

August 9, 2021

Imagine two countries that are in competition to "win the 21st century". The roads in the first country are unpaved and cars can't travel faster than 20 kilometers per hour. In contrast, the second country boasts a network of state-of-the-art expressways that permit safe speeds of up to 200 kilometres an hour. Which country would you bet on to win that competition?

In fact, the roads in the world's major countries are pretty similar. But significant differences are beginning to emerge in their information super-highways, in particular how quickly they are adopting the fifth-generation standard for broadband cellular networks (5G). As of the end of 2020, China had installed close to 700,000 5G base stations. By this June, that number had risen to just under a million, and 1.4 million are expected to be installed by the end of the year. In July, 10 key government bodies unveiled a three-year Action Plan for China's 5G development. As part of that plan, China aims to have 18 5G base stations installed for every 10,000 people — about 2.5 million in total — by the end of 2023. While it is difficult to obtain definitive information, the US had only installed something like 50,000 5G base stations by the end of last year (Figure 1).

Why is 5G so special?

According to the International Telecommunication Union (ITU) — the United Nations' specialized body for information and communication technologies — a 5G network will offer mobile users data at a rate of 100 megabits per second, or ten times faster than via 4G networks. The ITU says that 5G networks will be able to support 1 million devices per square kilometre, compared to 4G's 100,000 devices. Finally, the ITU estimates that it will only take one millisecond for data to go from your device to the main server and back again. That's down from 10 milliseconds for a 4G network. A 4G network essentially facilitates the exchange of information between people. Taking mobile communication a step further, 5G's superior capabilities will permit the rapid and accurate exchange of large quantities of data among machines. For example, your self-driving car will take you around town

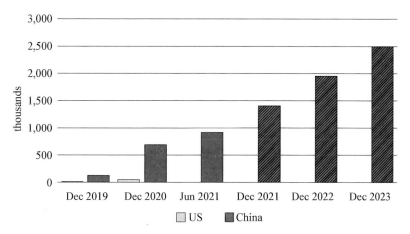

Figure 1   5G Base Stations Installed/To Be Installed

Source: Statista, Press Reports, Yicai

safely because it will be able to talk to other cars, to traffic signals and to satellites.

Given 5G's potential to create smart factories, smart cities and smart medicine, why aren't other countries rolling out the technology as fast as China?

There appear to be two main obstacles. First, there is a basic incentive-compatibility problem. A first-rate mobile network is a key piece of infrastructure that — like a highway system — offers significant returns to the entire economy. But only a small portion of these returns accrue to the telecom firms who create the network. Moreover, these firms need to make huge up-front investments in the face of uncertain revenues and it is not clear that they can make reasonable profits. So, there is a disconnect between the network's social and private returns. Second, 5G suffers from a sort of chicken-and-egg problem. Since the 5G system is not yet fully in place, few 5G-specific applications have been developed. And, since there aren't many applications, there is little demand for the network. Little demand for the network means that there are limits to how much the telecoms can charge for service, thus delaying 5G's development.

Much of the cost that telecoms incur arise from the purchase of the rights to use certain radio frequencies (spectrum). Eric Schmidt, Google's former Chief Executive and Chairman, worries that these expenses are retarding network development. In a *Financial Times* Op-Ed, Schmidt estimated that it would cost $70 billion to build the one million stations needed to give the US a functional 5G system. However, US telecoms are spending more than this on spectrum auctions alone. These, Schmidt suggests, are more focused on raising government revenue than creating infrastructure. He proposes that Congress use the proceeds from the spectrum auctions to provide funding for the 5G network.

A further complication arises from the US's lack of a homegrown telecommunication equipment provider. The world's five main players — Huawei, ZTE, Samsung, Nokia and Eriksson — are Chinese, South Korean, Finnish and Swedish. US telecoms face more regulatory hurdles when they purchase their equipment overseas.

China has solved the incentive-incompatibility problem by making 5G's development and commercialization a national priority. To capture 5G's potentially high social returns, it has catalyzed its telecoms, equipment providers and industrial firms. Pilot schemes were already envisaged during the 13th Five-Year Plan (2016 – 2020). More specific policy guidance was provided in 2019 for local governments to develop 5G-based "industrial internet". Being at the forefront of a new technology does mean undertaking a high-risk, high-return strategy. But this is a gamble that the Chinese government is willing to take. Liu Liehong — a Vice-Minister at the Ministry of Industry and Information Technology — estimated that China will need to spend CNY 1. 2 trillion ($187 billion) to 2025 on constructing its 5G network. If it is successful, Liu believes that investment could result in CNY 2. 9 trillion in additional economic value added. In an effort to get around the chicken-and-egg problem, July's Action Plan proposes a "demand-driven supply, supply-created demand" model. The government will proceed simultaneously along two tracks: (i) encouraging the development of the system through targets for base stations and user penetration and (ii) promoting 5G applications in various commercial sectors. The Action Plan hopes to build off of the early successes of using 5G in mining, farming, ports and factories.

Now imagine two countries that are cooperating to survive the 21st century. One country becomes the first to exploit a new technology. Do you think that there would be important lessons and positive spillovers for the second country?

5G 与赢得 21 世纪的竞争

2021 年 8 月 9 日

假设有两个国家竞争来"赢得 21 世纪"。第一个国家的道路没有铺砌,汽车的时速不能超过 20 千米。而另一个国家则拥有最先进的高速公路网络,安全时速可以达到 200 千米。你认为哪个国家能够在竞争中胜出?

事实上,世界上主要国家的路况非常相似,但它们在信息高速公路方面正呈现出很大的差异,尤其是在对第五代移动通信技术(5G)的普及速度上。截至 2020 年底,中国已建成近 70 万个 5G 基站,到今年 6 月底,这一数字已上升到略低于 100 万,预计到年底将达到 140 万。今年 7 月,中国十部门印发了《5G 应用"扬帆"行动计划(2021—2023 年)》(以下简称"行动计划")。作为该行动计划的一部分,中国计划到 2023 年底建设约 250 万个基站,即平均每万人 18 个基站。到去年年底,美国只建成了大约 5 万个基站(很难获得确切的信息)(见图 1)。

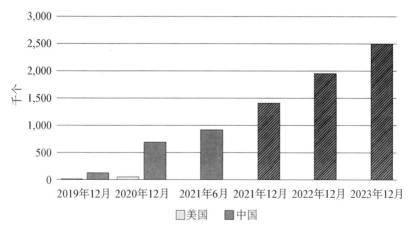

图 1　已建成/计划中的 5G 基站

数据来源:Statista 数据库、新闻报道、第一财经

5G 为什么这么特别？

根据国际电信联盟（简称 ITU，联合国负责信息和通信技术事务的专门机构）的数据，5G 网络将以每秒 100 兆比特的速度向移动用户提供数据，这比 4G 网络快 10 倍。5G 网络每平方千米内可以支持 100 万台设备接入互联网，而 4G 网络只能支持 10 万台设备。ITU 估计，数据从用户的设备传输到主服务器再返回只需要一毫秒。这比 4G 网络需要的 10 毫秒要低。4G 网络从根本上促进了人与人之间的信息交流。5G 在移动通信方面更进一步，其卓越的性能将允许机器之间快速准确地交换大量数据。例如，您的自动驾驶汽车将安全地带您在城市中四处转转，因为它可以与其他汽车、交通信号和卫星通话。

考虑到 5G 在打造智慧工厂、智慧城市和智慧医疗方面有如此潜力，为什么其他国家的技术推广速度不如中国？似乎有两大障碍。首先，存在一个基本的激励相容问题。一流的移动网络是基础设施的关键组成部分，就像高速公路系统一样，为整个经济带来显著回报。然而，这些回报中只有一小部分属于创建网络的电信公司。此外，这些公司在收入不确定的情况下需要进行大量的前期投资，不清楚能否获得合理的利润。因此，网络的社会回报和私人回报之间存在脱节。其次，5G 面临着先有鸡还是先有蛋的问题。因为 5G 系统尚未完全到位，所以很少有专门针对 5G 的应用。然后，由于应用不多，对网络的需求也很少。对网络的需求很少，意味着电信公司可以收取的服务费有限，从而延缓了 5G 的发展。

电信业产生的大部分成本来自购买某些无线电频率（频谱）的使用权。谷歌前首席执行官兼董事长埃里克·施密特（Eric Schmidt）担心这些费用正在阻碍网络的发展。在《金融时报》的一篇评论文章中，施密特估计，为美国提供功能齐全的 5G 系统所需的 100 万个基站将耗资 700 亿美元。然而，美国电信公司仅在频谱拍卖上的支出就超过了这一数额。施密特认为，这些拍卖更侧重于增加政府收入，而不是建设基础设施。他建议国会使用频谱拍卖的收益来为 5G 网络提供资金。另一个复杂的因素是美国缺乏本土电信设备供应商。世界五大厂商——华为、中兴、三星、诺基亚和爱立信分别来自中国、韩国、芬兰和瑞典。美国电信公司在海外采购设备时面临更多监管障碍。

通过将 5G 的开发和商业化作为国家优先事项，中国解决了激励不相容的问题。为了获得 5G 潜在的高社会回报，中国推动了国内电信、设备供应商和工业公司的发展。在"十三五"（2016—2020 年）规划期间，已经设想了试点方案。2019 年，中央为地方政府发展基于 5G 的"工业互联网"提供了更为具体的政策指引。站在新技术的前沿确实意味着采取了一种高风险、高回报的策略。但这是中国政府愿意冒的风险。时任工业和信息化部副部长刘烈宏估计,到 2025 年,中国将需要花费 1.2 万亿元(1,870 亿美元)来建设 5G 网络。他认为,如果成功,这些投资将带来 2.9 万亿元的额外经济增加值。为了解决鸡和蛋的问题,7 月份中国的行动计划提出了"需求牵引供给,供给创造需求"的模式。政府将同时沿着两条轨道开展工作:(1)通过基站和用户普及目标鼓励系统的发展;(2)推动 5G 在各个商业领域的应用。行动计划希望在采矿、农业、港口和工厂使用 5G 的早期成功基础上再接再厉。

现在想象两个国家正在合作度过 21 世纪。一个国家成为第一个开发新技术的国家。你认为这对第二个国家会有重要的教训和积极的溢出效应吗?

Is China's Investment Really That Unproductive?

July 30, 2020

Michael Pettis, a professor at Peking University's Guanghua School of Management recently posted an essay on the Carnegie Endowment for Peace's website in which he takes exception to the use of the Cobb-Douglas production function to analyse the Chinese economy. The Cobb-Douglas framework for the analysis of an economy's supply side has a venerable history. Charles Cobb and Paul Douglas published their "A Theory of Production" in the *American Economic Review* back in 1928. The Cobb-Douglas production function has been around so long because it is intuitive. It models GDP growth as a weighted average of the growth of the capital stock and the growth of labour plus the growth of total factor productivity (TFP). The great weakness of this framework is that TFP growth — the most important factor in an economy's long-term development — is calculated as a residual: GDP growth minus the capital contribution minus the labour contribution.

Professor Pettis makes it clear that he has no problem with the Cobb-Douglas approach in general. However, he objects to using it to understand China's growth. He says, "Most economists agree that China suffers substantially more from nonproductive investment than other countries do, and because this investment is not written down to the extent that bad investment is recorded in other countries, it should follow that China's GDP data is not comparable to that of other countries."

I disagree with Professor Pettis on both of his key points. I do not believe that there has been excessive unproductive investment in China, and I think that China's GDP data are broadly comparable to those of other countries. My disagreement with Professor Pettis on the first point is empirical. On the second, we disagree on the fundamentals of national income accounting.

Let's start with the second point first. Corporate and national income accounting differ in their treatment of investment. Investment is typically an expenditure on a long-lived productive asset. Corporations usually amortize the purchase of a productive asset over a number of years, reducing their profit by a fraction of the asset's cost in each year until it is fully amortized. Should the corporation realize that the asset was no longer useful and decide to write it off, then it would expense its unamortized value in the year the decision was made and reduce profits commensurately.

National income accounting does not work this way. In the calculation of GDP, the full cost of the asset is recorded in the investment account in the year in which it was acquired. There is no need to make adjustments in subsequent years should the asset become non-productive. That's because the National Accounts have already recorded its full cost. To make a subsequent adjustment to investment or GDP would be redundant. It would amount to paying for the asset twice. Indeed, I know of no country in which GDP is adjusted for the productivity of its capital stock.

Now let's consider if Chinese investment has really been so unproductive. China unquestionably invests much more than most other countries (Figure 1). This has been the case since the early 1980s, but the gap widened since 2000. Between 2000 and 2018, the ratio of investment to GDP was 43 percent in China, compared to 22 percent for advanced countries and 25 percent for emerging market and developing countries (EMDCs) ex-China.

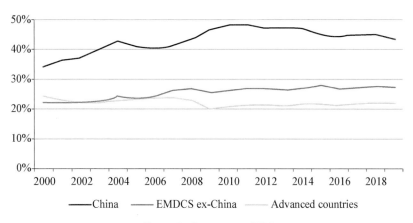

Figure 1   Investment/GDP

Source: CEIC, Yicai

With China's investment rate about double of what we see elsewhere, it has been a common assumption that the efficiency of Chinese investment must be pretty low and that many projects must be non-productive. Indeed, we have observed pockets of over-capacity in certain industries such as steel and solar panels and in certain regions, like Ordos, Inner Mongolia (which is actually no longer a ghost town). However, these are examples of micro-economic imbalances. The macro-economic data tell a very different story.

Unproductive investment should have low returns. However, in China's case, despite the very high investment rates, the marginal product of capital has been very high. The marginal product of capital is the amount of additional GDP that can be generated by a unit increase in capital. It can be calculated as a country's real GDP growth rate divided by the ratio of investment to GDP.

Figure 2 presents the marginal product of capital for China, EMDCs ex-China and advanced countries. It shows that China's marginal product of capital has fallen from 25 percent in the early 2000s to 14 percent more recently. Nevertheless, it remains superior to those of other countries. This suggests that, from a macroeconomic perspective, Chinese investment is relatively productive.

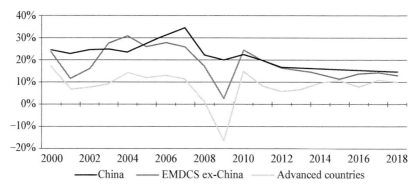

Figure 2　Marginal Product of Capital

Source: CEIC, Yicai

The question of over investment is an important one and one which interests me deeply. While Professor Pettis states that "… a large and rising share of economic activity in the country consists of nonproductive investment," he does not provide an estimate of how big the problem might be. Different approaches have been used in the literature to assess this question. My colleagues and I used sophisticated filtering techniques to determine the extent to which excessive credit growth led to over-investment in China between 1997 – 2015. We found over-investment peaked in 2014, when it accounted for about 1. 5 percent of GDP or about 3. 3 percent of total investment. GDP growth in 2014 was 7. 4 percent.

What would it mean, in the context of the Cobb-Douglas production function, if a fraction of investment spending was not productive?

Since it does not result in the creation of productive assets, non-productive investment spending would resemble the purchase of consumption goods. Like a fine meal, they would be consumed and have no effect on the capital stock. Nevertheless, the amount of spending in the economy in that period would be the same. It's just that its composition would change, with GDP being composed of more consumption and fewer investment goods.

In the current year, with the same amount of GDP being produced by an unchanged quantity of labour and a smaller capital stock, the Cobb-Douglas production function would suggest that TFP growth increased. Over time, however, the misallocation of resources resulting from unproductive investment would result in a fall in both measured GDP growth and TFP.

中国的投资真的没有收益吗？

2020 年 7 月 30 日

北京大学光华管理学院教授迈克尔·佩蒂斯（Michael Pettis）近期在卡内基国际和平基金会的网站上发表了一篇文章①。在这篇文章中，他对使用柯布-道格拉斯生产函数（the Cobb-Douglas production function）来分析中国经济提出了反对意见。用柯布-道格拉斯生产函数分析经济供给侧有着悠久的历史，该函数最早是由查尔斯·柯布（Charles Cobb）和保罗·道格拉斯（Paul Douglas）于 1928 年在《美国经济评论》上提出的。柯布-道格拉斯生产函数能使用如此长的时间是因为它的直观性。在函数中，GDP 增长是资本存量增长、劳动力增长加上全要素生产率（TFP）增长的加权平均值。这个函数最大的一个缺点是，在计算 TFP（经济长期发展的最重要的要素）时，得到的是差值，即 TFP 等于 GDP 增长减去资本投入和劳动力投入后得到的差额。

佩蒂斯教授认为柯布-道格拉斯生产函数总体上没有什么问题，但他反对用它来分析中国的经济增长。他说："很多经济学家认为中国的非生产性投资损失要比其他国家高很多，因为其他国家把非生产性投资计入不当投资，但中国没有。因此，中国的 GDP 数据与其他国家没有可比性。"

我不同意佩蒂斯教授所说的这两点。我不认为中国的无收益投资是过量的，中国的 GDP 数据与其他国家具有广泛的可比性。我不同意佩蒂斯教授说的第一点，我是有事实依据的。我们之间的第二个分歧在于国民收入核算的基本原理。

先看第二点。公司和国民收入核算两者处理投资的方式不同。投资是典型的对长期生产性资产的支出。公司通常将生产性资产的购置成本分若干年摊

---

① 中国经济需要的是制度改革，而不是追加资本（https://carnegieendowment. org/chinafinancialmarke ts/82362）。

销，每年在利润中减去该年摊销的部分，直到完全摊销。如果公司认为资产不再有用并决定将其冲销，那么就将尚未摊销的金额计入做出冲销决定当年的费用，并在利润中扣除相应的金额。

但这不是国家收入核算的计算方式。在计算 GDP 的时候，全部的资产购置成本被记入购置当年的投资账目下，即便以后资产变成了非生产性投资，在接下来的年份中也不需要做调整，因为国民账户中已经录入了全部的购置成本，再在投资或 GDP 中做后续的调整就多此一举了。如果后续再去调整，就相当于给这项投资付了两次钱。据我所知，没有哪个国家是根据资本存量的生产率来调整其 GDP 的。

让我们回到这个问题：中国的投资是否真的没有收益。毫无疑问，中国的投资确实比其他国家多（见图 1）。这种情况自 20 世纪 80 年代初期就出现了，但自 2000 年开始差距逐渐扩大。2000 年至 2018 年，中国投资占 GDP 的比重为 43%，而发达国家为 22%，中国以外的新兴市场和发展中国家为 25%。

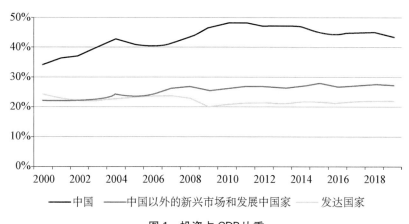

图 1　投资占 GDP 比重

数据来源：环亚经济数据、第一财经

中国的投资率几乎是其他国家或地区的两倍，一般会认为中国的投资效率会很低，很多投资项目没有收益。我们确实看到某些行业产能过剩，比如钢铁行业和太阳能电池板行业；以及某些地区产能过剩，比如内蒙古鄂尔多斯（现在已经不是"鬼城"①了）。但是也有微观经济失衡的情况。宏观经济数据所呈现的

---

① 中国最大的"鬼城"——鄂尔多斯市康巴什现状（https：//www. forbes. com/sites/wadeshepard/2016/ 04/19/an-update-on-chinas-largest-ghost-city-what-ordos-kangbashi-is-like-today/？ sh＝41dcf20f2327）。

情况截然不同。

无收益投资回报很低。但是,中国的情况是这样的,虽然投资率高,但资本边际产出却很高。资本边际产出是指每增加一个单位资本产生的额外 GDP,可以按照一个国家的实际 GDP 增速除以投资占 GDP 的比重来计算。

图 2 显示的是中国、除中国以外的新兴市场和发展中国家以及发达国家的资本边际产出。如图所示,中国的资本边际产出从 20 世纪初的 25% 降到最近的 14%,但仍比其他国家高。这说明从宏观经济的角度来看,中国的投资还是相对有收益的。

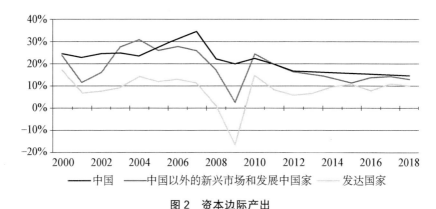

图 2　资本边际产出

数据来源:环亚经济数据、第一财经

过度投资是一个非常重要的问题,也是我非常感兴趣的话题。佩蒂斯教授说:"中国相当大一部分的经济活动包含非生产性投资,而且这一部分越来越多。"但他没有估算过这个问题到底有多大。文献中使用了很多方法来评估这个问题,我和同事们也用了很多成熟的过滤技术来判断 1997 年至 2015 年中国由过度信贷增长导致的过度投资情况。我们发现过度投资在 2014 年达到峰值[①],当时约占 GDP 的 1.5%,约占总投资的 3.3%。2014 年的 GDP 增速为 7.4%。

如果柯布-道格拉斯生产函数显示一部分投资支出是没有收益的,这意味着什么呢?

因为不会产生生产性资产,非生产性投资就类似于购买消费品。就像一顿美餐,最终会被消化掉,不会对资本存量产生影响。但是,同期的经济支出是不

---

① 中国能发展多快? 中国至 2030 年发展规划(https://www.bankofcanada.ca/wp-content/uploads/2016/04/swp2016-15.pdf)。

变的,变的只是支出结构,导致 GDP 中消费增多,投资品减少。

在本年度,相同数量的 GDP 由不变的劳动力数量和较小的资本存量产生,柯布-道格拉斯生产函数会显示 TFP 的增长加快。然而,随着时间的推移,无收益投资导致的资源分配不当将会导致 GDP 增速和 TFP 下降。

How Sustainable Is China's Debt?

January 7, 2021

To escape the middle income trap and become a moderately developed country in the next 15 years, China has to successfully manage a number of risks. Most economists would agree that foremost among these is China's rising indebtedness.

High macroeconomic leverage — the financing of economic development via the accumulation of large amounts of debt — is risky. While an economy can have good years and bad years, debts are supposed to be paid in full and on time. When debts cannot be paid, crises occur.

Economists have not been able to determine specific thresholds above which a country's debt becomes unsustainable. But it is fair to say that a country's debt is sustainable if it can be serviced under a wide range of adverse scenarios. So, in addition to the size of the debt, its currency composition, its maturity profile and the composition of the country's creditors are all important factors.

The evolution of China's non-financial sector debt, as a percent of GDP, is depicted in Figure 1. China's corporate sector has accounted for most of the country's borrowing, about 60 percent of the total as of September last year. Households accounted for 23 percent and governments for the remaining 17 percent.

China's indebtedness has undergone three distinct phases since the outbreak of the global financial crisis in 2008 (Table 1). Between December 2007 and December 2015, it rose by more than 80 percent of GDP. About two-thirds of this debt was accumulated by corporations. Initially, most of these liabilities were incurred as part of the government's CNY 4 trillion spending plan, which was designed to counter the depressive effects of the financial crisis. In subsequent years, a wider variety of firms were able to access credit, as China's shadow banking system grew in importance.

By the end of 2015, concern about the rise in leverage and the opacity of the shadow banking system's exposures led the authorities to pursue a policy of deleveraging. By 2017, addressing financial risks became a key priority — one of

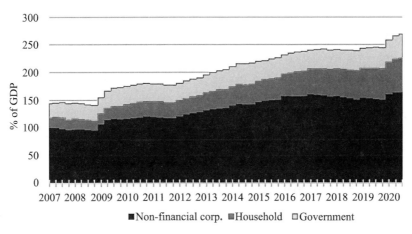

Figure 1   Macro Leverage Ratio: Non-Financial Sector

Source: Wind, Yicai

the "three tough battles" — along with alleviating poverty and tackling pollution.

Between December 2015 and December 2019, the debt of the non-financial corporate sector was essentially unchanged as a percent of GDP. Households accounted for almost all the increase in indebtedness in this period. Most of this was in the form of new mortgages.

The outbreak of the pandemic ushered in a third phase of indebtedness. Between December 2019 and September 2020, China's debt rose by close to 25 percent of GDP, as the country fought to maintain employment and output in the face of an unprecedented shock. The rise in indebtedness in these nine months was significantly larger than over the previous four years and about 20 percent of all the increase since 2007.

Table 1   Change in China's Non-Financial Sector Leverage: December 2007 - September 2020 (% of GDP)

	Total	Household	Non-Financial Corp.	Government
Dec. 07 to Dec. 15	82. 3	20. 4	55. 1	6. 8
Dec. 15 to Dec. 19	18. 1	16. 6	0. 1	1. 4
Dec. 19 to Sep. 20	24. 7	5. 6	12. 7	6. 4
Dec. 07 to Sep. 20	125. 1	42. 6	67. 9	14. 6

Source: Wind, Yicai

How does China's indebtedness compare to that of other countries?

Data from the BIS allow us to situate China's indebtedness with respect to those of the other G20 countries as at June 2020 (Figure 2). China ranks as the sixth most indebted G20 country, between the US and Italy.

While China's indebtedness is not "off of the charts" with respect to its G20 peers, it is high for a large, middle-income country. Indeed, as a percent of GDP, credit to the non-financial sector in China is about double the average of the other middle-income G20 countries.

Does that mean that China is too poor to be this levered?

Not necessarily. Compared to the other middle-income G20 countries, China has a larger and more diversified industrial base, which makes it more resilient to shocks. Moreover, many of those countries suffer from "original sin". Because of a history of unsustainable borrowing and high inflation, they find it difficult to borrow in their own currency. In contrast, almost all of China's debt is denominated in *renminbi* and it is largely held domestically. These factors are also positive for China's debt sustainability.

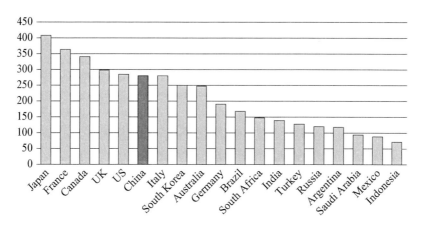

Figure 2　Credit to Non-Financial Sector (% of GDP)

Source: BIS, Yicai

Another way to think through debt sustainability is to look at they type of activity being financed. If a country borrows to improve its productive capacity, the increase in leverage is more likely to be sustainable than if debt is being accumulated to pay for consumption.

Capital goods are typically very expensive and need to be paid for over a number of years. It is not surprising to find that the increase in the leverage of China's non-financial sector tracks that of its capital stock, with both increasing rapidly since 2008 (Figure 3).

For debt to be sustainable, it is not sufficient that capital goods be financed. The investment has to be productive enough to service the debt. In a country as big

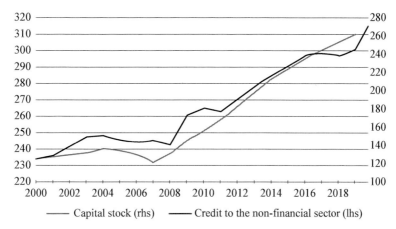

Figure 3   Non-Financial Sector Leverage and Capital Stock (% of GDP)

Source: Wind, Yicai

as China, one will certainly be able to find white elephant projects. Indeed, we have observed pockets of over-capacity in certain industries such as steel and solar panels and in certain regions, like Ordos, Inner Mongolia (which is actually no longer a ghost town). However, these are examples of micro-economic imbalances. The macro-economic data tell a very different story.

To assess the productivity of Chinese investment, we look at the marginal product of capital. This is the extra bit of GDP that you get from that last bit of investment. Figure 4 shows that China's marginal product of capital has fallen from extremely high rates in the early 2000s. Nevertheless, at close to 15 percent, it remains superior to those of advanced countries and other emerging market and developing countries (EMDCs). This suggests that, from a macroeconomic perspective, Chinese investment continues to be relatively productive.

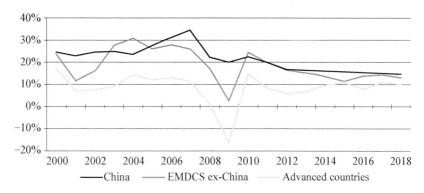

Figure 4   Marginal Product of Capital

Source: CEIC, Yicai

Ensuring that investment remains productive is one important way to increase the sustainability of China's debt. Other policies can also be helpful here.

China's non-financial corporations should be encouraged to finance themselves without incurring debt, for example via the equity market. The development of Shanghai's STAR market, which offers firms a quicker path to IPO, is a model that could be pursued more aggressively.

Chinese households are becoming more levered because of the high cost of housing and incentives to own rather than rent. It is encouraging that the recent Central Economic Work Conference called for promoting the construction of affordable rental properties and improving long-term rental policies, as this should relieve households of the need to become "mortgage slaves".

All of the increase in government indebtedness since 2007 was incurred at the local level. This is because local governments often lack the power to raise taxes and sustainably fund their expenditures. Indeed, as Figure 5 shows, China's general government revenue, as a percent of GDP, is lower than in most other G20 countries. A recurrent tax on residential property would not only boost local government revenues and reduce their borrowing needs, it would also dampen the speculative demand for apartments and improve housing affordability.

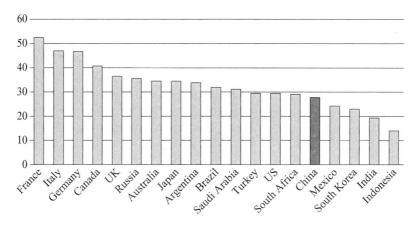

Figure 5　General Government Revenue (% of GDP)

Source: IMF, Yicai

China's explicit government debt is low, compared to that of other G20 countries. However, off the books liabilities loom at both the local and central government levels.

Due to limits on their borrowing, local governments have set up investment financing vehicles, which are designed to help raise capital for infrastructure projects. If the projects fail, these "firms" liabilities could end up on the local governments' books. Such contingent liabilities are not small — in its Staff Report for the 2019 China Article IV Consultation, the International Monetary Fund (IMF) estimated that they could be in the neighbourhood of 30 percent of GDP.

China's central government does not appear to have large hidden liabilities, but it has other worries. In particular, unfavourable demographics are putting pressure on the public pension system and China's Academy of Social Sciences has forecast that the pension system's reserves will be depleted by 2035. The government has been transferring shares in state-owned enterprises to the pension fund and it is considering raising the retirement age to address the situation. But it may have to borrow, on its own account, to mitigate remaining risks.

中国债务的可持续性如何？

2021 年 1 月 7 日

为了摆脱中等收入的陷阱，并在接下来的 15 年里成为一个中等发达国家，中国必须成功地管理一部分风险。大多数经济学家都会同意，在这些风险中首要的便是中国不断上升的债务。

较高的宏观经济杠杆率（即通过积累大量债务而为经济发展融资）是有风险的。虽然对一个经济体来说，年景有好有坏，但债务应该按时全额偿还。当无法偿债时，危机就发生了。

经济学家们还无法确定一个国家的债务超过哪个具体的门槛（红线）就变得不可持续。但恰当地说，如果一个国家的债务能在一系列不利的情境下仍得到偿还，则其便是可持续的。因此，除了债务规模之外，其货币构成，到期情况以及该国债权人的构成均是重要因素。

中国非金融行业债务的演变（占 GDP 的百分比）如图 1 所示。截至 2020 年

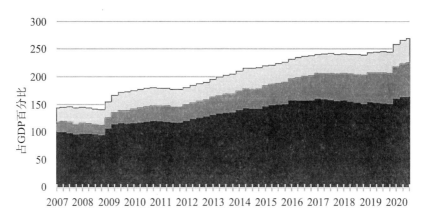

图 1　宏观杠杆率：非金融行业

数据来源：万得资讯、第一财经

年 9 月,中国企业相关行业已占中国借贷总额的 60% 左右。家庭于该项的占比为 23%,而政府则占剩余的 17%。

自 2008 年全球金融危机爆发以来,中国的债务经历了三个不同的阶段(表 1)。在 2007 年 12 月至 2015 年 12 月期间,它的增长量超过了 GDP 的 80%。这部分债务中的大约三分之二是由公司积累的。最初,这些债务中的大部分是作为政府 4 万亿元支出计划的一部分而产生的,该计划旨在应对金融危机的负面影响。在随后的几年里,随着中国影子银行体系重要性的日益增强,更多种类的企业能够获得信贷额度。

表 1　中国非金融行业杠杆率变化:自 2007 年 12 月至 2020 年 9 月(占 GDP 百分比)

	总数	家庭	非金融企业	政府
2007 年 12 月至 2015 年 12 月	82.3	20.4	55.1	6.8
2015 年 12 月至 2019 年 12 月	18.1	16.6	0.1	1.4
2019 年 12 月至 2020 年 9 月	24.7	5.6	12.7	6.4
2007 年 12 月至 2020 年 9 月	125.1	42.6	67.9	14.6

数据来源:万得资讯、第一财经

到 2015 年底,对杠杆率上升和影子银行系统风险敞口不透明的担忧导致政府部门推行去杠杆政策。到 2017 年,防范化解重大风险成为了一个关键的优先事项,与精准脱贫及污染防治并称为"三大攻坚战"。

在 2015 年 12 月至 2019 年 12 月期间,非金融企业行业的债务占 GDP 的百分比基本没有变化。家庭几乎成了这一时期债务增加的全部来源,这其中的大部分是以新型抵押贷款的形式。

新冠肺炎疫情的爆发导致了债务出现第三个阶段。在 2019 年 12 月至 2020 年 9 月期间,面对前所未有的冲击,中国努力维持就业和经济产出,因此中国的债务增长接近 GDP 的 25%。这 9 个月间的债务增长明显大于之前 4 年,且约占 2007 年以来全部增长的 20%。

中国的债务与其他国家相比如何?

根据国际清算银行的数据,我们可以得出截至 2020 年 6 月中国和二十国集团(以下简称 G20)其他国家的债务状况(图 2)。中国位列美国和意大利之间,是负债最多的 G20 国家第六位。

尽管与其他 G20 国家相比,中国的债务并非"超常",但对于一个中等收入

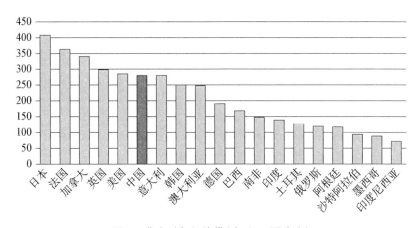

图 2　非金融部门信贷（占 GDP 百分比）

数据来源：国际清算银行、第一财经

的大国而言，债务负债率很高。的确，占中国 GDP 百分比的非金融部门信贷约为其他 G20 中等收入国家平均水平的两倍。

这是否意味着中国太穷而无法这样加杠杆？

并不一定。与其他中等收入 G20 国家相比，中国拥有更大、更多样化的工业基础，这使其更能抵御冲击。此外，这些国家中许多都遭受"原罪"之苦。由于不可持续的借贷和高通货膨胀的历史，它们发现很难以自己的货币借贷。相比之下，中国几乎所有的债务都以人民币计价，并且主要在国内持有。这些因素也对中国的债务可持续性有利。

通过债务可持续性进行思考的另一种方法是查看债务融资活动的类型。如果一个国家借钱来提高其生产能力，那么杠杆增加的可持续性比累积债务来支付消费的可能性更大。

资本货物通常非常昂贵，需要支付数年的费用。毫不奇怪的是，中国非金融部门的杠杆率增长追随其资本存量的增长，并且自 2008 年以来二者都迅速增长（图 3）。

为了使债务可持续，仅对资本货物进行融资是不够的。投资必须有足够生产力以偿还债务。在像中国这样大的国家，人们一定能够找到"白象"项目。实际上，我们已经观察到一些产能过剩，某些行业，例如钢铁和太阳能电池板，以及某些地区，例如内蒙古的鄂尔多斯市（实际上不再是鬼城）。但是，这些都是微观经济失衡的例子。宏观经济数据则大为不同。

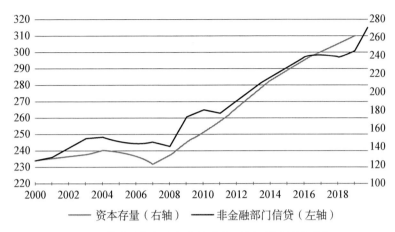

图 3　非金融部门杠杆及资本存量(占 GDP 百分比)

数据来源：万得资讯、第一财经

　　为了评估中国投资的生产率，我们看一下资本边际产出。这是从最后一点投资中获得的 GDP 额外收益。图 4 显示，中国的边际资本产出已从本世纪初期的极高水平下降。但是，它接近 15%，仍然优于发达国家、其他新兴市场和发展中国家。这表明，从宏观经济角度看，中国的投资仍然相对富有成效。

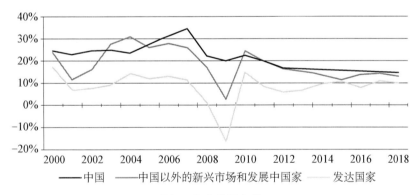

图 4　资本边际产出

数据来源：环亚经济数据、第一财经

　　保证投资的生产力是提高中国债务可持续性的重要途径之一。其他政策在这方面也会有所帮助。

　　中国应鼓励非金融公司在不借债的情况下自筹资金，比如发行股票。科创板的发展为公司提供了更快的 IPO 途径，企业可以更积极地采用这种方式。

由于高昂的住房成本和租房不如买房的观念,中国的家庭杠杆率不断升高。令人鼓舞的是,最近召开的中央经济工作会议呼吁推动保障性租赁住房建设,完善长租房政策,让居民不再需要为了买房而成为"房奴"。

2007 年以来,中国政府新增债务均为地方政府性债务。这是因为地方政府通常无权提高税收和持续拨款覆盖支出。如图 5 所示,中国的一般政府收入占 GDP 的比重要确实比大多数其他 G20 国家要低。征收住房保有税不仅可以增加地方政府的收入,减少其借贷需求,还可以抑制投机性的炒房需求并提高住房购买力。

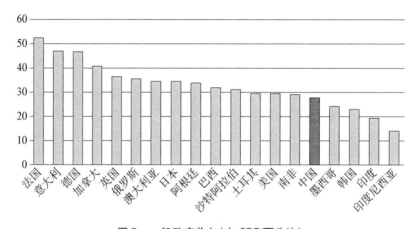

图 5　一般政府收入(占 GDP 百分比)

数据来源:国际货币基金组织、第一财经

与其他 G20 国家相比,中国的显性政府债务水平较低,但其地方和中央政府都受到隐性债务的影响。

由于借款限制,地方政府设立了投资融资平台,用于帮助基础设施项目筹集资金。如果项目失败,这些"公司"债务可能最终会进入地方政府的账簿。国际货币基金组织(IMF)在 2019 年中国第四条磋商-工作人员报告中估计,中国此类或有负债数额不小,约占 GDP 的 30% 左右。

中国中央政府似乎没有很大的隐性负债,但有其他担忧。特别是人口结构的不利因素给公共养老金体系带来的压力,据中国社会科学院预测,中国养老金累计结余将于 2035 年耗尽。政府目前在划拨国有资产充实养老金,并开始考虑通过延长退休年龄来解决养老金问题。但中央政府可能不得不自己借钱来应对残余风险。

China Needs More Defaults and More Meaningful Credit Ratings

November 26, 2020

November has been a turbulent month for China's corporate bonds. Three high-profile defaults have roiled the market which, at $4. 2 trillion, is the world's second largest. Bond prices have fallen as investors re-assess risks and the market wonders just how bad things can get.

A recent Bloomberg article notes that bond defaults through November 24 this year, totalled CNY 104 billion ($16 billion). That would make 2020 the third consecutive year in which corporate defaults topped CNY 100 billion.

In the midst of China's bond market panic, it is important to note that default rates are not particularly high. Figure 1 shows that defaults on Chinese corporate bonds have, indeed, risen sharply since 2017. However, in recent years, the amount of defaulted corporate bonds is only 0. 5 percent of the amount outstanding. This is about one-third the rate seen in the US.

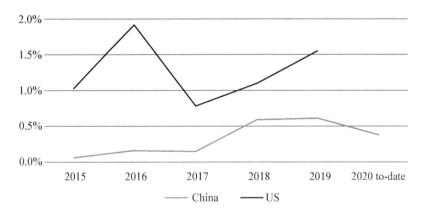

Figure 1　Defaulted Amount as a % of Outstanding Corporate Bonds

Source: Bloomberg, SIFMA, S&P, Wind, Yicai

If this year's default rate is neither particularly high historically nor internationally, why is the market so concerned?

It is perhaps significant that the coal miner, the integrated circuit maker and the car manufacturer which defaulted this month are all state-owned companies (SOEs). In previous years, private companies have accounted for close to four-fifths of China's corporate bond defaults. There were only 5 SOE defaults, on average. So far this year, 10 SOEs have defaulted and they have accounted for more than half the amount of defaulted debt. Chinese credit markets have typically operated on the tacit assumption that SOEs, which can benefit from government support, are better credit risks than private companies. This assumption creates "moral hazard". On the creditor side, funds are lent on the expectation of a government rescue should the issuer's fortunes sour. On the firm's side, excessively risky projects may be undertaken, if it is assumed that the government will not let the firm fail. Moral hazard undermines the efficiency of Chinese financial markets. Its reduction should be seen as a welcome development, even if it is painful for some investors in the short run.

Why is moral hazard being addressed now?

It is likely a sign that policymakers believe that the recovery is on track and the economy is strong enough to withstand financial stress. Indeed, with its employment objective being met, the government is returning to its pre-COVID policy of containing financial risks by increasing bond market efficiency and reining in excessive investment.

These defaults could also be evidence of local governments lack of the resources needed to keep loss-making firms afloat. State-owned asset managers do appear to be scrambling. Yongcheng Coal's default was, in part, induced by the transfer of its cash holdings to its parent, Henan Energy. Similarly, a month before its default, Huachen Automotive Group transferred its stake in Brilliance China Automotive Holdings to a subsidiary, to keep this valuable asset out of its creditors' hands.

The actions of state-owned asset managers have not escaped the attention of the State Council's Financial Stability and Development Committee. In its November 21 meeting, which was chaired by Vice Premier Liu He, the Committee noted the need to protect bond market investors from fraud, malicious asset transfers and the misappropriation of funds. Moreover, it expressly called for the prevention of moral hazard. In the near term, we may see more SOEs default on their bonds. We should take this as a sign that the Committee's instructions are being followed.

Policy makers have long sought to increase the role of China's capital markets. Expanding the bond market could broaden borrowers' access to finance as well as provide investors with a deeper pool of fixed income assets. Credit assessment in well-functioning bond markets depends critically on transparent information that is available on a timely basis. Credit rating agencies have a key role to play here.

It is important to note that both Huachen Automotive and Yongcheng Coal were rated AAA just prior to their defaults. Elsewhere, AAA credits do not default.

Figure 2 presents the experience of the global bonds rated by S&P between 1981 and 2019. It shows that bonds rated AAA never defaulted in the year they obtained that rating. Moreover, the default rate of firms that had been rated AAA 15 years earlier was only 1 percent. In comparison, 3 percent of the firms rated B defaulted in the year they obtained the rating and 15 percent defaulted over the next 15 years.

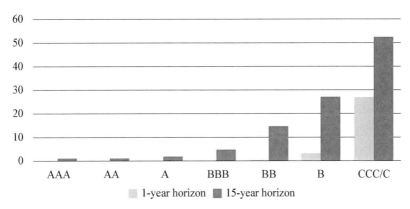

Figure 2　Global Corporate Bond Default Rates 1981 to 2019 Average (%)

Source: S&P, Yicai

Now circumstances do change over time and firms' creditworthiness can deteriorate. Rating agencies will reflect this deterioration in their ratings. According to S&P, the median US corporate rating fell to B 24 months prior to default, to B− seven months prior to default, and to CCC+ two months prior to default. This reduction in ratings provides important information to bond holders.

China has nine domestic firms which are licenced to provide credit ratings in the onshore bond market. In addition, foreign rating agencies have established wholly-owned subsidiaries that have been allowed to rate onshore bonds. Clearly, a domestic AAA rating does not mean the same as one obtained from the international agencies. For example, as end-July 2019, there were 109 Chinese issuers which were rated AAA by the domestic rating agencies. Fitch did not rate any of them AAA or even AA. It classified 57 of them as A and 41 as BBB. In fact, Fitch was unable to give the remaining 11 AAA issuers investment grade ratings.

There appear to be three takeaways from this month's bond market turmoil.

First, the sky is not falling and default rates remain low. Second, policymakers feel secure enough in the macroeconomic situation to address the moral hazard associated with lending to SOEs. That may mean more SOE defaults in the future but that's a price worth paying to increase the efficiency of the bond market. Third, it is imperative that the ratings on Chinese bonds meaningfully reflect firms' financial risks.

中国债券市场需要更多"违约"和更有意义的信用等级评定

2020 年 11 月 26 日

对中国企业债市场而言,2020 年 11 月并不平静。三起备受关注的违约事件在这个价值 4.2 万亿美元的世界第二大债券市场中引发动荡。由于投资者重估风险并为未来市场的走向感到不安,债券价格普遍下跌。

据近期彭博社的一篇报道,截至 2020 年 11 月 24 日,中国企业债年内违约金额共计 1,040 亿元(折合 160 亿美元),这是企业债券违约金额连续第三年超过 1,000 亿元。

在这场中国债券市场恐慌中,需要着重指出的是:中国债券市场整体违约率其实并不高。图 1 显示,虽然中国企业债违约率在 2017 年之后显著上升,但近年来企业债违约金额只占债券余额的 0.5%,这约为美国三分之一的水平。

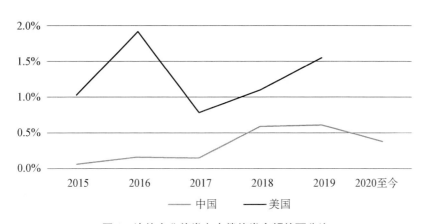

图 1 违约企业债券占未偿债券余额的百分比

数据来源:彭博社、美国证券与金融市场协会、标准普尔、万得资讯、第一财经

既然 2020 年的市场违约率水平无论是从历史上还是国际上看都不算高,那为什么市场会如此担忧呢?

一个可能的原因是本月违约的主体(采矿企业、集成电路制造商、汽车制造商)大多是国有企业。过去,中国企业债违约主体的八成都是私营企业,平均每年国企违约的次数大约只有 5 次。然而截至 2020 年 11 月底,当年已出现了 10 家国企债券违约,占比超过一半。在中国信贷市场,往往默认国企背后有着政府支持,信贷风险较私人企业更低,而这种"默认"会产生"道德风险"。对债权人来说,他们认为国企债券发行人如果出现偿债困难,政府会出手救助,所以会更倾向于向这些企业进行借款。对企业来说,如果它们坚信政府不会放任企业破产,就更可能投资风险过高的项目。道德风险削弱了中国金融市场的效率,减少"道德风险"虽然短期对投资者不利,但长期来看却有好处。

为什么现在要解决"道德风险"?

这可能是一个信号,表明决策者认为经济复苏已步入正轨,足以抵御一定的金融压力。确实,在实现了就业目标的背景下,政府正在恢复新冠肺炎疫情之前的政策,即通过提高债券市场效率和抑制过度投资来控制金融风险。

此类违约行为也可能意味着地方政府难以继续维持亏损企业的运转。永城煤电控股集团有限公司之所以违约,部分原因是将现金转移给了母公司河南能源化工集团;华晨汽车集团在违约前一个月,将其在华晨中国汽车控股有限公司的股份转让给了一家子公司,从而使该资产脱离了债权人控制。

这些行动引起了国务院金融稳定发展委员会(以下简称金融委)的关注。2020 年 11 月 21 日,国务院副总理、金融委主任刘鹤主持了金融委第四十三次会议。会议指出,要依法严肃查处欺诈发行、虚假信息披露、恶意转移资产、挪用发行资金等各类违法违规行为,严厉处罚各种"逃废债"行为,保护投资人合法权益。此外,金融委还明确要求"切实防范道德风险"。短期内可能会看到更多的国企债券违约,我们应该视其为金融委要求得到落实的一个信号。

长期以来,政策制定者一直试图增强中国资本市场的作用。扩大债券市场规模可以拓宽企业融资渠道,也可为投资者提供更多的固定收益类投资标的。在良好运行的债券市场中,信用评估的关键取决于及时准确获取信息,其中信用评级机构可以发挥关键作用。

需要注意的是,华晨汽车和永城煤电在违约前的评级都是 AAA 级,而在其他市场,拥有 AAA 级评级的企业是"不会违约"的。

图 2 显示的是标准普尔评级的债券在 1981 年至 2019 年之间的违约情况。评级为 AAA 的债券在获得该评级后的一年内从未违约,即便是企业在获得 AAA 级评级后的 15 年内,违约率也仅为 1%。评级为 B 的公司中在获得评级

的当年违约率为 3%,此后 15 年中出现违约的概率为 15%。

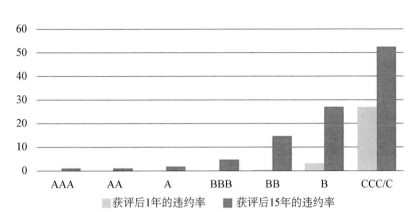

图 2 1981 年至 2019 年全球企业债违约率平均值(%)

数据来源:标准普尔、第一财经

企业的状况随着时间推移而改变,企业的偿债能力可能会降低,评级机构会将这种变化反映在评级中。根据标准普尔的数据,在美国公司违约事实发生的前 24 个月,评级中位数为 B,在前 7 个月降至 B−,在前两个月降至 CCC+。评级的下调为债券持有人提供了重要信息。

中国目前有 9 家公司拥有境内债券市场信用评级牌照,国外评级机构也设立了可以对中国境内债券进行评级的全资子公司。显然,国内与国际上的 AAA 评级仍不对等。举例来说,截至 2019 年 7 月底,中国有 109 家债券发行人被国内评级机构评为 AAA 级,但国际评级机构惠誉对这些公司的评级没有一家是 AAA,也没有一家是 AA。惠誉给其中 57 家的评级为 A 级,41 家的评级为 BBB 级,剩余 11 家惠誉无法给出投资级以上的评级。

11 月债券市场的动荡带来了三点启示。首先,天没有塌下来,违约率仍然很低。其次,政策制定者在当前宏观经济形势下感到足够安全,可以着手解决与向国企放贷相关的“道德风险”问题,这可能意味着未来会有更多的国企违约,但为了提高债券市场的效率,这个代价是值得的。第三,让中国债券评级有效地反映企业财务风险已成为当务之急。

Is China Facing a Demographic Crisis?

June 1, 2021

On May 11, the National Bureau of Statistics released the results of its seventh National Census. These once-a-decade enumerations of China's population provide the most comprehensive picture of the nation's demographics. Media reports focused on the slow growth in the overall number of people and the aging of Chinese society. They warned that China faced a "demographic crisis". Indeed, from a macroeconomic perspective, the news was not good. The key data point was the decline in the population aged 15 – 59, from 940 to 894 million since the previous census in 2010. This is China's "working-age" population. The five percent drop in the pool of potential workers — 0. 5 percent per year — represents the loss of a key input for building GDP. Looking ahead, the news only gets worse. The decline in China's working age population is expected to accelerate over the coming decades. Projections from the United Nations suggest that between 2020 and 2050, the amount of 15 – 59 year-olds will fall by 23 percent, or 0. 9 percent per year.

What does this mean for GDP growth?

According to standard models, a 1 percentage point decline in employment translates into a fall in GDP growth of 0. 55 percentage points. If a constant share of the working-age population is employed, then the projected decline in the 15 – 59 year-old group would shave 0. 5 percentage points off of annual GDP growth over the next 30 years.

China will likely grow between 4 – 5 percent per year over the next 15 years and perhaps between 2 – 3 percent per year over the following 15 years. So, losing ½ a percentage point in growth due to unfavourable demographics should not prevent Chinese people from increasing their standard of living.

However, with workers comprising a falling share of the population, their earnings will have to be spread more widely in order to support an increasing number of dependents.

Figure 1 shows the outlook for China's dependency rates to 2050, based on projections by the United Nations. China reached its demographic peak in 2008. At that time, the working-aged comprised close to 70 percent of the population, with the young and the old together accounting for the remaining 30 percent. The share of those 60 and over is expected to rise rapidly and reach 35 percent by 2050. Those under 15 will fall to 14 percent and the working-aged will account for 51 percent of the total population.

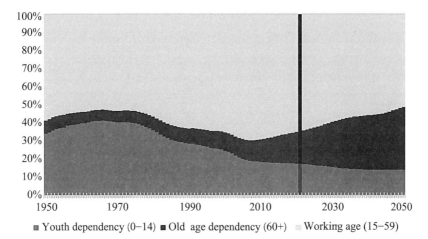

Figure 1　Distribution of China's Population

Source: UN, Yicai

China is not alone in facing this sort of demographic challenge, although its transition over the next three decades is predicted to be among the most extreme. Figure 2 shows the working-age population (here we use 15 – 64) as a share of the total population for the G20 countries in 2020 and in 2050.

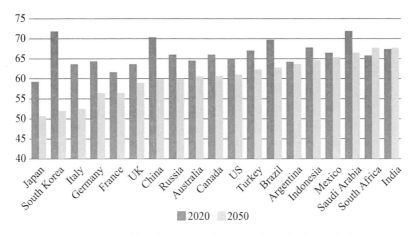

Figure 2　Working Age Population as a % of Total Population

Source: UN, Yicai

In 2020, the Chinese economy benefited from a relatively high share of working-age people. It ranked third after Saudi Arabia and South Korea. However, by 2050 China's ranking will fall to seventh lowest. Only South Korea and Italy are expected to experience more precipitous increases in dependency.

So, what can be done to manage this demographic decline?

One obvious policy response would be to increase the retirement age. In China, female workers currently retire at 55 and males at 60. These low retirement ages appear to be an artifact of earlier years, when the priority was to ensure the employment of young people. Around the world, governments are worried about the effect of poor demographics on their pension systems and they are trying to find ways to keep people employed longer. There is no reason why China cannot be part of this trend. Raising the retirement age by five years would give the Chinese economy access to a pool of close to 80 million additional workers. However, even the 15 – 64 age group is expected to decline over time (Figure 3). Suppose China gradually phased in a five-year increase in the working age over the next 30 years, consistent with the dashed line in Figure 3. The resulting decline in the working-age population would only be 10 percent, compared to the 23 percent fall in the 15 – 59 age group. Thus, raising the retirement age by five years doesn't eliminate the problem of demographic decline, but it cuts it by more than half.

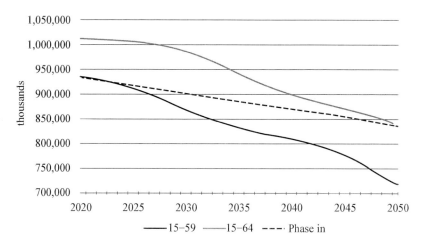

Figure 3　Effect of Raising the Retirement Age

Source: UN, Yicai

With labour increasingly at a premium, China needs to make the best possible use of its workforce. Yet, the large differences in productivity across the three broad sectors of the economy suggest potentially large gains from reallocating workers.

Figure 4 shows productivity — real GDP per worker — in agriculture, manufacturing and services. Productivity in each of these sectors has increased over time. Still, it remains much lower in agriculture than in manufacturing and services.

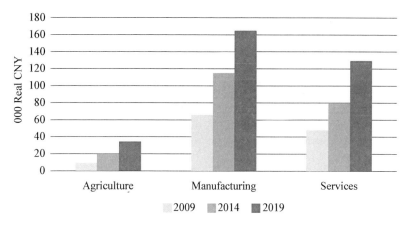

Figure 4   Real GDP per Worker

Source: Wind, Yicai

Agriculture employs about a quarter of China's workforce. What kind of productivity increase might we expect if some of these farm workers shifted to more productive undertakings? Let's do a thought experiment. Let's assume that current levels of productivity and the overall size of the labour force are unchanged. Now, let's reduce the share of workers in agriculture from 25 percent to 10 percent. This is not an extreme assumption. Agriculture's share of China's workforce actually fell by 25 percentage points over the last two decades. Moreover, in OECD countries, agriculture only employs 5 percent of the workforce. We now re-employ these workers in the service industry, where productivity is close to four times as high. In this thought experiment, the reallocation of labour raises GDP by 12 percent. If we would allow this transition to take place over 30 years, the increase in annual growth would be 0. 4 percent — enough to offset much of the impact of the decline of the 15 – 59 year-olds.

In the preceding thought experiment, we left productivity unchanged. However, it is likely that productivity will continue to increase such that a Chinese worker 30 years from now will be capable of supporting more dependents than a worker today.

One of the key channels through which productivity increases is education. According to economic theory, workers become more productive as they accumulate "human capital", which is modelled as proportional to the number of years of education. The recent census shows that China's educational attainment continued to increase. In 2020, those aged 15 and above had, on average, 9.9 years of schooling. That was up from 9.1 years in 2010 (Figure 5).

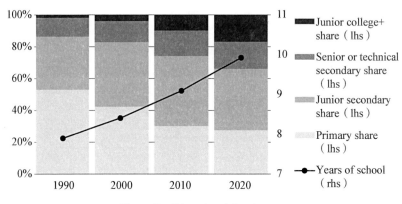

Figure 5   Educational Attainment

Source: Wind, NBS, Yicai

Over the next 30 years, it is reasonable to expect that educational attainment will increase further. Let's assume that average years of schooling rises to 12.2 years by 2050. That's where South Korea is today. By comparison, Germany is at 14.2 and Canada, Switzerland and the US are at 13.4. If human capital increases one-for-one with years of education, that means that after 12.2 years of schooling, the average worker would be 23 percent more productive than one today. Thus, the increase in productivity would fully offset the effect of the decline in the population aged 15 – 59.

The results of the census have already caused a re-think of China's population policies. This week, the government relaxed restrictions and allowed families to have three children. However, encouraging couples to have more children is likely to be difficult, especially in cities, given the high costs of living. Moreover, policies to increase the retirement age are liable to be unpopular, as Chinese grandparents provide important non-paid work, which facilitates their children's participation in the labour force. However, the good news is that further educating the workforce and reallocating it more efficiently are potentially very effective tools for managing China's demographic decline.

中国是否面临人口危机？

2021 年 6 月 1 日

　　中国的人口普查每十年一次，对中国人口情况做出最全面的统计。2021 年 5 月 11 日，中国国家统计局公布了第七次全国人口普查结果。媒体的报道聚焦总人口数量增长缓慢和中国社会老龄化问题，并警告说中国已面临"人口危机"。的确，从宏观经济角度来看，这个消息并不乐观。关键的数据是，自上次人口普查（2010 年）以来，中国的"劳动年龄"人口——15—59 岁人口从 9.4 亿下降到 8.94 亿，降幅为 5%（每年 0.5%），这意味着创造 GDP 的关键投入遭受损失。展望未来，这一消息则变得更糟。中国劳动年龄人口预计在未来几十年会加速下滑。联合国的预测表明，从 2020 年到 2050 年，15—59 岁人口的数量将下降 23%（每年 0.9%）。

　　这对 GDP 增长意味着什么？根据标准模型，就业每下降 1 个百分点意味着 GDP 增长下降 0.55 个百分点。如果劳动年龄人口的就业比例不变，那么 15—59 岁人口的预期减少将使未来 30 年的 GDP 年增长率减少 0.5 个百分点。未来 15 年，中国的 GDP 可能每年增长 4%—5%，之后的 15 年可能每年增长 2%—3%。因此，由于不利的人口结构而失去 0.5 个百分点的增长，应该不会妨碍中国人提高生活水平。然而，随着劳动人口在总人口中占比下降，他们的收入将不得不分配给越来越多的受抚养人。图 1 显示了联合国预测的中国到 2050 年的抚养比前景。中国在 2008 年达到了人口高峰。当时，劳动年龄人口占总人口近 70%，儿童和老人合计占剩余的 30%。预计 60 岁及以上人口的比例将迅速攀升，到 2050 年达到 35%。15 岁以下人口将下降到 14%，而劳动年龄人口将占总人口的 51%。

　　中国并不是唯一面临着人口挑战的国家，但预计未来 30 年中国的转型将是最极端的。图 2 显示了 2020 年和 2050 年 G20 国家劳动年龄人口（此处为 15—64 岁）占总人口的比例。

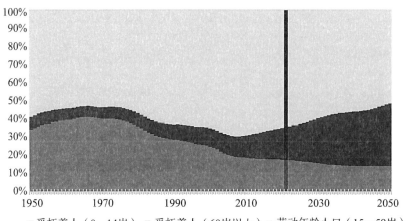

图 1　中国人口年龄分布

数据来源:联合国、第一财经

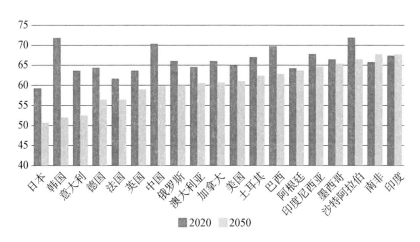

图 2　劳动年龄人口占总人口的比例(%)

数据来源:联合国、第一财经

2020 年中国经济从人口红利(相对较高的劳动年龄人口比例)中获益,中国劳动年龄人口比例位列 G20 国家第三,居沙特阿拉伯和韩国之后,但是到 2050 年,中国的排位将下降到倒数第七,届时只有韩国和意大利可能会面临受抚养人口的激增。

那么,我们该如何应对人口下降呢? 有一个很明显的办法就是延迟退休年龄。目前中国的退休年龄是女性 55 周岁,男性 60 周岁。这样的低退休年龄是早年的产物,当时的首要任务是确保年轻人的就业。各国政府现在都在担心糟糕的人口结构会影响其养老系统,都在想尽办法延长就业年限,中国自然也在其中。如果退休年龄能延迟 5 年,就可以给中国经济增加 8,000 万劳动力。但是,15—64 岁的人口也在随着时间的推移减少(见图 3)。假如中国在未来 30 年内(按照图 3 中虚线所示)逐渐推行退休年龄延迟 5 年的计划,那么劳动年龄人口只会下降 10%,而 15—59 岁人口将下降 23%。因此,虽然将退休年龄提高 5 年并不能消除人口下降的问题,但是能够将劳动年龄人口下降速度减慢一半以上。

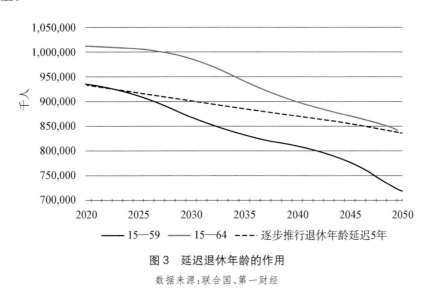

图 3　延迟退休年龄的作用

数据来源:联合国、第一财经

随着劳动力的价格越来越高,中国需要尽可能充分利用劳动力。经济的三个主要部门生产率的巨大差异说明可以从重新分配劳动力中获得巨大收益。图 4 显示的是农业、制造业和服务业的生产率(劳动者人均实际 GDP)。三个部门的生产率是随着时间推移提高的,但是农业部门的生产率要比其他两个部门低很多。

农业部门大概拥有中国四分之一的劳动力。如果能将这些劳动力转移到生产效率更高的工作中去,生产率可以提高多少呢? 我们来做一个假想实验。假设目前的生产率水平和整体的劳动力规模不变,然后把农业部门的劳动力比例从 25% 减少到 10%。其实这个假设并不极端,因为中国农业部门的劳动力比例在过去 20 年里确实下降了 25 个百分点。在经合组织国家,农业只雇用了 5% 的劳动力。现在,在服务业重新雇用这些劳动力,那里的生产率近乎是农业部门的四倍。在这个假想实验中,劳动力的再分配使 GDP 提高了 12%。如果我们

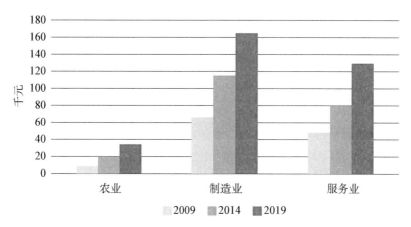

图 4 三部门劳动者人均实际 GDP

数据来源:万得资讯、第一财经

允许这种转变持续 30 年,那么年增长率将达到 0.4%,足以抵消 15—59 岁人口下降的大部分影响。

在上述假想实验中,我们假定生产率不变。但是,实际的情况是生产率是会不断提高的,30 年后一个中国劳动者将有能力养活比现在更多的受抚养人。

提高生产率的一个重要途径是教育。根据经济学理论,当劳动者积累"人力资本"时,他们的生产率就会提高,而"人力资本"与受教育年限成正比。最近的人口普查显示,中国人口受教育程度在不断提高。2020 年,全国人口中,15 岁及以上人口的平均受教育年限由 2010 年的 9.1 年提高至 9.91 年(图 5)。

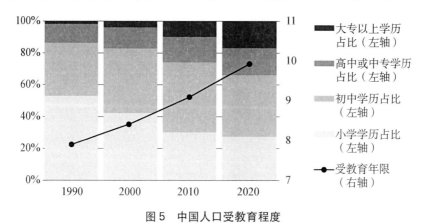

图 5 中国人口受教育程度

数据来源:万得资讯、中国国家统计局、第一财经在未来 30 年中,我们有理由相信中国人口受教育程度会进一步提高。假设到 2050 年,中国人口平均受教育年限上升到 12.2 年,就达到了现在韩国的水平。目前,德国人口平均受教育年限为 14.2 年,加拿大、瑞士和美国为 13.4 年。如果人力资本随着受教育年限的增加而一对一增加,就意味着受教育 12.2 年后,普通劳动者的生产率将比今天高出 23%。因此,生产率的提高将完全抵消 15—59 岁人口下降的影响。

人口普查的结果已经引起了中国对人口政策的重新思考。本周,中国政府放宽了限制,允许一对夫妻生育三个孩子。然而,鉴于生活成本高昂,尤其是在城市,鼓励夫妇生育更多孩子可能会很困难。此外,延长退休年龄的政策可能不受欢迎,因为在中国,祖父母和外祖父母会无偿为子女工作(比如照看孩子),以支持子女参与劳动力市场。好消息是,继续提高劳动力受教育水平并更有效地重新分配劳动力,可能是应对中国人口下降的非常有效的工具。

How Can China Promote a Sustainable Increase in Household Consumption?

March 4, 2021

The IMF's January World Economic Outlook forecasts that the global economy will grow by 5. 5 percent this year, after having declined by 3. 5 percent in 2020. Despite this rebound, the IMF expects economic activity in China's trading partners to remain quite subdued. Figure 1 compares the IMF's current GDP forecasts (the solid lines) with the one made a year ago (the dotted lines). In both Advanced Economies (AEs) and Emerging Market and Developing Economies (EMDEs) excluding China, the IMF expects that GDP will only barely return to their end-2019 levels late this year. Perhaps more importantly, the level-difference between the IMF's current forecast and the one it made a year ago is huge. For both AEs and EMDEs ex-China, the gap represents about two and a half years of lost growth.

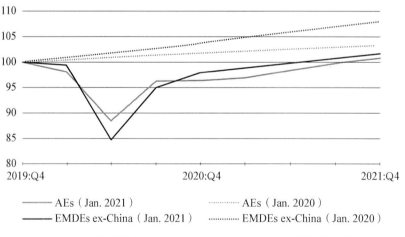

Figure 1   IMF GDP Forecast Comparisons (Indices, 2109Q4 = 100)

Source: IMF, Yicai

Despite the weakness in foreign GDP, Chinese exports were robust last year. Special factors were at work. The pandemic led foreign demand to shift from services to goods. The demand for information and communication technology and personal protective equipment was particularly strong. Since it was able to get its supply chains up and running quickly, China was particularly well placed to meet this demand. The risk is that China's trading partners have already gone on a shopping spree and their future demand for Chinese goods could weaken. Moreover, with foreign supply chains increasingly in working order, China is bound to face more export competition. Over the medium term, it will be difficult to sustain foreign demand without strong GDP growth in China's trading partners. Should the weakness abroad persist, China's household consumption will have to play a larger role in driving its economy.

Economic theory suggests that there are two ways to sustainably stimulate consumption — by reducing savings and by increasing incomes.

Government policy can lead households to reduce their savings by adjusting prices or changing risk perceptions. Such policies can allow households to feel comfortable spending more at current levels of income. Relative to policies that raise incomes, those aimed at reducing savings are more likely to have a rapid impact on spending.

Figure 2 shows that, even before the pandemic, Chinese households' expenditures grew somewhat less rapidly than their incomes. This led their already high savings rate to increase. Then, in the face of the uncertainty caused by the virus, the savings rate spiked last year. While much of that increase seems to be temporary, there appears to be room for policy to address the high rate of household saving.

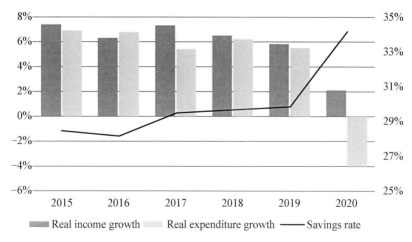

Figure 2　Chinese Household Income, Expenditure and Savings

Source: Wind, Yicai

One of the reasons that Chinese families save so much is to buy a home. The cost of housing in China's cities, relative to income, is exceptionally high. While expensive housing is largely a function of fundamentals, the government has scope to improve housing affordability. One factor that drives families to buy their apartments rather than rent is uncertainty over the future stream of their rental payments. The economics of renting often compares very favorably with those of owning. However, leases in Chinese cities are typically only one year long and there is no limit on how high a landlord can raise the rent once it has expired. Improving long-term rental policies, by adopting international best practice, could eliminate much of the uncertainty over future rental payments. This would support the market for rental properties and address a major cause of high savings.

Many apartments in Chinese cities are purchased as investments but are left vacant, rather than rented out. This is because holding costs are very low. A recurrent tax on residential property would be a good way to keep these apartments occupied and rental costs low, in line with the government's long-stated principle "housing is for living, not for speculation".

Another of households' key motivations to save is to insure themselves against unforeseen events, such as job losses or debilitating illnesses. One way to reduce such precautionary savings is through risk pooling, like employment and medical insurance. While China does have such programs, the number of people covered and the amount of coverage can be expanded. Such an expansion of the social safety net need not involve an outlay of public resources. It could be entirely funded via employee and employer contributions.

The Chinese tax system penalizes consumption and rewards saving. It relies heavily on consumption taxes. Compared to taxing incomes, taxing consumption is regressive, since poorer households spend a relatively large fraction of their incomes. A rebalancing of tax policy could redistribute income from savers to spenders and support consumption with no fiscal cost.

The government can also implement policies to raise incomes, thereby, encouraging spending. In the long run, income growth depends on improved productivity. Government policies can raise productivity by providing public goods — like high-quality education — and enhancing economic efficiency. The payoff from policies to increase productivity typically only cumulates slowly over time. It is unlikely to result in a quick boost to consumption. Nevertheless, if well-implemented, such policies are likely to be sustainable since the rise in incomes they create should support the costs of the initial investment. To increase productivity, the government could undertake policies which ensure that resources flow to their most productive ends. In particular, it should reduce barriers to the creation of a vibrant private sector by eliminating red tape and lowering costs.

In recent years, regulatory reforms have markedly improved China's business environment. According to the World Bank's Doing Business Report, China now ranks 31st out of 190 countries in terms of the ease of doing business, just ahead of France and behind Spain. In 2014, it ranked 96th, between the Maldives and the Solomon Islands.

However, the report notes that China's ranking in paying taxes (105th) and getting credit (80th) are relatively low. Doing better here would certainly help increase productivity, raise incomes and support consumption.

Policies to stimulate household consumption can have positive effects on aggregate demand. However, such demand management must be undertaken prudently. It is important to be on guard against two risks.

The first is an excessive increase in household debt. As the People's Bank of China has recently said, it is not appropriate to rely on consumer finance to expand consumption. This is because consumption itself does not generate the income needed to service the debts incurred.

The second risk is an unwarranted use of government subsidies. Consumption subsidies could be useful in some instances. Indeed, last year, 170 Chinese local governments issued consumption vouchers worth CNY 19 billion ($2.9 billion). These subsidies gave a needed boost to local economies in early 2020, when pandemic-related uncertainty was at its peak. However, vouchers cannot deliver a sustainable increase in household consumption. Fiscal resources are limited. They are best used to invest in public goods that will increase productivity or reduce uncertainty.

Last week, the Party's top leadership met to discuss the draft 14th Five-Year Plan (2021 – 2025). One of the key structural areas considered was the strategy of expanding domestic demand. It will be interesting to see what measures policymakers adopt to unleash the power of the Chinese consumer, when the Plan is unveiled later this month.

如何促进中国家庭消费的可持续增长？

2021 年 3 月 4 日

国际货币基金组织在 2021 年 1 月发布的《世界经济展望报告》中预测，2020 年全球经济下降 3.5％，2021 年将增长 5.5％。尽管出现了反弹，但国际货币基金组织预计，中国的贸易伙伴的经济活动仍将相当低迷。图 1 将国际货币基金组织目前的 GDP 预测（实线）与一年前的预测（虚线）进行了比较。国际货币基金组织预计，到今年年底，发达经济体（AEs）与除中国以外的新兴市场和发展中经济体（EMDEs ex-China）的 GDP 才能勉强恢复到 2019 年底的水平。或许更重要的是，国际货币基金组织目前的预测与一年前存在巨大差异。对于发达经济体和除中国以外的新兴市场和发展中经济体，这一差异意味着了大约两年半的增长损失。

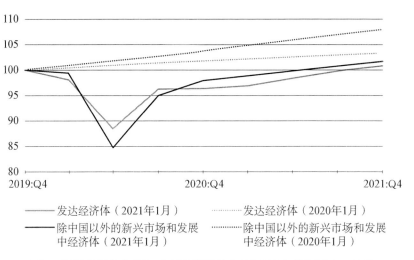

图 1 国际货币基金组织对 GDP 预测的差异（2019 年第四季度＝100）

数据来源：国际货币基金组织、第一财经

　　虽然国外经济疲软,但中国 2020 年的出口却很强劲。这是特殊因素在起作用。新冠肺炎疫情导致国外需求从服务转向商品。对信息和通信技术以及个人防护设备的需求尤其强劲。因为中国能够迅速建立和运行供应链,所以在满足这种需求方面有很大优势。风险在于,中国的贸易伙伴已经疯狂采购了一番,未来它们对中国商品的需求可能会减弱。此外,随着国外供应链日趋正常,中国必然会面临更多的出口竞争。从中期来看,如果中国的贸易伙伴没有强劲的 GDP 增长,外需将难以持续。如果国外的疲软状况持续下去,中国的家庭消费将不得不在拉动经济方面发挥更大的作用。

　　经济理论表明,有两种方法可以持续刺激消费:减少储蓄和增加收入。政府政策可以通过调整价格或改变风险认知来引导家庭减少储蓄。此类政策可以让家庭在目前的收入水平下更放心地消费。相对于提高收入的政策,旨在减少储蓄的政策更有可能对支出产生快速影响。图 2 显示,即使在新冠肺炎疫情之前,中国家庭支出的增长速度也略低于收入。这导致它们已经很高的储蓄率不断上升。随后,面对病毒带来的不确定性,2020 年储蓄率飙升。虽然大部分增长似乎是暂时的[①],但似乎还有政策空间来解决家庭储蓄率高的问题。

图 2　中国家庭的收入、支出和储蓄增速

数据来源:万得资讯、第一财经

　　中国家庭储蓄这么多的原因之一是为了买房。与收入相比,中国城市的住

[①] 中国的复苏是不平衡和不可持续的吗(https://www.yicaiglobal.com/opinion/mark.kruger/is-china-recovery-unbalanced-and-unsustainable)?

房成本极高。虽然昂贵的住房在很大程度上取决于基本面,但政府在提高住房负担能力方面仍有空间。促使家庭买房而不是租房的一个因素是未来租金流的不确定性。租房往往比买房更经济。然而,中国城市的租约通常只有一年,而且一旦到期,对于房东可以将房租提高多少没有限制。通过采用国际最佳做法来改进长期租赁政策,可以消除未来租金支付的大部分不确定性。这将支持租房市场,并解决导致高储蓄的一个主要因素。

中国城市的很多公寓是作为投资购买的,但却一直空置,而不是出租。这是因为持有成本很低。征收住房保有税将是保持这些公寓使用和降低租金成本的好方法,这也符合政府长期以来的原则,即"房子是用来住的、不是用来炒的"。

家庭储蓄的另一个主要动机是确保自己免受意外事件的影响,如失业或导致身体衰弱的疾病。减少这种预防性储蓄的一种方法是风险共担,比如就业和医疗保险。虽然中国有这样的项目,但覆盖的人数和保险金额还可以扩大。社会安全网的扩大不需要涉及公共支出,完全可以通过雇员和雇主的缴费来实现。

中国的税收制度有利于储蓄而不利于消费。其在很大程度上依赖于消费税。与所得税相比,消费税是累退的,因为较贫困的家庭花费了他们收入中相对较大的一部分。税收政策的再平衡可以将储蓄者的收入重新分配给消费者,并在没有财政成本的情况下支持消费。

政府还可以实施政策来提高收入,从而鼓励消费。从长远来看,收入增长取决于生产率的提高。政府可以通过提供公共产品(如高质量教育)和提高经济效率来提高生产率。提高生产率的政策所带来的回报通常只会随着时间慢慢累积。它不可能导致消费的快速增长。然而,如果实施得当,这些政策可能是可持续的,因为它们产生的收入增长可以承担初始投资的成本。为了提高生产率,政府可以出台政策,确保资源流向最富成效的地方。尤其应该消除繁文缛节、降低成本,从而减少障碍以创建充满活力的私营部门。

近年来,监管改革显著改善了中国的营商环境。根据世界银行《营商环境报告》,在 190 个国家中,中国的营商便利度排名第 31 位,排在西班牙之后,法国之前。2014 年中国排名第 96 位,在马尔代夫和所罗门群岛之间。然而,报告指出,中国在纳税(第 105 位)和获得信贷(第 80 位)方面排名相对较低。在这些方面做得更好,肯定有助于提高生产率,增加收入,支持消费。

刺激家庭消费的政策可以对总需求产生积极影响。然而,这种需求管理必须审慎进行。重要的是,需警惕两个风险。

第一个风险是家庭债务的过度增加。正如中国人民银行最近所指出的,不宜靠发展消费金融来扩大消费。^①因为消费本身并不产生偿还债务所需的收入。

第二个风险是政府补贴的不当使用。在某些情况下，消费补贴可能是有用的。事实上，2020 年中国有 170 个地方政府发放了价值 190 亿元(29 亿美元)的消费券。^②这些补贴在 2020 年初为地方经济提供了必要的提振，当时与疫情相关的不确定性达到了顶峰。然而，消费券无法实现家庭消费的可持续增长。财政资源是有限的，最好将其投资于可以提高生产率或减少不确定性的公共产品。

2 月 26 日，中共中央政治局召开会议，讨论了"十四五"(2021—2025 年)规划草案，涵盖的关键结构领域之一即是扩大内需战略。该规划在 3 月晚些时候公布后，可以看看决策者采取哪些措施来释放中国的消费潜力。

---

① 央行：不宜靠发展消费金融来扩大消费（https://m. 21jingji. com/article/20210208/herald/434cbce4c096ac423bc0f8521cacd3dd. html）。
② 国务院联防联控机制 5 月 8 日新闻发布会文字实录（http://www. gov. cn/xinwen/gwylflkjz116/index. htm）。

Mooncake Madness

September 25, 2020

On October 1, Chinese people will celebrate the Mid-Autumn Festival. The Festival falls on the 15th day of the 8th month of the Chinese calendar, the first full moon after the autumn equinox. On this night, the moon is at its largest and fullest.

Like Thanksgiving in North America, the Mid-Autumn Festival is a time for families to reunite. Those who cannot be together take solace in going outside, looking up and admiring the same moon at the same time as their loved ones.

Mooncakes are the Festival's traditional food. These round pastries are flavoured with a variety of sweet or savoury fillings. I am partial to Chinese date, while most of my colleagues at the Yicai Research Institute prefer egg and lotus paste.

Giving mooncakes to key business associates has become *de riguer* and firms often offer mooncakes to their employees as a holiday perk. While mooncakes come at all price points, those offered to impress contacts can sell for CNY 50 – 100 per box. First-class mooncakes are not only made with the best ingredients but are also extravagantly wrapped. Indeed, the Chinese authorities have explicitly called for limiting wasteful packaging.

Even though the Mid-Autumn Festival period is short, the imperative to give mooncakes makes these little pastries big business. In 2019, China produced 1. 4 billion mooncakes worth CNY 19. 7 billion ($2. 8 billion). Figure 1 shows that the value of mooncake sales rose by 50 percent in the last five years.

It can be very profitable to produce mooncakes and every year thousands of new mooncake bakeries are registered. About 80 percent of the mooncake bakeries are small Mom and Pop operations, with less than CNY 1 million in capital. Foreign firms are also players in this market, with mooncakes from Starbucks, Haagen Dazs and KFC being particularly sought after.

It is not unusual for people to receive a dozen boxes of mooncakes from their contacts, employers, friends and relatives. While people like to eat a mooncake or two, these delicacies are quite rich — some say that a mooncake has the same

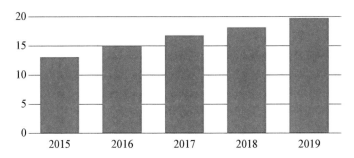

Figure 1   Value of Mooncake Sales (CNY billion)

Source: iiMedia, Yicai

calories as four bowls of rice. So, many people pass on their unwanted mooncakes, giving the best quality ones to their parents and grandparents and the lower quality ones to friends and acquaintances, many of whom are already trying to get rid of the mooncakes they have received. With everyone receiving so many mooncakes in such a short period of time, the mooncake market is typically in excess supply, as the premium put on giving exceeds the market's capacity to digest these gifts.

The rebalancing of the supply of and demand for mooncakes has been ingeniously solved through the creation of the mooncake coupon. In many cases, paper coupons are given instead of the actual confections. The coupons can be redeemed at the issuing bakery or hotel for a box of mooncakes. The portability of these coupons has also facilitated the creation of a vibrant secondary market.

As the Mid-Autumn Festival approaches, large groups of middlemen station themselves around the outlets of the most popular purveyors of mooncakes, the places people go to redeem their coupons. As market-makers, these middlemen offer to purchase your mooncake coupon at a discount or sell you a mooncake coupon should you wish to pick up one of the more prestigious brands at a great price.

The excess supply of mooncakes in the primary market has not been lost on the bakeries. They know that a significant portion of the public would accept a discount for their coupon rather than consume the mooncakes. So, they intentionally sell a volume of coupons that is in excess of their productive capacity and begin an incredible series of transactions in which everyone seems to come out better off:

- The bakery prints a CNY 100 mooncake coupon and sells it to the distributer for CNY 65.
- I buy the coupon from the distributer for CNY 80 and give it to my mother-in-law.
- She has more than enough mooncakes and sells my coupon to a middleman

for CNY 40.

- The bakery then buys back the coupon from the middleman for CNY 50.

When all the transactions are complete, the bakery earned CNY 15, the distributer earned CNY 15, the middleman earned CNY 10, I impressed my mother-in-law with a fancy gift at only a fraction of the face value and she pocketed CNY 40. We all enjoy a happy Mid-Autumn Festival, and no one had to go to the trouble of baking a mooncake!

月饼狂热

2020 年 9 月 25 日

2020 年 10 月 1 日,中国人将迎来中秋节。中秋节在农历八月十五日,即秋分后的第一个满月。这个夜晚月亮最大最圆。

与北美的感恩节一样,中秋节是个家人团聚的日子。那些不能团聚的人可以走出去,与亲人共同赏月,从而得到慰藉。

月饼是中秋的传统食物。这些圆形糕点用各种甜味或咸味的馅料制成。我喜欢红枣泥馅,而第一财经研究院的大多数同事则喜欢蛋黄莲蓉月饼。

向重要的商业伙伴赠送月饼已经成为惯例,公司也经常将月饼作为员工的节日福利。虽然月饼有各种价位,但用来送礼的月饼可以卖到每盒 50 到 100 元。一流的月饼不仅选用最好的材料制作,而且包装也很奢华。其实,政府已经明确要求限制过度包装。

中秋节虽然短暂,但送月饼势在必行,这让小糕点做成大生意。2019 年,中国生产了 14 亿个月饼,价值 197 亿元(28 亿美元)。图 1 显示,月饼销售额在过去 5 年中增长了 50%。

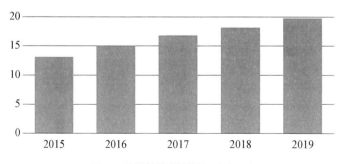

图 1　月饼销售额(单位:十亿元)

数据来源:艾媒咨询、第一财经

生产月饼利润很高，每年都有成千上万家新的月饼店注册。大约 80% 的月饼店是资本不到 100 万元的小型家庭作坊①。外国公司也是这个市场的参与者，星巴克、哈根达斯和肯德基的月饼尤其受追捧。

人们从熟人、老板、朋友和亲戚那里收到十几盒月饼是很平常的。虽然大家喜欢吃一两个月饼，但这些美食却相当油腻，有人说一个月饼的热量相当于四碗米饭。所以，很多人把不想要的月饼转送出去，质量最好的给父母和祖父母，质量较差的送给朋友和熟人，而很多熟人也想把他们收到的月饼处理掉。所有人在这么短的时间内收到如此多的月饼，月饼市场通常供大于求，因为对送礼的重视超过了市场消化这些礼物的能力。

月饼券的诞生，巧妙地解决了月饼供需的再平衡问题。在许多情况下，人们赠送纸质兑换券而不是实物。兑换券可在发行的烘焙店或酒店兑换一盒月饼。其便携性也促进形成了一个充满活力的二级市场。

随着中秋节的临近，大批"黄牛"驻扎在最受欢迎的月饼供应商的门店附近，人们去那里兑换月饼。作为做市商，这些"黄牛"会以折扣价购买你的月饼券，或以优惠的价格向你出售更知名品牌的月饼券。

烘焙店也注意到月饼在一级市场上供大于求。它们知道，相当一部分人更愿意折价卖掉月饼券，而不是消费月饼。因此，它们故意出售超过其生产能力的月饼券，并开始了一系列令人难以置信的交易②，而且最后大家都赚钱了。

- 烘焙店打印了一张 100 元的月饼券，65 元卖给了经销商。
- 我花 80 元从经销商那里买了这张券并送给了我的岳母。
- 她已经收到太多月饼，就将这张券 40 元卖给了一个"黄牛"。
- 烘焙店从"黄牛"那里 50 元买回了这张月饼券。

当所有的交易完成后，烘焙店赚了 15 元，经销商赚了 15 元，"黄牛"赚了 10 元，我花不到面值的钱送了岳母一件精美礼物，她则赚了 40 元。大家都过了个愉快的中秋节，没有人需要为制作月饼烦恼！

---

① 行业报告预测今年中秋月饼售价或小幅提升　我国连续五年新增月饼相关企业超过 1,000 家（https://finance.sina.com.cn/roll/2020-08-24/doc-iivhuipp0380604.shtml）。
② 月饼是一门怎样的生意（https://www.lianxianjia.com/zixun/149819.html）。

American Families Only Half as Rich as Those in Chinese Cities

May 12, 2020

There has been a lot of chatter in the press about the Chinese government's setting a growth target for this year and whether or not it will be able to achieve its longstanding goal of doubling incomes from 2010 to 2020.

While this year's economic prospects are clouded by uncertainty, a recent study by researchers at the People's Bank of China (PBOC) indicates that China has already achieved its objective of building a moderately prosperous society — at least in its cities.

The study, published in the latest issue of *China Finance*, highlights the results of a comprehensive survey of urban families' finances conducted at the end of 2019. It reports that median household net worth stood at RMB 1. 41 million or close to $200,000.

The US's own Survey of Consumer Finances was last conducted by the Federal Reserve (Fed) in 2016. If I adjust its findings for inflation, then median US household net worth was about $104,000 in 2019 dollars. Thus, one can say that the typical US household is only about half as rich as the typical Chinese urban family.

Since per capita GDP in the US is close to five times higher than in China, how can we explain such a surprising result?

The very unequal distribution of wealth in the US is a big part of the story. Figure 1 shows that while median US household wealth is about half that of Chinese urban families, average US household net worth is about 80 percent higher than China's $413,000.

The ratio of average to median net worth is a measure of how equally wealth is distributed. If everyone's wealth was exactly the same, the ratio of the two net worth measures would be 1. 0. China's mean household net worth is double its median. The ratio in the US is seven times, pointing to a much more unequal distribution of wealth.

Since it lies right in the middle of the wealth distribution, we can think of the

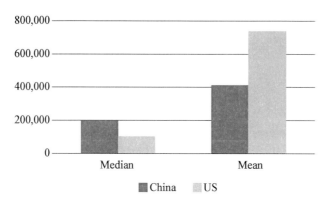

Figure 1　Household Net Worth (US $)
Source: PBOC, US Federal Reserve, Yicai

median household as "typical". Half the families are richer and half the families are poorer than it is. On average, American families are wealthier than Chinese ones. There are a lot of really wealthy American families that pull that average up. But the typical American household remains poorer than its Chinese urban counterpart. Note that I am making these comparisons in 2019 US dollars and am not accounting for the fact that a US dollar buys more in China than it does in the US.

A second reason that Chinese urban households are relatively wealthy is that home ownership is quite widespread. According to the PBOC study, 96 percent of urban households own residential property. The corresponding figure for the US is only 64 percent. The gap between US and Chinese in home ownership is even more striking at the low end of the income distribution. In the US, only one-third of the families in the lowest income quintile own a home. In China, 89 percent do.

In fact, many Chinese families own more than one property: 31 percent of them have two and 11 percent have three or more. On average, each urban family owns 1. 5 residential properties.

Chinese family wealth does not simply rest on inflated real estate values. Residential property represents just under 60 percent of household assets, with financial assets and other real assets (shops, productive equipment, vehicles, etc.) each accounting for close to 20 percent. Moreover, from the information in the study, I estimate that the price-to-income ratio of these households' residential property holdings at 3. 7. This is fairly close to the median house price-to-income ratio in the US, 3. 6, according to Demographia's most recent survey.

The third reason for Chinese urban households' high net worth is their relatively low indebtedness. Seventy-seven percent of US households have assumed some sort of financial liability (a mortgage, a car loan, student debt, etc.). In

China, only 57 percent of the urban households have incurred such liabilities. Not only do fewer Chinese households carry liabilities, but what debts they owe are small relative to their assets. The debts of the median Chinese household, which does have liabilities, only amounts to 16 percent of its assets. In contrast, the median indebted American household has a leverage ratio of 36 percent of its assets.

The final piece of the puzzle is understanding how Chinese urban households can have such a high rate of home ownership and such a low rate of indebtedness.

Chinese households do have much higher savings rates than their US counterparts and that is an important factor. But more important was the way in which the housing stock was privatized. Up until the late 1990s, almost all residential property belonged to state-owned institutions, which provided low-rent accommodation to their employees. As part of the state-owned enterprise reform program, the government relieved firms of the burden of providing housing for their workers. Urban households were able to purchase their apartments from their employers at reasonable prices, leading to today's high rate of home ownership and supporting urban prosperity.

美国家庭只有中国城市家庭一半富有

2020 年 5 月 12 日

关于中国政府 2020 年的增长目标,以及能否实现 2010 年至 2020 年收入翻番的长期目标,媒体上有很多讨论。

尽管 2020 年的经济前景充满不确定性,但中国人民银行最近的一项研究表明,中国至少在城市已经实现了建设小康社会的目标。

该研究发表在最新一期的《中国金融》上,重点介绍了 2019 年底对城市家庭财务状况进行的全面调查结果。报告称,中国家庭净资产中位数为 141 万元,接近 20 万美元。

美国联邦储备系统(以下简称"美联储")最近一次消费者财务调查是在 2016 年进行的。如果根据通货膨胀调整其调查结果,那么 2019 年美国家庭的净资产中位数约为 10.4 万美元。因此,可以说典型美国家庭的财富只有中国城市家庭的一半左右。

然而,美国的人均 GDP 比中国高近五倍,我们如何解释这个出人意料的结果?

美国的财富分配极度不均衡,这是其中一个重要原因。图 1 显示,虽然美国家庭财富中位数约为中国城市家庭的一半,但其平均净资产则比中国的 41.3 万美元高出约 80%。

家庭净资产的平均数与中位数之比是衡量财富分配平均程度的指标。如果每个人的财富完全相同,那么两个数值的比率将是 1.0。中国家庭平均净资产是中位数的两倍,美国是七倍,表明其财富分配更不平等。

由于恰好位于财富分布的中间位置,我们可以把中位数家庭视为"典型"。一半的家庭比它富有,另一半比它贫穷。平均而言,美国家庭比中国家庭富裕。美国有很多相当富有的家庭,这拉高了平均水平。但典型的美国家庭仍然比中国城市家庭更穷。请注意,我是在 2019 年美元基础上进行比较的,并没有考虑

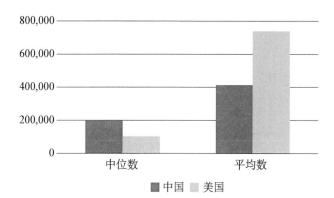

图1 中美家庭净资产(单位:美元)

数据来源:中国人民银行、美联储、第一财经

美元在中国的购买力比在美国强这一事实。

中国城市家庭相对富裕的第二个原因是住房拥有相当普遍。根据中国人民银行的调查,96%的城市家庭拥有房产。在美国,这一比例仅为64%。在低收入群体中,中美在住房拥有方面的差距更加显著。在美国,收入最低的20%家庭中只有三分之一拥有住房。在中国,这一比例高达89%。

事实上,许多中国家庭拥有不止一套房产。31%的家庭拥有两套房子,11%拥有三套或更多房子。平均每个城市家庭拥有1.5套房子。

中国家庭的财富并不仅仅依赖于膨胀的房地产价值。住宅资产占家庭资产的比例不到60%,而金融资产和其他实体资产(店铺、生产设备、车辆等)各占近20%。另外,根据央行研究中的信息,我估计这些家庭的房价收入比为3.7。这与Demographia最新调查①的美国房价收入比的中位数(3.6)非常接近。

中国城市家庭净资产高的第三个原因是它们的负债率相对较低。77%的美国家庭有金融债务(房屋抵押贷款、汽车贷款、学生债务等),而中国只有57%的城镇家庭有这种债务。整个中国家庭负债的占比很小,而且它们所欠的债务相对于资产来说比较少。中国的中位数家庭的确有负债,但债务仅占资产的16%。相比之下,美国中位数家庭的负债占其资产的比例高达36%。

谜底的最后一部分是弄清楚为何中国城市家庭有如此高的房屋拥有率和如此低的负债率。

① 16th Annual Demographia International Housing Affordability Survey(http://demographia.com/dhi16-intro.pdf)。

中国家庭的储蓄率确实比美国高得多,这是一个重要因素。但更重要的是其住房存量私有化的方式。直到 20 世纪 90 年代末,中国几乎所有的房产仍然属于国有单位,这些单位为员工提供低租金的住宿。作为国企改革计划的一部分,政府减轻了企业为员工提供住房的负担。城镇家庭得以用合理的价格从雇主那里购买公寓,从而造就了今天的高房屋拥有率,并为城市繁荣添砖加瓦。

How Should We Think About Rising Home Prices?

June 24, 2021

It seems like they are everywhere. Mostly male, they are dressed in black trousers, white shirts and dark ties. They typically have whiteboards on which they list apartments' dimensions, their number of rooms and the asking price.

When I linger to look at the information — I'm a numbers guy after all — they approach eagerly and ask if I'm looking to buy. When I tell them I already have a place, they ask if I want to sell.

China's always vibrant property market has gone into overdrive this year. The National Bureau of Statistics recently reported that in the first five months of the year, sales of newly constructed residential property were just under 600 million square metres (Figure 1). That's up by more than a fifth from pre-pandemic levels.

Notwithstanding the surge in sales, the increase in new home prices has been modest. According to the 100-city data compiled by the China Index Academy, home prices were up just over 4 percent year-over-year in May, well below the recent peak of 19 percent in January 2017.

Home prices have not spiked, in part, because developers have been able to satisfy demand by selling out of inventory. In the past three years, the volume of newly-started projects well-exceeded sales, which had peaked in 2018 (Figure 1). With supply exceeding demand, price pressures have been contained.

The concern is that this inventory may dry up soon and home price inflation could return to the high rates recorded five years ago. The data show that we could, indeed, be at a turning point.

To illustrate demand pressures, I have constructed a "sales gap" measure, which is the monthly volume of sales minus the volume of starts, expressed as a percentage of sales. I smooth the series by taking a 12-month moving average. An increase in the sales gap implies rising excess demand for housing. The year-over-year change in the 100-city price index has tracked the sales gap fairly well since 2012 (Figure 2). The recent rise in the sales gap suggests that we should brace ourselves for higher home price inflation in the coming months.

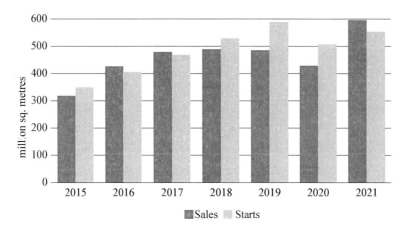

Figure 1　Newly Constructed Residential Property (Jan. – May)

Source: Wind, Yicai

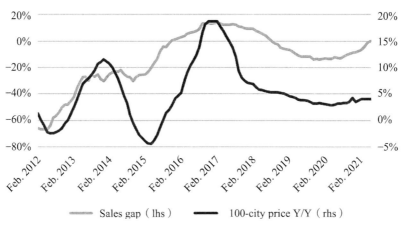

Figure 2　Sales Gap and Home Prices

Source: Wind, Yicai

Senior Chinese officials are also concerned about emerging price pressures. Guo Shuqing, the Chairman of the China Banking and Insurance Regulatory Commission, warned of serious real estate bubbles, in some areas, during the recent Lujiazui Forum.

In order to get a more nuanced picture of home price dynamics, we turn to data collected by RIWI, which uses patented, machine-learning technology to reach the broadest possible set of respondents by continuously drawing in populations otherwise not included in surveys.

In China, anyone using the Web could be randomly exposed to a RIWI survey. The vast majority of RIWI's Chinese respondents have never or rarely taken surveys before. Typically, Chinese surveys only draw on those living in key urban centres and on habitual, incentivized survey respondents. Or they use content drawn from social media. RIWI's surveys are anonymous, continuous, random and do not collect personally identifiable information, increasing the likelihood that respondents will answer authentically.

Between January and June 2021 (and ongoing), we used RIWI technology to randomly engage respondents from China's Web-using population to answer questions about their economic behavior, including how the value of their homes had changed over the past 12 months. The resulting data were gathered 24/7 and on a continuous basis. The responses came from all over China, including all tiers of cities. RIWI's respondents are un-incentivized. They answer the survey because the questions seem interesting.

Based on close to 11,000 responses, the RIWI data show an average home price increase of 5.5 percent for the period January – May. This compares to 4.0 percent for the China Index Academy. RIWI respondents likely reported the change in their existing homes, while the China Index Academy's 100-city data covers new-home prices.

We sorted the sample into six groups by home-price change: those whose prices fell, those that remained the same, and those whose prices rose by 5, 10, 15 or 20 percent and more. We also divided the respondents into three regions: Beijing, Shanghai and everywhere else in China.

The distribution of the price groups was strikingly similar across all three regions (Figure 3). This suggests that price dynamics are driven by intra-rather than inter-regional factors. Most of the responses cluster around a zero price change. However, the distribution has a "fat tail" with 15 percent of respondents reporting a price change of 20 percent or more.

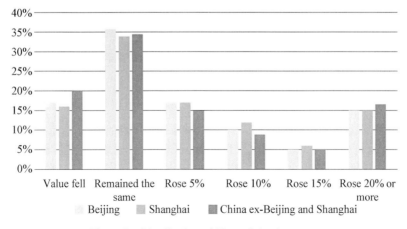

Figure 3   Distribution of Home Price Increases

Source: RIWI, Yicai

We estimate that the properties in the fat tail had an outsized influence on the aggregate price change. This relatively small group contributed 64 percent to the price increase in Shanghai, 68 percent to the price increase in Beijing and it accounted for three-quarters of the price increase elsewhere in China (Figure 4).

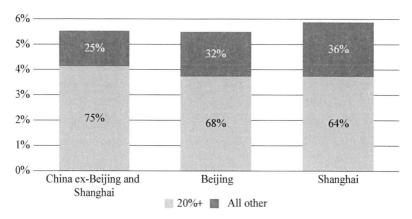

Figure 4　Jan. – May Home Price Inflation: Contributions by Price Change Group

Source: RIWI, Yicai

The RIWI data imply the price pressures we are seeing are narrowly based in a relatively small share of properties. What do we know about the people who own these homes?

It turns out that their owners earn higher incomes, are better educated and are more likely to own their own companies than those in the rest of the sample. From these characteristics, we can assume that they live in better housing. The relatively rapid increase in the price of better housing suggests that the demand for upgrades is what's driving home price inflation.

This is not surprising. Many Chinese apartments are small. Relatively few have elevators, with the six-floor walk up being a popular configuration. And there is a strong demand for apartments in good school catchment areas, which sell at premium prices. With the strong increase in incomes in recent years, it is understandable that Chinese families are willing and able to spend more on housing.

If the demand for upgrades is driving home price inflation, there are implications for policy as well. Implementing broad-based measures may be inappropriate should the authorities want to manage rising price pressures. Instead, they may want to focus more narrowly on policies which increase the supply of and reduce the demand for higher-end real estate.

For many observers, China's demographic decline means that the country has already reached "peak housing". However, the implication of the granular data provided by RIWI's surveys is that the demand for upgrades could be a source of strength for years to come. And that's good news for all those guys with the whiteboards.

我们应该如何看待房价不断上涨？

2021 年 6 月 24 日

这些人似乎无处不在。大多是男性，身着黑色长裤、白色衬衫和深色领带。他们通常带着白板，上面列出房屋面积、房间数量和报价。

当擅长和数字打交道的我停下来看这些信息的时候，他们热切地走过来问我是否想买房。我告诉他们我已经有房子了，他们又问我是否想卖。

2021 年，中国一向活跃的房地产市场进入超速发展期。中国国家统计局最近发布报告称，2021 年前 5 个月，全国新建住宅的销售面积略低于 6 亿平方米（图 1）。[①] 这比新冠肺炎疫情前的水平高出了五分之一以上。

尽管销量激增，但新房价格的涨幅不大。根据中指研究院编制的百城数据[②]，5 月份房价同比上涨略高于 4%，远低于 2017 年 1 月 19% 的近期峰值。

房价没有飙升，部分原因是开发商通过出售库存就能满足需求。近三年，新开工项目量远超销量，而销量早在 2018 年就达到峰值（图 1）。由于供大于求，价格压力得到了控制。

令人担忧的是，这些库存可能很快就会枯竭，而房价涨幅也会回到 5 年前的高位。数据显示，或许我们确实正处于一个转折点。

为了解释需求压力，我构建了一个"销售缺口"指标，即每月销量与开工量之差占销量的百分比。通过取 12 个月的移动平均值来显示平滑曲线。销售缺口的扩大意味着对住房的过度需求上升。自 2012 年以来，百城价格指数的同比变化很好地追踪了销售缺口（图 2）。最近销售缺口的扩大表明，我们应该为未来几个月的房价上涨做好准备。

---

① 2021 年 1—5 月份全国房地产开发投资和销售情况（http://www. stats. gov. cn/tjsj/zxfb/202106/t20210616_1818430. html）。

② 中指研究院百城价格指数（https://academy. cih-index. com/en/reports. html）。

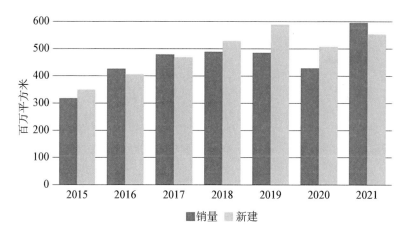

图1 新建住宅(1—5月)

数据来源:万得资讯、第一财经

图2 销售缺口和房价

数据来源:万得资讯、第一财经

监管部门也对新出现的价格压力感到担忧。中国银行保险监督管理委员会(以下简称"银保监会")主席郭树清在最近的陆家嘴论坛上警告称,一些地区存在严重的房地产泡沫。[1]

为了更细致地了解房价动态,我们求助RIWI公司[2]收集的数据,该公司利用专利机器学习技术,通过不断吸引原本不包括在调查范围内的人群,来覆盖尽

---

① 郭树清陆家嘴论坛金句频现,暗讽美国大量印钞、苦口婆心劝投资者理智(https://finance.sina.cn/hy/2021-06-10/detail-ikqcfnca0222269.d.html?from=wap)。

② RIWI官网(www.riwi.com)。

可能广泛的受访者群体。

在中国,任何使用互联网的人都可能随机接触到 RIWI 的调查。RIWI 中的绝大多数中国受访者以前从未或很少接受过调查。通常,中国的调查只针对生活在主要城市中心的人,以及有调查习惯的、受礼品激励的受访者,或者使用社交媒体的内容。RIWI 的调查是匿名、连续和随机的,不收集个人身份信息,增加了受访者真实回答的可能性。

2021 年 1—6 月(仍在进行中),我们使用 RIWI 技术,从中国网络用户中随机抽取受访者询问有关他们经济行为的问题,包括房产价值在过去 12 个月中的变化。由此产生的数据全天候持续收集。受访者来自中国各地,涵盖所有级别的城市。RIWI 的受访者没有拿任何奖励。他们参与调查是因为这些问题看起来很有趣。

基于近 11,000 份回复,RIWI 的数据显示,1—5 月平均房价涨幅为 5.5%,而中指研究院的数据为 4.0%。RIWI 的受访者很可能报告了他们现有住房的价格变化,而中指研究院的百城数据则涵盖了新房价格。

我们根据房价变化将样本分为 6 组:房价下跌、房价不变、房价上涨 5%、10%、15% 以及房价上涨 20% 及以上。我们还将受访者分为 3 个区域:北京、上海和中国其他地区。

在这 3 个地区,价格变化组的分布情况惊人地相似(图 3)。这表明价格动态是由区域内而不是区域间因素驱动的。大多数的反馈都集中在价格不变附近。不过,这一分布情况拖着一个"肥尾",有 15% 的受访者报告其房价上涨了 20% 或更多。

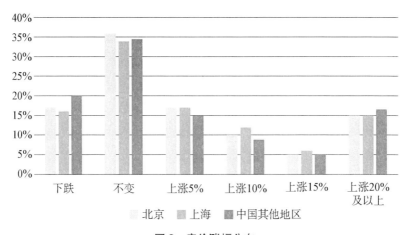

图 3　房价涨幅分布

数据来源:RIWI、第一财经

我们估计,肥尾组的房产对总的房价变化产生了巨大影响。这个相对较小的价格组贡献了上海64%的房价上涨,北京68%的上涨,以及中国其他地区四分之三的上涨(图4)。

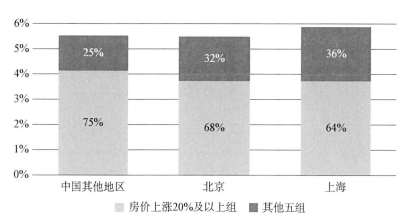

图4 1—5月房价上涨:各价格变化组的贡献

数据来源:RIWI、第一财经

RIWI的数据意味着,我们所看到的价格压力仅源于少数房产。我们对拥有这些房产的人了解多少呢?

事实证明,与样本中的其他人相比,这些房产的所有者收入和受教育程度更高,更有可能拥有自己的公司。根据这些特征,我们可以假设他们住在更好的房子里。这类住房价格的相对快速上涨表明,对房屋升级的需求是推动房价上涨的原因。

这并不奇怪。中国的很多公寓都很小。有电梯的相对较少,没有电梯的6层住宅楼很常见。优质学校学区房的需求旺盛,而且售价极高。随着近年来收入的大幅增长,中国家庭愿意也有能力在住房上花费更多,这是可以理解的。

如果升级房屋的需求在推动房价上涨,那么政策也会受到影响。如果监管部门想要应付价格上涨的压力,实施广泛的措施可能不大合适。相反,它们可能希望更小心地专注于增加高端房地产供应并减少对其需求的政策。

对于许多观察人士来说,中国劳动年龄人口的减少[1]意味着它已经达到了"住房高峰"。然而,RIWI调查提供的详细数据表明,升级住房的需求可能是未来几年的动力来源。这对那些在街边拿着白板的中介来说是个好消息。

---

[1] 中国是否面临人口危机(https://www.yicaiglobal.com/opinion/mark.kruger/is-china-facing-a-demographic-crisis)?

Property Developers' Debt: Taking Aim at the Grey Rhino

July 29, 2021

Property developers are having a tough year.

In the first half of 2021, there have been several high-profile defaults: China Fortune Land in February, Chongqing Sincere Property in March and Sichuan Languang Development this month. Now, all eyes are on China Evergrande Group, which is the country's most indebted developer and whose stock and bond prices have fallen sharply. At first glance, the timing of the developers' difficulties seems odd. The market for residential property is red-hot. The volume of new home sales in the first half of the year is up close to 30 percent from last year and close to 20 percent from a pre-pandemic 2019. But developers' problems are structural, not cyclical. Their business model involves borrowing large sums to acquire land and then constructing apartment blocks, which typically take three years to complete. Over time, land prices have risen rapidly, increasing the amount developers must finance and putting pressure on their debt-fueled business model. Moreover, competitive pressure has led to more industry concentration. There are close to 100,000 property developers in China, but the share of sales accounted for by the top-three and top-thirty firms has almost tripled over the last ten years (Figure 1).

Even as the business of property development has become more challenging, the authorities have become increasingly concerned about developers' indebtedness and its implications for financial stability. Last August, Guo Shuqing, the Chairman of the China Banking and Insurance Regulatory Commission, called real estate the biggest threat to China's financial stability. He referred to it as a "grey rhino" — a highly probable and potentially high-impact risk, but one that attracts insufficient attention. While the authorities have always been mindful of the property market, last autumn, they asked developers to comply with a series of guidelines to improve their creditworthiness. These guidelines are limiting their ability to borrow and making their financial stress more acute.

How big is the grey rhino? How much do property developers' owe and who are

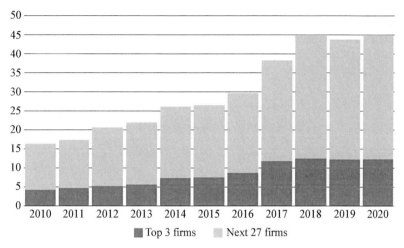

Figure 1   Sales Concentration Ratios (%)

Source: Wind, Yicai

their creditors?

According to the National Bureau of Statistics, developers' total liabilities amounted to CNY 76 trillion in 2019. That's a huge number. To put it in context, GDP that year was CNY 99 trillion. It is important to note that a large portion of developers' liabilities represent advanced purchase payments that homebuyers have made for their apartments. These liabilities do not bear interest. They are a type of interest-free loan to the developers. Moreover, they do not have a specific maturity. The buyers assume the risk for construction delays, which extends the time between their prepayment and move-in dates.

Let's do an add up of developers' interest-bearing liabilities, which are largely funded by the banks, the trust companies and the bond markets. As at the end of 2020, Chinese banks had CNY 49.5 trillion in real estate-related loans outstanding. Of these, CNY 34.4 trillion were personal mortgage loans. The remaining CNY 15.1 trillion — about 11 percent of the banks' overall loan book — appear to be loans for property development. Trust companies have a somewhat larger exposure to developers. As at the end of 2020, 14 percent of trusts' funds were invested in real estate, a total of CNY 22.8 trillion. The International Capital Markets Association (ICMA) estimates that, at end-2020, developers' outstanding bonds in the onshore market totalled CNY 2.1 trillion. According to ICMA, developers also had $165.5 billion (CNY 1.1 trillion) outstanding in offshore bonds. While their exposure in the onshore market is about 6 percent of the value of all bonds outstanding, their offshore exposure accounted for just under a quarter of the entire market.

Adding up the funds raised from these four sources, we estimate that property developers' interest bearing liabilities amounted to CNY 41. 1 trillion at the end of last year (Figure 2). This is still a very large sum, equal to 40 percent of GDP and about a quarter of all non-financial corporate finance outstanding.

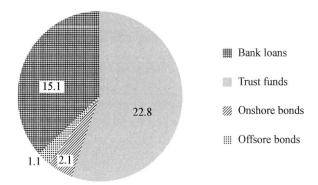

Figure 2　Property Developers' Interest-Bearing Liabilities (end – 2020, CNY trillion)
Source: Wind, ICMA, Yicai

The authorities are concerned about developers' leverage for three reasons. First, the sheer size of their liabilities represents financial stability risks — especially to the banks and the trusts. Second, the developers' ability to borrow increases the cost of housing. This is because it allows developers to bid aggressively against each other at land auctions, driving up the price of land and the cost of the finished apartment. Third, the significant resources currently devoted to property development are not available to invest in projects that are more likely to increase the long-run productivity of the economy.

To address these concerns, the authorities have, for some time, put rules around how much banks could lend to property developers and the uses to which these funds could be put. Last fall, a new and colourful framework was introduced to reinforce the health of developers' balance sheets. Called the "Three Red Lines", this framework links the amount of borrowing a developer can undertake to its ability to respect thresholds for three financial ratios: liabilities (less prepayments for apartments) divided by assets, net debt divided by equity and cash divided by short-term debt (Table 1). A developer who is able to respect all three thresholds, is classified as "green" and is permitted to increase its debt by a maximum of 15 percent per year. In contrast, one that breaches all three thresholds is classified as "red" and is not permitted to increase its borrowings.

Table 1   Three Red Lines Framework

Red Lines	Financial Ratio	Threshold
Leverage	Liabilities (ex-buyers' prepayments)/Assets	<70 percent
Gearing	Net debt/Equity	<100 percent
Liquidity	Cash/Short-term debt	>100 percent

Classification	Number of Red Lines Breached	Max. Annual Debt Growth
Red	3	0 percent
Orange	2	5 percent
Yellow	1	10 percent
Green	0	15 percent

Source: The People's Bank of China, Ministry of Housing and Urban-Rural Development

The framework was first applied to the largest developers, which have three years to fully comply with the three red lines. However, it is expected to be gradually expanded to smaller- and medium-sized developers over time.

Developers are implementing the framework by cutting the prices of new apartments to increase cashflow, selling non-core assets and seeking operational efficiencies. Indeed, it appears that they are making progress. In April, Bloomberg reported that 33 of the 66 major developers it tracks met all three of the thresholds. This was an improvement from only 14 developers in October. While Evergrande is deleveraging, it still doesn't meet any of the thresholds. It recently stated that it reduced its interest-bearing debt from CNY 717 billion, as at the end of 2020, to around CNY 570 billion. Last year, it committed to reducing its interest-bearing debt by CNY 150 billion a year over three years and to achieving a "green" rating by 2022. Meanwhile, the authorities are taking no chances. They reportedly asked the banks to stress test their exposures to Evergrande and assess the impact on their capital of potential losses on their loans to the developer.

While these are clearly difficult times for China's property developers, at least they can take advantage of the cyclical strength of sales to facilitate their deleveraging. Moreover, it is a good sign that the macroeconomic recovery is sufficiently robust and China can focus on reining in financial risks.

It's challenging to protect the system from black swans. By their nature, these risks are hard to quantify and difficult to predict. However, it is only prudent to take aim at grey rhinos once conditions permit.

房地产开发商债务：瞄准"灰犀牛"

2021 年 7 月 29 日

房地产开发商正在度过艰难的一年。

2021 年上半年发生了几起备受瞩目的违约事件：2 月华夏幸福，3 月重庆协信地产，以及本月四川蓝光发展。现在，所有的注意力都集中在中国负债最多的房地产开发商恒大集团身上。到目前为止，该集团的股价和债券价格大幅下跌。乍一看，房地产开发商遭遇困难的时机似乎有些奇怪。楼市依然火热，今年上半年新房销售量同比增长近 30%，比新冠肺炎疫情前的 2019 年增长了近 20%。但开发商的问题是结构性的，而不是周期性的。它们的商业模式包括借入大量的资金购买土地，然后建造公寓楼，通常需要 3 年时间才能完工。随着时间的推移，土地价格快速上涨，这增加了开发商必须通过融资获得的资金量，并对其债务驱动的商业模式造成压力。此外，竞争压力导致了更高的行业集中度。中国有近 10 万家房地产开发商，在过去 10 年中，前 3 名和前 30 名公司的销售份额几乎增加了两倍（图 1）。

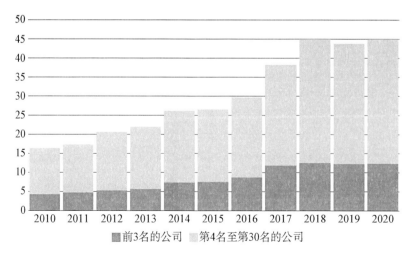

图 1　销售额集中度（%）

数据来源：万得资讯、第一财经

随着房地产开发业务变得更具挑战性,监管部门越来越担心开发商的债务问题及其对金融稳定的影响。去年8月,银保监会主席郭树清表示,房地产是中国金融稳定的最大威胁。他称之为"灰犀牛"——一种没有引起足够关注,但极有可能发生,并且具有潜在高影响的风险。监管部门一直关注着房地产市场,去年秋天,它们要求开发商遵守一系列准则来提高自己的信用度。这些准则限制了它们的借贷能力,使它们的财务压力更加严重。

灰犀牛有多大?房地产开发商欠多少钱?它们的债权人是谁?国家统计局的数据显示,2019年开发商负债总额达到76万亿元。这是一个巨大的数字。那一年,中国的GDP是99万亿元。值得注意的是,开发商的负债很大一部分是购房者为其公寓支付的预付款。这些负债不支付利息。这是开发商的无息贷款。此外,它们没有具体的到期时间。买家承担施工延误的风险,这将延长他们提前付款和入住之间的时间。

让我们来计算一下开发商的有息负债,主要由银行、信托公司和债券市场提供资金。截至2020年底,中国各银行的房地产相关贷款余额49.5万亿元。其中,个人住房抵押贷款34.4万亿元,剩下的15.1万亿元(约占银行贷款总额的11%)似乎是房地产开发贷款。信托公司对开发商的敞口要大一些。截至2020年底,14%的信托资金投向房地产,总额22.8万亿元。国际资本市场协会(ICMA)估计,2020年底,在岸市场开发商未偿还债券总额为2.1万亿元。该协会称,开发商未偿还的离岸债券达1,655亿美元(约1.1万亿元人民币)。尽管它们在在岸市场的敞口仅约为所有未偿债券价值的6%,但它们在离岸市场的敞口占整个市场的近四分之一。

将这四个渠道筹集的资金相加,我们估计2020年底房地产开发商的有息负债为41.1万亿元(见图2)。这仍然是一个非常大的数额,相当于GDP的40%,约占所有非金融企业未偿融资的四分之一。

监管部门之所以担心开发商的杠杆问题,有三个原因。首先,这些开发商庞大的债务规模意味着金融稳定风险——尤其是对银行和信托机构而言。其次,开发商的借款能力增加了住房成本。这是因为它允许开发商在土地拍卖中积极竞标,推高土地价格和竣工公寓的成本。第三,目前用于房地产开发的大量资源无法用于投资那些更有可能提高经济长期生产率的项目。

为了解决这些问题,监管部门此前对银行可以向房地产开发商提供多少贷款以及这些资金的用途做出了规定,并在去年秋天引入了一个全新的丰富多彩的框架,从而使开发商的资产负债表更加健康。这个框架被称为"三道红线",将

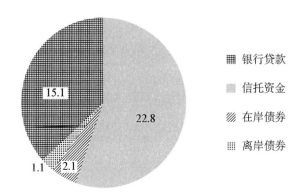

图例：
- ▦ 银行贷款
- ▧ 信托资金
- ▨ 在岸债券
- ▥ 离岸债券

图2　房地产开发商的有息负债(截至 2020 年,万亿元)

数据来源:万得资讯、国际资本市场协会、第一财经

开发商的可贷金额与它们遵守三个财务比率标准的能力联系起来。这三个标准是:剔除预收款项后的资产负债率、净负债率和现金短债比(见表1)。满足全部标准的开发商被归入"绿色"档,负债年增速不得超过 15%。三道红线均触线的公司则被归入"红色"档,不得新增有息负债。

表1　"三道红线"框架

红线	财务比率	标准
杠杆	剔除预收款项后的资产负债率	<70%
杠杆	净负债率	<100%
流动性	现金短债比	>100%

档位	触及红线数	最大有息负债规模年增速
红色	3	0%
橙色	2	5%
黄色	1	10%
绿色	0	15%

数据来源:中国人民银行、中国住房和城乡建设部

　　该框架首先应用于最大的开发商,它们有 3 年的时间进行调整,以完全遵守三条红线。但随着时间的推移,有望逐步扩展到中小开发商。

　　开发商正在通过降低新公寓的价格以增加现金流、出售非核心资产和寻求

提高运营效率来落实该框架。事实上，它们似乎已经取得了进展。2021 年 4 月，彭博社报道称，在其追踪的 66 家主要开发商中，有 33 家达到了全部三个标准，这比 2020 年 10 月只有 14 家开发商达到的情况有所改善。恒大虽然正在去杠杆，但还是不符合任何标准。恒大最近表示，已将有息负债从 2020 年底的 7,170 亿元降至约 5,700 亿元。2020 年，恒大承诺在 3 年内每年减少 1,500 亿元有息负债，到 2022 年实现"绿色"评级。同时，监管部门并不冒险。据报道，它们要求银行对恒大的风险敞口进行压力测试，并评估其潜在损失对资本的影响。虽然现在是中国房地产开发商的艰难时期，但至少它们可以利用销售的周期性优势来推动去杠杆化。此外，这预示着足够强劲的宏观经济复苏，中国可以专注于控制金融风险。保护系统免受黑天鹅攻击是一项挑战。就其性质而言，这些风险难以量化和预测。然而，一旦条件允许，瞄准灰犀牛是明智的。

Why Not Eliminate Corporate Income Taxes?

April 4, 2021

The US is looking to build a global consensus for a minimum corporate tax rate of 21 percent.

From the US's perspective, it is easy to see why such a proposal makes sense. The Biden Administration is looking to spend $2.3 trillion on infrastructure projects over the next eight years. It wants to finance these projects by raising corporate income taxes. The Administration worries that higher tax rates could encourage firms to move from the US to lower-tax jurisdictions. Getting international agreement on a high minimum corporate tax rate reduces that risk.

In many countries, including Hungary (9 percent), Ireland (12.5 percent) and Lithuania (15 percent), the corporate tax rate is well below 21 percent (the dotted line in Figure 1). Should a consensus form around the US's proposal, these countries would be forced to overhaul their tax systems.

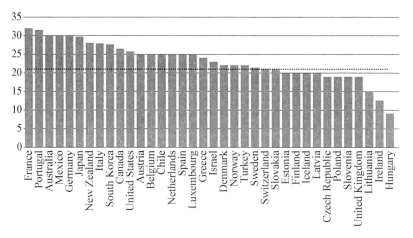

Figure 1 Corporate Income Tax Rates

Source: OECD, Yicai

However, agreement on a minimum statutory rate will not ensure that the effective corporate tax rate is harmonized among countries. This is because governments give tax breaks to nudge corporations in desired directions. For example, governments often offer tax deductions for undertaking research and development or investing in new plant and equipment.

In the G7 countries, the effective tax rate is, on average, 3 percentage points below the statutory rate. Moreover, as Figure 2 shows, the gap varies widely by country. This suggests that countries like Italy and France make greater use of tax incentives than the US and the UK. It also means that ensuring a globally-agreed upon minimum tax is not straightforward.

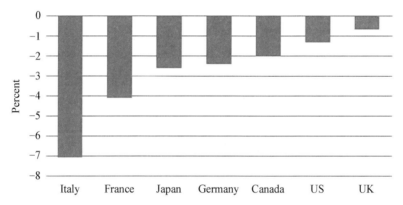

Figure 2   Difference Between Effective and Statutory Corprorate Tax Rates (2019)

Source: OECD, Yicai

If the US really wants to avoid tax-jurisdiction arbitrage, it could try to build a consensus for a statutory rate of zero. As Figure 3 shows, OECD governments are not especially dependent on corporate income tax to fund their expenditures. Between 2000 and 2018, corporate income tax only represented 10 percent of government tax revenue and 3 percent of GDP.

Eliminating the corporate income tax sounds like a radical proposal. However, moving to a zero corporate tax rate could enhance economic stability, improve the efficiency of a country's economy and address income inequality.

While a corporation's interest expenses are tax-deductible, its dividends are paid after-tax. This makes equity a relatively expensive form of corporate finance. As a result, firms prefer increasing leverage to taking on additional equity. It is no wonder that US corporate borrowing has risen from 30 to 80 percent of GDP over the last 70 years.

Excessive debt leads to corporate fragility and greater risk of bankruptcy in times of stress. In addition, corporations can use their debts to shift profits and

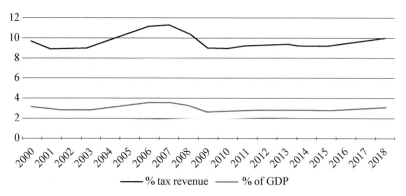

Figure 3　Corporate Income Tax in OECD Countries

Source: OECD, Yicai

avoid taxes. A zero corporate tax rate would reduce the incentive to over-borrow and increase economic stability.

A country's corporate income tax system is typically complex and it is expensive for firms to comply with the tax regulations. For example, a study by the US's Internal Revenue Service estimated that it cost American firms between $92 and $110 billion annually in compliance costs. This amounts to about one-third of the actual corporate tax paid.

In addition to heavy compliance costs, firms have the incentive to devote significant time and energy to tax avoidance strategies. Eliminating the corporate income tax would allow firms to put the resources devoted to minimizing and then paying taxes to more productive uses. Or the cost savings could be passed on to consumers in the form of lower prices. Freeing firms from paying income taxes could go some way to reverse the slowdown we have seen in global productivity growth.

The optics of eliminating corporate taxes are bad because it appears that the government is giving a tax break to the wealthy. However, some research shows that taxing corporations can actually be regressive, with workers bearing a substantial portion of the corporate tax burden through lower wages. One study found that increasing corporate taxes to raise one euro of revenue would lower wages by 65 cents. The low-skilled, women, and young workers are particularly hard hit.

Eliminating the corporate income tax need not worsen the income distribution. Governments can replace their lost revenue through progressive taxes on incomes or wealth. Indeed, in many jurisdictions, individuals pay a lower rate on dividends and capital gains than on labour income. This is justified because corporate income is taxed twice — once at the firm and again at the individual level. Eliminating the corporate income tax would allow governments to, at the same time, remove these benefits for the propertied.

China's government is much more reliant on corporate income taxes than those of OECD countries. In 2019, Chinese corporations paid CNY 3. 7 trillion in tax, which accounted for 24 percent of national tax revenue and 4 percent of GDP. Moreover, as Figure 4 shows, the importance of corporate income tax as a source of government revenue has grown in recent years.

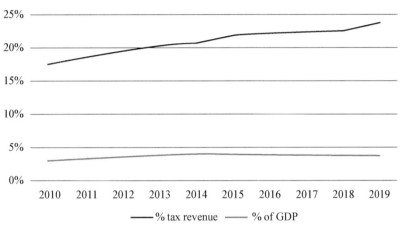

Figure 4   Corporate Income Tax in China

Source: Wind, Yicai

Still, even in China, tax reform would make it possible for the country to enjoy the advantages of a zero corporate tax rate without running a huge deficit. The key would be imposing a recurrent tax on residential property to replace the lost corporate tax revenue.

While China taxes the sale of residential property, it does not have a recurrent property tax. I estimate that China's stock of residential property is worth something like CNY 500 trillion, about five times GDP. If the government were to levy a recurrent property tax at 0. 75 percent, a rate similar to what we see in North America, it could fully replace the revenue lost from eliminating corporate taxes.

Property taxes are simple to collect, difficult to evade and are inexpensive to pay. Analysis done by the OECD suggests that recurrent property taxes are the least harmful to economic growth because they do not affect saving and investment decisions. In addition, such a tax would likely be progressive because the distribution of property is typically skewed to rich households.

In China, a property tax would have the added benefit of increasing the supply of apartments and improving housing affordability. Many apartments in Chinese cities are purchased as investments but are left vacant, rather than rented out. A recurrent property tax would be a good way to keep these apartments occupied and rental costs low, in line with the government's long-stated principle "housing is for living, not for speculation".

Around the world, governments have become increasingly concerned about companies that operate globally but choose to "locate" in low tax jurisdictions. Governments are looking to harmonize their tax rules but there will always be incentives to use the tax code strategically.

Setting the corporate income tax rate to zero minimizes "base erosion and profit shifting". It removes tax-induced incentives to lever up. It reduces spending on tax avoidance and tax compliance. In the context of wider tax reform, it need not worsen — and it might even improve — the distribution of income.

Despite these many benefits, governments face strong political pressures to keep these taxes in place. Perhaps governments could build an international consensus to support them in upgrading their fiscal systems.

So, why not eliminate corporate income taxes?

何不取消企业所得税？

2021 年 4 月 4 日

美国正寻求就 21% 的最低企业税率达成全球共识。[1]

从美国的角度来看，很容易发现这一提议是有道理的。拜登政府计划未来 8 年中在基础设施项目上花费 2.3 万亿美元[2]，希望通过提高企业所得税来为这些项目提供资金。拜登政府担心，税率提高可能会促使企业从美国转移到税收较低的司法管辖区。就较高的最低企业税率达成国际协议可以降低这种风险。

许多国家的企业税率远低于 21%（图 1），包括匈牙利（9%）、爱尔兰（12.5%）和立陶宛（15%）。如果就美国的提议达成共识，这些国家将被迫大改税收制度。

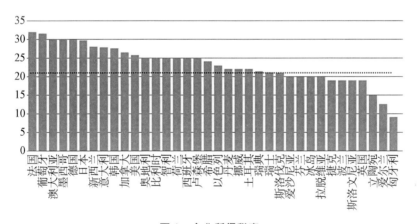

图 1 企业所得税率

数据来源：经济合作与发展组织、第一财经

---

① 美国在全球企业税谈话中提出新计划（https://www.ft.com/content/847c5f77-f0af-4787-8c8e-070ac6a7c74f）。

② 拜登 2.3 万亿美元基建计划目标广泛（https://www.wsj.com/articles/biden-set-to-unveil-2-trillion-infrastructure-plan-11617181208?mod=article_inline）。

然而,就最低法定税率达成协议并不能确保各国实际企业税率保持一致。这是因为,政府会给予税收减免以推动企业朝着理想的方向发展。例如,政府通常会为研发或投资新工厂和设备提供税收减免。

在七国集团(以下简称 G7)国家,实际税率比法定税率平均低 3 个百分点。此外,如图 2 所示,差值因国家而异。这表明,意大利和法国等国家比美国和英国更好地利用了税收优惠。这也意味着就最低税率达成全球共识并非易事。

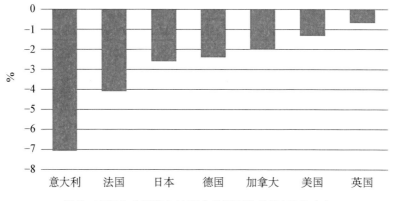

图 2　实际企业税率与法定企业税率的差值(2019 年)

数据来源:经济合作与发展组织、第一财经

如果美国真想避免司法管辖区之间的税收差异,可以尝试就法定税率为零达成共识。如图 3 所示,经合组织国家并不特别依赖企业所得税为其支出提供资金。2000 年至 2018 年,企业所得税仅占政府税收的 10%,占 GDP 的 3%。

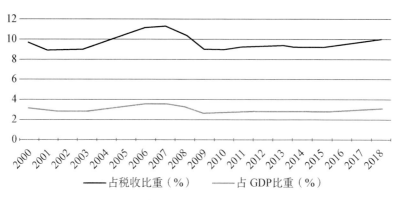

图 3　经济合作与发展组织国家企业所得税

数据来源:经济合作与发展组织、第一财经

取消企业所得税听起来像是一个激进的提议。然而,零企业税率可以增强经济稳定性,提高国家的经济效率,解决收入不平衡的问题。

虽然企业的利息支出可以免税,但其股息是在税后支付的,这使得股权成为一种相对昂贵的企业融资形式。因此,企业更愿意增加杠杆而不是承担额外的股权。难怪在过去的 70 年里,美国企业借款占 GDP 的比例从 30% 上升到 80%。①

过多债务会导致企业的脆弱性以及在困难时期更大的破产风险。此外,企业可以利用债务转移利润②和避税。零企业税率会减少过度借贷的诱因,增强经济稳定性。

一个国家的企业所得税制度通常很复杂,企业税收合规的成本很高。例如,美国国税局的一项研究估计,美国企业每年的合规成本在 920 亿至 1,100 亿美元之间。③ 这相当于实际缴纳的企业税的三分之一左右。

除了高昂的合规成本外,企业还有动力在避税策略上投入大量时间和精力。取消企业所得税能使企业将投入资源最小化,从而将税收支出用于更具生产性的用途。或者,节省的成本可以以更低的价格惠及消费者。免除企业所得税可能会在一定程度上扭转我们所看到的全球生产力增长放缓的局面。

取消企业税看上去很糟糕,因为政府似乎是在为富人减税。然而,研究表明④,对企业征税实际上可能是累退的,因为工人通过较低的工资承担了很大一部分企业税收负担。一项研究发现,每增加 1 欧元的企业税会使工人工资减少 65 欧分。低技能工人、女性和年轻工人受到的影响尤其严重。

取消企业所得税不一定会使收入分配变糟。政府可以通过对收入或财富征收累进税来弥补损失的收入。实际上,在许多司法管辖区,个人缴纳的股息和资本收益税低于劳动所得税。这是有道理的,因为企业收入被征了两次税,一次是在公司层面,一次是在个人层面。取消企业所得税将使政府得以同时取消富人的这些福利。

---

① 我们应该结束商业利息支付的税收减免吗(https://www.ft.com/content/426c1465-9561-4300-8d3e-2430e4124c93)?

② "这是个公平问题":向跨国公司征更多税(https://www.ft.com/content/40cffe27-4126-43f7-9c0e-a7a24b44b9bc)。

③ 企业和合作伙伴的纳税人合规成本:新面貌(https://www.irs.gov/pub/irs-soi/12rescontaxpaycompliance.pdf)。

④ 企业税收的发生率及其对税收累进性的可能影响(https://voxeu.org/article/incidence-corporate-taxation-and-implications-tax-progressivity)。

中国政府比经合组织国家更依赖企业所得税。2019 年,中国企业纳税 3.7 万亿元,占国家税收的 24%,占 GDP 的 4%。此外,如图 4 所示,近年来企业所得税作为政府收入来源的重要性有所增加。

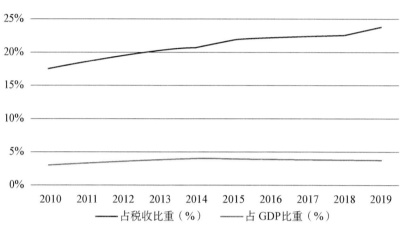

图 4 中国企业所得税

数据来源:万得资讯、第一财经

尽管如此,即使在中国,税收改革也能使其享受到零企业税率的优势,而不会出现巨额赤字。关键在于征收住房保有税,以弥补失去的企业税收。

虽然中国对住宅房地产的销售征税,但是没有住房保有税。笔者估计中国的住宅存量价值约 500 万亿元,约为 GDP 的 5 倍。如果政府征收 0.75% 的住房保有税,这一税率与北美税率类似,它可以完全弥补因取消企业税而损失的收入。

房产税易于征收,难以逃避且支付费用低廉。经合组织的分析表明,住房保有税对经济增长的危害最小,因为它不会影响储蓄和投资决策。① 此外,这种税收应该是累进的,因为房产分配通常倾向于富裕家庭。

在中国,房产税还会带来额外的好处,即增加公寓供应和提高住房负担能力。中国城市的许多公寓都是作为投资购买的,但却一直空置而不出租。定期征收住房保有税是保持这些公寓使用率和降低租金成本的好方法,这符合中国政府长期以来的原则:"房子是用来住的,不是用来炒的。"

① 不动产税收改革(https://www.oecd-ilibrary.org/sites/9789264254053-5-en/index.html? itemId = /content/component/9789264254053-5-en)。

在世界各地,政府越来越关注在全球运营但选择位于低税收管辖区的企业。各地政府正在寻求协调它们的税收规则,但总会有激励措施来战略性地使用税法。

将企业所得税税率设置为零可以最大限度地减少"税基侵蚀和利润转移"。它消除了税收引发的加杠杆动机,减少了避税和税收合规的支出。在更广泛的税收改革背景下,它不会恶化甚至可能改善收入分配。

尽管有这些好处,政府仍面临着保留这些税收的强大政治压力。或许各国政府可以达成国际共识,以支持其财政体系的升级。

那么,为什么不取消企业所得税呢?

How Can China Achieve Carbon Neutrality by 2060?

November 1, 2020

As a result of its immense population and the highly industrial nature of its GDP, China is the world's largest emitter of CO_2, accounting for close to 30 percent of global emissions in 2019.

However, Chinese people do not lead particularly carbon-intensive lifestyles. Figure 1 shows that on a per person basis, China's emissions are about half American levels and about 7 percent lower than what we see in Europe. It is just that there are almost twice as many Chinese as there Americans and Europeans combined.

Industry and construction account for a much larger share of China's economy than those of the US or Europe. While the share of services in the Chinese economy is increasing, China's industry is by no means shrinking and it continues to have significant energy needs. Indeed, industry accounts for two-thirds of China's energy consumption.

In addition, China is the world's largest exporter. Exports account for about a fifth of the economy and a significant portion of China's emissions comes from the transformation of raw materials into goods that are consumed by people living in other countries.

President Xi Jinping recently committed China to go carbon neutral by 2060. This will entail a massive structural change in the economy. As Figure 1 shows, emissions in China continue to grow, whereas they are declining in the US and Europe. This is, in large part, due to China's GDP growing about three times as fast as those of the other major economies.

China has not yet published a detailed roadmap for how it will attain carbon neutrality by 2060. However, there appear to be three margins upon which it can operate to achieve its goal.

First, it can reduce the energy-intensity of its output. Even if we assume that the economy grows at modest rates for the next 40 years, it is likely to be more than twice as large as it is today. So, carbon neutrality implies a massive reduction in the

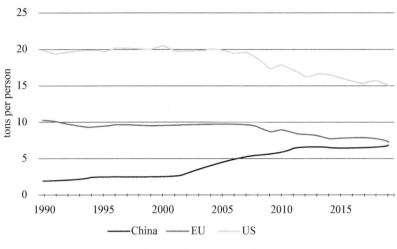

Figure 1   Per Capita CO$_2$ Emissions

Source: BP, UN, Yicai

amount of energy needed to produce 1 RMB of GDP.

A lot can happen in 40 years. Indeed, 35 years ago, when I was studying Chinese in Tianjin, it took more than three times as much energy to produce 1 RMB of GDP as it does today (Figure 2). As recently as 2008, producing a unit of GDP took 50 percent more energy than it does today. China has steadily become much more energy efficient over time and it will need to continue this trend into the future.

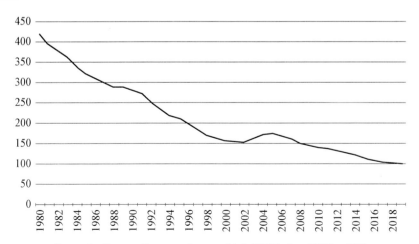

Figure 2   Energy Consumption per Unit GDP Index (2019＝100)

Source: BP, Wind, Yicai

A slower pace of urbanization will support a less energy-intensive economy. In recent years, China built myriad structures and transportation systems to accommodate the hundreds of millions of people that moved into its cities. The steel and cement needed for these investments required huge amounts of energy. With much of the urban infrastructure now in place and a more stable urban population, this demand for energy should fall. A declining population and a more service-based economy will also help reduce future energy intensity.

The second margin upon which China can work is the carbon-intensity of its energy supply. By relying less on fossil fuels, China can reduce the amount of emissions from producing a given amount of energy. China still burns coal for almost 60 percent of its energy needs. However, hydro, nuclear and renewables — like wind, solar and biofuels — only generate a small fraction of the CO_2 coal does to produce the same amount of energy.

Figure 3 shows a projection, by Tsinghua University's Institute of Energy, Environment and Economy, of what China's energy mix in 2060 might look like, compared to what it was in 2019. The share of energy generated from fossil fuels will fall from 85 to 13 percent. Nuclear's share will rise from 2 to 19 percent and that of renewables will jump from 5 to 53 percent.

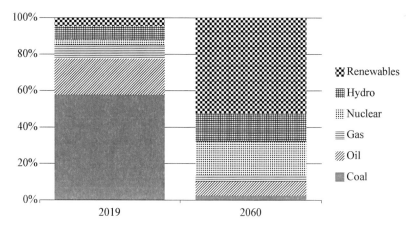

Figure 3 Energy Generation by Fuel Source

Source: BP, Bloomberg, Yicai

A transition of this magnitude will require enormous investments. Hector Pollitt, head of modelling at Cambridge Economics, estimates that investment in the power sector alone will be $4 trillion (undiscounted) above baseline over 40 years. That's close to 30 percent of China's GDP last year.

As Figure 3 shows, China will still consume some fossil fuels in 2060 and, given the size of its economy, it will likely emit a significant amount of carbon. So, the third margin China needs to explore is the increased use of carbon sinks. Options include carbon capture and storage, reforestation, a greater use of wood in construction and more sustainable farming techniques.

China's commitment to carbon neutrality is significant. According to Climate Action Tracker, which independently monitors countries' climate-related activities against the Paris Agreement's goals, China's going carbon neutral by 2060 will reduce global warming by 0. 2 to 0. 3 degrees centigrade to 2100.

Unfortunately, China's commitment, on its own, is not enough for the world to achieve the Paris goals. Climate Action Tracker estimates that the world's temperature will still rise by 2. 4 to 2. 5 degrees centigrade by 2100. Nevertheless, what China's commitment has done is incite others to follow up. Just this week, Japan's new prime minister, Yoshihide Suga, committed his country to a carbon-neutral society by 2050. Japan is the world's fifth-largest emitter of CO_2.

I am a technology optimist. I think that potentially great advances could be made in the use of hydrogen fuel cells for transportation. And I recently read that scientists were able to capture thermal motion from graphene and convert it to electricity. This opens the possibility of potentially limitless, clean, low-voltage power.

While we cannot plan for technology to bail us out of the climate change crisis, technological solutions are more likely to be found if policymakers have committed themselves to addressing the problem.

中国如何在 2060 年前实现碳中和？

2020 年 11 月 1 日

由于人口众多，且 GDP 高度工业化，中国是世界上最大的二氧化碳排放国，2019 年的排放量占全球排放量的近 30%。

然而，中国人的生活方式并不那么高碳。图 1 显示，按人均计算，中国的碳排放量约为美国的一半，比欧洲低约 7%。中国的人口数量几乎是美国和欧洲之和的两倍。

与美国或欧洲相比，在中国经济中，工业和建筑业所占的比重要大得多。虽然服务业在中国经济中的比重不断增加，但中国的工业并没有萎缩，仍然有大量的能源需求。事实上，工业占中国能源消耗的三分之二。

此外，中国是世界上最大的出口国，出口约占经济总量的五分之一。中国碳排放的很大一部分来自将原材料转化为商品，供其他国家的人们使用。

习近平主席最近承诺中国要在 2060 年前实现碳中和。[①] 这将导致经济结构发生巨大变化。如图 1 所示，中国的碳排放量持续增长，而美国和欧洲的排放量正在下降。这在很大程度上是因为中国的 GDP 增速大约是其他主要经济体的三倍。

中国尚未公布如何在 2060 年前实现碳中和的详细蓝图，似乎可以从三个方面着手实现目标。

首先，可以降低产品的能源强度。即使我们假设未来 40 年经济将以温和的速度增长，其规模也可能是目前的两倍多。因此，碳中和意味着生产 1 元 GDP 所需的能源数量大幅减少。

40 年可以发生很多事情。的确，35 年前，我在天津学习汉语的时候，生产 1

[①] 习近平主席表示中国将在 2060 年前实现碳中和（https://www.caixinglobal.com/2020-09-23/china-will-be-carbon-neutral-by-2060-president-xi-says-101608820.html）。

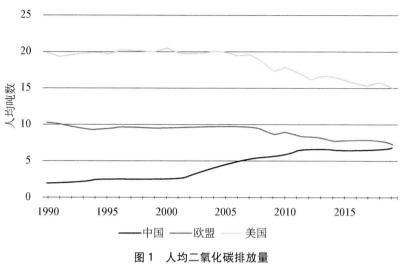

图 1　人均二氧化碳排放量

数据来源:英国石油公司、联合国、第一财经

元 GDP 所需的能源是现在的 3 倍多(图 2)。2008 年,单位 GDP 所消耗的能源比现在高 50%。随着时间的推移,中国的能源效率稳步提升,未来需要继续保持这一趋势。

图 2　单位 GDP 能耗指数(2019 年＝100)

数据来源:英国石油公司、万得资讯、第一财经

　　城镇化步伐放缓将支持能源强度较低的经济。近年来,中国建造了无数的建筑和交通系统,以容纳数亿迁入城市的人口。这些投资所需的钢铁和水泥需要大量能源。随着大部分城市基础设施到位,城市人口更加稳定,对能源的需求

应该会下降。人口减少和服务型经济也将有助于降低未来的能源强度。

中国可以利用的第二个方面是其能源供应的碳强度。通过降低对化石燃料的依赖,中国可以减少生产一定数量能源的排放量。中国仍有近60%的能源需求来自煤炭。然而,氢能、核能和可再生能源(如风能、太阳能和生物燃料)产生的二氧化碳,仅为生产相同数量能源的煤炭产生的二氧化碳的一小部分。

图3显示了清华大学能源环境经济研究所对2060年中国能源结构与2019年相比的预测[①]。化石燃料产生的能源占比将从85%下降到13%,核能占比将从2%上升到19%,可再生能源占比将从5%跃升至53%。

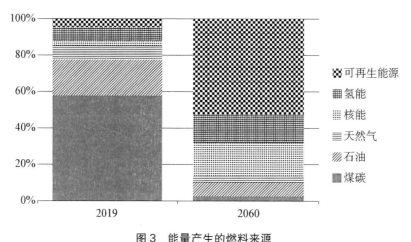

图3 能量产生的燃料来源

数据来源:英国石油公司、彭博、第一财经

如此大规模的转型需要大量投资。剑桥经济咨询公司(Cambridge Economics)建模主管赫克托·波利特(Hector Pollitt)估计,未来40年,仅电力部门的投资就将超过基线4万亿美元(未贴现)。[②] 这接近于中国2019年GDP的30%。

如图3所示,到2060年,中国仍将消耗一些化石燃料,而且,鉴于其经济规模,中国可能会排放大量碳。因此,中国需要探索的第三个方面是增加碳汇的使

[①] 中国顶级气候科学家绘制了实现2060年目标的路线(https://www.bloomberg.com/news/articles/2020-09-28/china-s-top-climate-scientists-lay-out-road-map-to-hit-2060-goal? cmpid = BBD092820 _ GREE NDAI LY&utm_medium = email&utm_source = newsletter&utm_term = 200928&utm_campaign = greendaily&sref = ZkcNToNQ)。

[②] 分析:在2060年前实现碳中和"将使中国更富裕"(https://www.carbonbrief.org/analysis-going-carbon-neutral-by-2060-will-make-china-richer)。

用。可选项包括碳捕获和储存、重新造林、在建筑中更多地使用木材,以及更可持续的耕作技术。

中国对碳中和的承诺意义重大。据独立监测各国气候相关活动违反《巴黎协定》目标的气候行动追踪组织的数据显示,中国在 2060 年前实现碳中和,到 2100 年能使全球变暖减少 0. 2—0. 3 摄氏度。[①]

不幸的是,中国的承诺本身并不足以让世界实现《巴黎协定》的目标。气候行动追踪组织估计,到 2100 年,全球气温仍将上升 2. 4—2. 5 摄氏度。不过,中国的承诺是在鼓励其他国家效仿。2020 年 10 月 26 日,日本新任首相菅义伟承诺日本将在 2050 年前实现碳中和。[②] 日本是世界第五大二氧化碳排放国。

我是一个技术乐观主义者。我认为在使用氢燃料电池[③]进行运输方面可能会取得巨大进步。我最近读到,科学家们能够从石墨烯中捕获热运动[④]并将其转化为电能。这开启了潜在无限、清洁、低压电力的可能性。

虽然我们无法规划技术来帮助我们摆脱气候变化危机,但如果政策制定者致力于解决这个问题,就更有可能找到技术解决方案。

---

① 中国在 2060 年前实现碳中和将使变暖预测降低约 0. 2—0. 3 摄氏度(https://climateaction tracker. org/press/china-carbon-neutral-before-2060-would-lower-warming-projections-by-around-2-to-3-tenths-of-a-degree/)。

② 世界第三大经济体日本承诺在 2050 年前实现碳中和(https://www. washingtonpost. com/world/japan-climate-emissions/2020/10/26/b6ea2b5a-1752-11eb-8bda-814ca56e138b_story. html)。

③ 中国的氢能(https://www. cleantech. com/hydrogen-in-china/)。

④ 物理学家构建出电路,可用石墨烯生产出清洁、无限的能量(https://www. sciencedaily. com/releases/2020/10/201002091029. htm)。

Part II

Data and Analytic Techniques

第二部分

数据及分析技巧

China's Economy:
The View From the IMF

January 18, 2021

On January 8, the International Monetary Fund (IMF) released its Staff Report for the 2020 China Article IV Consultation. As part of the IMF's Articles of Agreement, the authorities of member countries must engage in discussions with the IMF Staff on a regular basis. During these discussions, the Staff offer an analysis of the country's economic performance and suggestions for the policies to be pursued going forward. The views of the country's authorities are also reflected in the Reports.

The Article IV Reports are required reading for any one who wants to truly understand a country's economy and the challenges it faces. Having worked in the IMF for a few years in the mid-2000s, I can attest to the professionalism and the depth of analysis that goes into preparing these documents.

At 125 pages, the 2020 China Article IV Report is a wealth of information. Its central narrative is accompanied by numerous charts, tables, boxes and appendices. While the Report's scope might appear daunting to the casual reader, the Staff's key conclusions and policy recommendations are summarized in a two-page Appraisal.

It is easy to agree with many of the Report's common sense recommendations. Rather than re-state the Appraisal, let me pick on a couple of points where my view differs from those of the Staff.

Notwithstanding the speed of China's recovery, which has been much more rapid than in other countries, the Staff emphasize that growth has been unbalanced — heavily reliant on policy support rather than domestic consumption — and that the risks are to the downside.

They forecast that growth in 2020 will come in at 1. 9 percent, followed by an acceleration to 7. 9 percent in 2021. Thus, they are significantly more downbeat than the 21 Chief Economists surveyed by the Yicai Research Institute, who see GDP growth in 2020 and 2021 at 2. 4 and 8. 8 percent respectively.

Part of the difference in these two forecasts can be attributed to timing. The

Chief Economists were surveyed more recently and their forecasts benefitted from seeing the strong data released in December. Indeed, Helge Berger, the Fund's mission chief for China, suggested that these data presented an upside risk to the Staff's forecast. But something more fundamental is likely at play here as well.

Figure 1 compares the Staff's forecast for China's GDP in its 2020 Article IV report to the one released a year earlier. It is striking that the level of GDP implied by the current forecast remains below the pre-pandemic projection all the way out to 2024. While the economy's rate of growth over 2022 - 2024 is the same as projected in 2019, some of the output lost in 2020 — about 2 percent of GDP — is never recovered.

Indeed, the Staff see the pandemic as having permanent effects on the supply side of China's economy. They attribute this to labour market scarring from employment losses, public investment in low productivity projects and the costs of workplace safety and hygiene practices.

The Staff see the output gap — the difference between the economy's actual output and the amount it could potentially produce — as large in 2021 and only narrowing gradually over the medium term. In contrast, China's authorities are more optimistic. They see the output gap closing sometime this year.

My analysis of the monthly data on economic activity is even more positive. It suggests that the economy already returned to the level of activity we might have expected before the pandemic. Indeed, the National Accounts for the fourth quarter, which were released on January 18, reported that GDP was up 6.5 percent year-over-year. This means that the output gap had, indeed, closed.

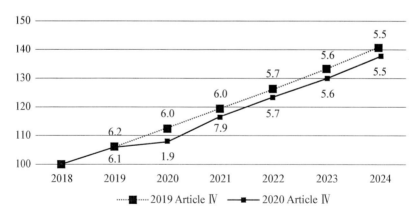

Figure 1　IMF Forecasts: China GDP Indices (2018 = 100)

Source: IMF, Yicai

The analysis of the output gap is not an academic exercise. The output gap features prominently in deciding the course of macroeconomic policy. The Staff, seeing a large output gap, recommend that "macro policy should remain moderately expansionary in 2021". If the gap is already closed, policy should begin to tighten, with an eye to addressing financial risks.

One of the Report's key recommendations is that fiscal policy should be reoriented from infrastructure spending to strengthening the social safety net.

The Staff characterize China's social safety net as "woefully inadequate". They note that only one in three urban workers is covered by unemployment insurance and that, at 3. 5 percent of GDP, China's health and welfare expenditures are well below the 6 percent of GDP that other emerging market countries spend. In the Staff's view, China's thin social safety net leads households to hold excessive precautionary savings and devote too little of their incomes to consumption.

At the same time, the Staff believe that China's increase in public investment threatens to reverse the progress toward "balanced growth". They point out that China's stock of public capital is quite high, relative to GDP, and suggest that further traditional infrastructure investment could suffer from diminishing returns.

China's authorities agree on the need to enhance the social safety net and I suspect that greater social protection will be a key part of the 14th Five-Year Plan. Nevertheless, I think that China will continue to aggressively lever the benefits of public investment.

Both in the context of the pandemic and during the global financial crisis, China was able to rapidly roll out public spending projects, which helped support employment while providing useful capital. In contrast, policy in many other countries appears to consist of "pushing on strings", as they wait for private investment to take advantage of ultra-low interest rates.

While it is likely true that the benefits of infrastructure investment will diminish as the public capital stock grows, I wonder how well these benefits are measured and if they still remain large enough, from a social perspective, to warrant continued spending.

Consider this example.

Last year, China suffered from record rainfalls that resulted in severe flooding in the southern part of the country. But thanks to significant investments in water management, the damage was much less severe than in 1998, when a smaller amount of rain led to widespread death and devastation. I wonder if our economic data can accurately account for the social benefits from the years spent planning trees and creating sponge cities.

Clearly, no one would advise China to build bridges to nowhere. But, as the Staff admit, knowledge spillovers suggest that there is a strong case for public investment in basic R&D. Moreover, the Staff see a role for the government to support China's transition to a low carbon future. At the same time, the Staff should be aware that China's infrastructure investment has moved into new areas like 5G and satellite communications.

At a time when the global economy is weak and private spending is depressed, I would have liked the Staff to have taken a step back and distill the lessons — both in terms of smoothing the business cycle and improving productivity — that China's public investment programme might have for other countries.

As I noted, it is hard to disagree with many of the Report's recommendations. Let me emphasize a couple, which strike me as particularly important.

The Staff make a convincing argument for lowering the minimum social security contribution rates. The high minimum contributions often discourage formal employment among the lowest-paid. Instead, the workers are hired "under the table". Neither they, nor their employers, contribute to the system, which ends up failing the people that need the protection the most.

The Staff note that fiscal consolidation will be needed to stabilize the public debt-to-GDP ratio and put public finances on a sustainable footing. I strongly support their recommendation that a nation-wide, a recurrent tax on residential property would be an effective way to raise government revenue and stabilize the debt, while increasing the progressivity of the tax system.

One need not always agree with the Staff's suggestions. Still, the publication of the IMF's Article IV Report is an excellent way to foster informed debate on the state of the Chinese economy and the best course for its macroeconomic and financial policy.

中国经济：国际货币基金组织如是观

2021 年 1 月 18 日

2021 年 1 月 8 日，国际货币基金组织发布了 2020 年中国第四条磋商-工作人员报告（以下简称"第四条磋商报告"）。作为国际货币基金组织协议条款的一部分，成员国当局必须定期与国际货币基金组织的工作人员进行讨论。在讨论中，工作人员将对该国的经济表现进行分析，并为今后的政策提出建议。报告中也会反映该国当局的观点。

如果想要真正了解一个国家的经济及其所面临的挑战，那就必须阅读第四条磋商报告。21 世纪初期的中间几年，我在国际货币基金组织工作，可以证明这些文件的专业水平和分析深度。

中国 2020 年第四条磋商报告共 125 页，内容丰富。它的中心叙述有大量的图表、表格、方框和附录。这份报告可能会让普通读者望而生畏，所以将工作人员的主要结论和政策建议总结为两页的评估报告。

对该报告中的许多常识性建议，我们很容易表示赞同。在此我不想重述评估报告的内容，而是挑出我与工作人员不同的几个观点。

尽管中国的复苏速度比其他国家要快得多，但工作人员强调，增长一直不平衡，严重依赖于政策支持而不是国内消费，这种风险是不利的。

他们预测，2020 年的增长率将达到 1.9%，随后在 2021 年将加速至 7.9%。而第一财经研究院调研的 21 位首席经济学家认为，2020 年和 2021 年的 GDP 增长率分别为 2.4% 和 8.8%。因此，与这 21 位首席经济学家相比，他们的预测要悲观许多。

这两种预测间的差异一部分可归因于调研时间的不同。第一财经研究院的首席经济学家们参与调研的时间要近一些，他们的预测得益于 2020 年 12 月公布的势头强劲的数据。确实，国际货币基金组织中国事务负责人海格·佰杰尔（Helge Berger）认为他们的数据对工作人员的预测构成了上行风险。但一些更基本的东西也可能对结果产生了影响。

图1将工作人员在2020年第四条磋商报告中对中国GDP的预测与一年前发布的预测进行了比较。令人惊讶的是,目前预测所示的GDP水平低于新冠肺炎疫情发生前对截至2024年的预测水平。虽然2022—2024年的经济增长率与2019年的预测相同,但2020年损失的部分产出(约占GDP的2%)则永远无法恢复。

工作人员认为新冠肺炎疫情对中国经济的供给侧有着永久性的影响。他们将此归因于劳动力市场因失业而留下的创伤、在低生产效率项目上的公共投资以及为维持工作场所安全和卫生所需的措施的成本。

工作人员认为2021年的产出差距,即经济体实际产出与潜在产出之间的差额很大,且仅会在中期内逐渐缩小。相比之下,中国当局则更加乐观。它们预计在今年某个时候产出差距将缩小。

而我对月度经济活动数据的分析则更为积极。数据表明,经济已经恢复到我们在新冠肺炎疫情发生前本可能预测的活跃水平。实际上,2021年1月18日公布的2020年第四季度国民经济核算报告显示,GDP同比增长6.5%。这意味着,产出差距确实已缩小。

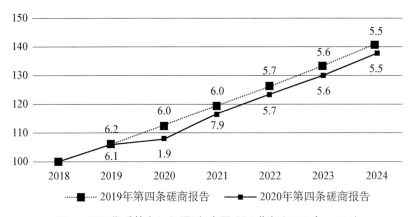

图1　国际货币基金组织预测:中国GDP指标(2018年＝100)

数据来源:国际货币基金组织、第一财经

分析产出差距不是一个学术问题。在决定宏观经济政策的过程中,产出差距尤为突出。工作人员看到了巨大的产出差距,建议"宏观政策应在2021年保持适度扩张"。如果差距已经消除,则应开始收紧政策以应对财务风险。

报告中最主要的建议之一是财政政策的重心应该从基础设施支出转到加强

社会保障上来。

工作人员认为中国的社会保障体系"严重能力不足"。他们指出只有三分之一的城镇职工缴纳了失业保险,中国的健康卫生和社会福利支出仅占 GDP 的 3.5%,远低于其他新兴市场国家 6% 的水平。工作人员认为中国薄弱的社会保障体系导致家庭预防性储蓄过多,消费占收入比例过低。

同时,工作人员认为公共投资的增加会对中国在"平衡发展"道路上取得的成就产生消极影响。他们指出中国的公共资金存量相对 GDP 而言过高,认为进一步投资传统基础设施的回报会减少。

中国当局认同加强社会保障体系的必要性,我认为加强社会保障将成为中国"十四五"计划的关键内容。尽管如此,我仍然认为中国还会继续积极利用公共投资的杠杆。

无论是在新冠肺炎疫情中还是在全球金融危机期间,中国都能够迅速推出公共支出项目,这有助于在支持就业的同时提供有用资本。相比之下,许多其他国家的政策似乎都已失效,因为它们在等待以超低利率吸引私人投资。

虽然随着公共资本存量的增长,基础设施投资的效益很可能会减少,但我想知道如何衡量这些效益,以及从社会角度看,它们是否仍然足够庞大,值得持续的投资。

请看这个例子。

2020 年,中国降水破历史纪录,导致南部地区发生严重洪灾。但是,由于在水资源管理方面投入了大量资金,损失远不如 1998 年严重,当时更少的降水量造成大面积的死亡和广泛破坏。我想知道我们的经济数据能否准确说明这些年植树造林、建造海绵城市所带来的社会效益。

显然,没有人会建议中国采取成本超出效益的举措。但是,正如工作人员所说,知识溢出效应表明,有充分理由在基础研发方面进行公共投资。此外,工作人员认为政府在支持中国向低碳未来的过渡中扮演着重要角色。同时,工作人员应注意,中国的基础设施投资已经进入 5G 和卫星通信等新领域。

在全球经济疲软、私人支出低迷之际,我本希望工作人员能退一步,提炼出中国的公共投资计划在平滑商业周期以及提高生产力方面对其他国家可能的经验教训。

正如我所指出的,很难不同意报告中的许多建议。让我强调两点,这两点在我看来特别重要。

工作人员在降低最低社会保障费率方面提供了令人信服的论据。较高的最低缴款额往往阻碍低收入者的正式就业。相反,这些工人是"私下"雇佣的。他们和他们的雇主都没有为这个体系做出贡献,最终让那些最需要保护的人失望。

工作人员指出,要稳定公共债务与 GDP 之比,并使公共财政处于可持续的基础上,就需要进行财政整顿。我强烈支持他们的建议,即在全国范围内征收住房保有税,将是增加政府收入和稳定债务的有效途径,同时增加税收制度的累进性。

不必总是同意工作人员的建议。尽管如此,国际货币基金组织第四条磋商报告的发布,是促进有关中国经济状况有见地辩论的绝佳方式及其宏观经济和金融政策的最佳路线。

Are Central Banks Behind the Curve on Inflation?

May 25, 2021

The global economy has begun to recover from the ravages of the pandemic. Yet monetary policy remains very accommodative. Central banks continue to purchase massive amounts of financial assets and maintain rock-bottom interest rates. Around the world, commodity prices, producer prices and consumer prices are all rising. Are we in for a bout of 1970's style inflation?

Former US Treasury Secretary Larry Summers, one of the most vocal critics of lax monetary policy, has accused the Federal Reserve of "dangerous complacency". He warns that once the Fed appreciates how entrenched the inflationary pressures are, it will be forced to raise interest rates sharply, imperiling both the recovery and financial stability.

When central banks consider how they ought to respond to rising prices, they first need to be clear about the source of the inflation. Broadly speaking, prices rise either because there is too much demand or because there is insufficient supply. Monetary policy is an effective demand management tool, but changes in monetary conditions have relatively little impact on the supply side of the economy. At any given time, a complex mix of demand and supply factors are usually at play and central banks need to weigh numerous pros and cons before they act.

It appears that the price pressures we are currently seeing are largely the result of supply constraints. While demand certainly is recovering, and prices are rising, it is likely that inflation will moderate as more supply comes on stream.

The IMF's April World Economic Outlook provides a bird's eye view of the global economy (Figure 1). Demand does not appear to be particularly strong. The level of global GDP this year is only expected surpass 2019's by 2. 6 percent. Annual growth of 1. 3 percent, over 2020 – 21, is well below the 3. 4 percent the global economy registered between 2014 – 19.

The IMF expects that the level of GDP this year will be 4 percent lower than the pre-pandemic trend. This gap narrows to 3 percent but it persists to 2026, implying that the pandemic left significant scars on global supply. While there is

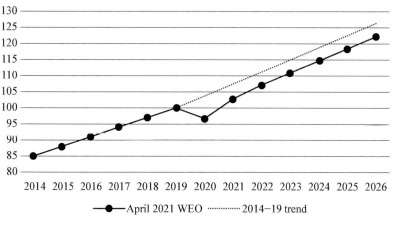

Figure 1　GDP Indices (2019＝100)

Source: IMF, Yicai

little evidence of overheating at the global level, the picture becomes more nuanced if we differentiate between services and goods. While there are encouraging signs that the rollout of vaccines is beginning to contain the spread of the virus, fear of infection and public health measures have depressed the demand for and the supply of services.

In contrast, the manufacturing sector is picking up (Figure 2). Global industrial production in January and February was about 3 percent higher than the same period in 2019. This represents an acceleration from December 2019, when the two-year growth rate was 2. 2 percent.

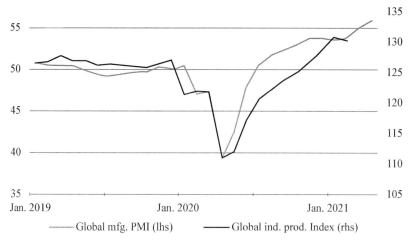

Figure 2　Global Manufacturing Indicators

Source: Wind, CPB, Yicai

The global manufacturing Purchasing Managers' Index (PMI), which is available through April, suggests that goods production around the world remained strong in the spring.

While factories are humming, the oilwells and mines that supply them with inputs have responded less nimbly. This has led to a sharp rise in the prices of primary commodities, which has fed inflationary fears. However, it appears that commodity producers are resolving their supply constraints and that prices should stabilize later this year.

This dynamic is, perhaps, most clearly seen in the global oil market. Figure 3 shows that the consumption of liquid fuels dropped sharply in early 2020. To balance the market, the OPEC + oil producing countries agreed to cut production by 9. 7 million barrels per day, close to 10 percent of global consumption. More recently, the increase in consumption has outstripped that of production and prices have begun to rise. At their April 1 meeting, OPEC + agreed to reduce the cuts to 5. 8 million barrels per day for the May to July period. Analysts expect that the global oil market will essentially be back in balance by year end.

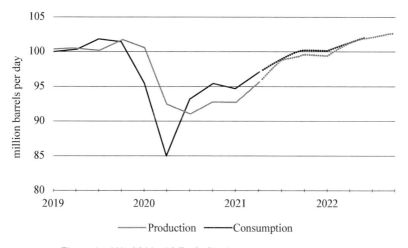

Figure 3　World Liquid Fuels Production and Consumption

Source: US Energy Information Administration

A similar story can be told for iron ore and copper (Figure 4), commodities whose prices have risen sharply in recent months. Iron ore production dropped last year due to a dam bursting in Brazil and mine auction delays in India. This year, supply is expected to be 2 percent higher than the pre-pandemic level, followed by 4 percent growth to 2024.

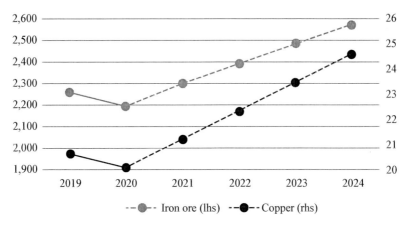

Figure 4　Iron Ore and Copper Production（million tones）
Source: Global Data, Yicai

The production of copper fell in 2020, as COVID-related restrictions disrupted supply in Chile and Peru. Production this year should exceed 2019's by 3 percent and then grow by 5 percent annually to 2024.

Supply constraints are also playing a role in US labour markets. Figure 5 presents the labour force participation rate for prime-age workers (those between 25 and 54). It shows that a significant share of prime-age workers left the labour force in early 2020. While some have returned, many have chosen not to look for work. The fear of becoming infected, an inability to find child care and the availability of extended unemployment benefits are cited as reasons for the US's worker shortage and rising wages.

Figure 5　US Labour Prime Age Force Participation Rate（%）
Source: FRED, Yicai

Supply constraints can affect prices in unexpected ways. There is currently a global shortage of computer chips. This is a confluence of many factors including a pandemic-induced demand for laptops, cell phones and game consoles and supply constraints such as a fire halting production in a Japanese chip factory, unseasonably cold weather shutting down plants in Texas, and droughts in Taiwan. Computer chips are an important input into the production of cars, where they are used for brake, power steering, information and entertainment systems. The chip shortage has resulted in reduced new car production. This, in turn, led US consumers to buy an unusually large number of used cars. Used car prices were up 21 percent, year-over-year, in April.

Most central banks monitor commodity and producer price markets closely but are focused on ensuring stable consumer prices. In China, producer price inflation rose to 6. 8 percent in April, the highest reading since October 2017. Still, consumer prices remain well-behaved with headline and core (ex-food and energy) inflation only 0. 9 and 0. 7 percent, respectively. Indeed, headline consumer price inflation remains well below the rates seen in early 2020, when the African swine fever ravaged the pig herd and drove up pork prices (Figure 6).

April consumer prices in the Euro Area rose at their fastest rate since November 2018. But, at 1. 6 percent, do not seem like a cause for concern.

Consumer price Inflation appears more problematic in the US, where it jumped to 4. 2 percent in April, the fastest rate since September 2008. Stripping out the volatile food and energy components, core inflation only rose by 3. 0 percent. Core inflation was inflated by the "base effect", which comes from the fall in the level of core prices in April 2020. The base effect contributed 0. 6 percentage points. The contribution of higher used car prices is worth another 0. 6 percentage points. This leaves "underlying" inflation at 1. 8 percent, which does not appear to be excessive.

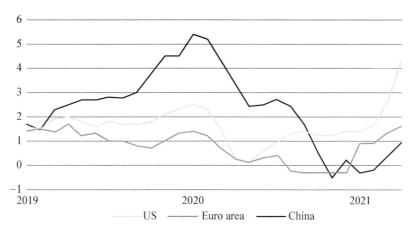

Figure 6   Headline Consumer Price Inflation (%)

Source: Wind, Yicai

The calculation a central bank has to make is a difficult one, as it must weigh information that often points in different directions. Moreover, monetary policy has to be forward looking and think about where inflation is going as well as its recent causes. The manufacturing sector is recovering quickly and this is causing shortages in those parts of the supply chain that can only respond slowly. Rising prices are part of this process. Monetary policy is a blunt instrument and it does not seem appropriate to use it to cool the manufacturing sector while the service sector remains weak. While global interest rates will have to rise over time, it is important for central banks to be patient, monitor the process of the supply constraints working themselves out and communicate clearly with the public.

中央银行在通胀问题上落后了吗？

2021 年 5 月 25 日

全球经济已经开始从新冠肺炎疫情的打击中恢复,但是货币政策仍然维持宽松。各国中央银行继续大规模购入金融资产并维持最低利率。世界范围内的商品价格、生产价格以及消费价格都在上升。我们是否将面临一场 1970 年式的通货膨胀?

美国前财政部长拉里·萨默斯(Larry Summers)是宽松货币政策最直言不讳的批评者之一。他指责美联储"自满的状态很危险",并警告一旦美联储意识到通货膨胀压力是根深蒂固的,就会被迫大幅加息,这将损害经济复苏和金融稳定。

央行在思考价格上升的应对政策时,首先应当认清通胀的根源。广义地说,价格升高的原因要么是需求过高,要么是供给不足。货币政策是一个非常有效的需求管理工具,但是货币状况的变化对经济的供应端影响相对较小。在任何特定的时间,通常都是供需混合因素的影响在发挥作用,央行在采取措施前一定要权衡好利弊。

我们目前面临的价格压力似乎主要是因为供给紧张。需求确实是在恢复中,价格在升高,随着供给逐渐增加,通胀情况会有所缓和。

国际货币基金组织四月份的《世界经济展望报告》提供了一份全球经济的"鸟瞰图"(图 1)。需求似乎没有那么强,预计 2021 年全球 GDP 仅比 2019 年增长 2.6%,2020—2021 年的年均增长率为 1.3%,远低于 2014—2019 年间 3.4% 的增速。

国际货币基金组织预计 2021 年全球 GDP 会比疫情前的趋势水平低 4%,未来该数值会降到 3% 并持续至 2026 年,说明疫情对全球供给的破坏非常严重。虽然缺乏全球经济过热的证据,但是如果我们把服务和商品分开看的话,情况会有略微不同。种种迹象表明接种新冠疫苗已经开始显现出对于疫情传播的

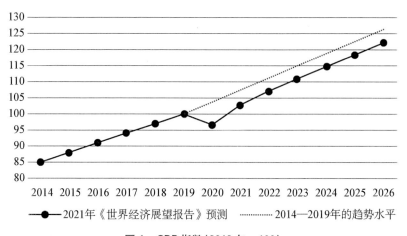

图 1　GDP 指数(2019 年 = 100)

数据来源:国际货币基金组织、第一财经

抑制作用,但是对于感染的恐惧和公共卫生防控措施抑制了服务业的需求和供给。

相比较而言,制造业正在回暖(图 2)。2021 年 1—2 月的全球工业生产比 2019 年同期高 3%,表明其自 2019 年 12 月以来增速加快,过去两年的增速为 2.2%。截至 2021 年 4 月的全球制造业采购经理人指数(PMI)表明 2021 年春季全球商品生产旺盛。

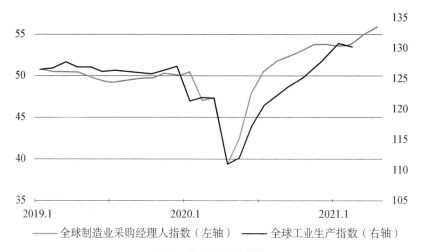

图 2　全球制造业指数

数据来源:万得资讯、CPB 数据、第一财经

　　工厂生产活跃的同时,其生产资料供应来源——油井和矿山在供应上却没有跟上,这导致主要商品的价格飙升,引发对通胀的担忧。但是,商品生产商正在想办法解决供应紧张的问题,商品价格预计在 2021 年晚些时候就能稳定下来。

　　这种动态或许在全球石油市场上最为明显。图 3 显示,2020 年初液态燃料消费骤降。为平衡市场,欧佩克 + 的石油生产国同意将日产量降低 970 万桶,接近全球石油消费的 10%。最近,石油消费增长已经超过了产量,石油价格开始回升。欧佩克 + 在 2021 年 4 月 1 日的成员国会议上达成一致,将 5 至 7 月的日产量缩减值调整为 580 万桶。分析师认为全球石油市场预计在 2021 年年底恢复平衡。

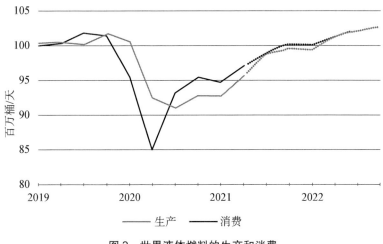

图 3　世界液体燃料的生产和消费

数据来源:美国能源信息署

　　铁矿石和铜也有类似的情况(图 4),这些商品的价格近几个月大幅上涨。由于巴西大坝决口和印度矿山推迟拍卖,2020 年铁矿石产量下降。2021 年供应量预计将比新冠肺炎疫情前增长 2%,到 2024 年增长 4%。

　　2020 年铜产量下降,因为新冠肺炎相关的限制扰乱了智利和秘鲁的供应。2021 年的产量应该会比 2019 年增长 3%,然后到 2024 年每年增长 5%。

　　美国劳动力市场中也出现供应受限的情况。图 5 显示了黄金劳动年龄人口(25—54 岁之间)的劳动力参与率。在 2020 年初,有很大一部分黄金劳动年龄人口离开了劳动力市场。虽然有些人已经重返就业,但许多人选择不找工作。他们担心感染疫情,找不到托儿服务以及无法获得长期失业救济,这些因素被认为是美国工人短缺和工资上涨的原因。

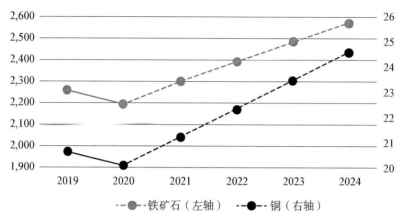

图 4　铁矿石和铜产量(百万吨)

数据来源:全局数据、第一财经

图 5　美国黄金劳动年龄人口的劳动力参与率(%)

数据来源:美国联邦储备经济数据库、第一财经

供应受限可能以意想不到的方式影响价格。目前全球范围内出现了计算机芯片的短缺,这是许多因素共同作用的结果,包括新冠肺炎疫情引起的对笔记本电脑、手机和游戏机的需求,以及供应受限,如日本芯片工厂由于火灾导致停产,极端寒冷天气下美国得克萨斯州的工厂关闭,以及中国台湾的干旱。计算机芯片是汽车生产中的一项重要部件,用于制动、动力转向、信息和娱乐系统,芯片短缺导致了新车产量下降。这反过来又使得美国消费者购买了异常多的二手车。2021 年 4 月,二手车价格同比增长了 21%。

大多数央行会密切关注商品和生产者价格市场,但重点放在保障消费者价格的稳定。中国 2021 年 4 月的生产者价格指数上涨 6.8%,为 2017 年 10 月以来的最高水平。尽管如此,消费者价格仍然表现良好,总体和核心(食品和能源除外)通胀率分别仅为 0.9% 和 0.7%。的确,总体消费者价格通胀仍远低于 2020 年初的水平,当时受非洲猪瘟影响,生猪养殖业受到冲击并拉高了猪肉价格(图 6)。

欧元区 2021 年 4 月的消费者价格指数以 2018 年 11 月以来最快速度上涨,但 1.6% 的增长率似乎并不令人担忧。

美国的消费者价格通胀问题看上去更为突出,该指数 2021 年 4 月猛增 4.2%,为 2008 年 9 月以来的最高增速。剔除波动性较大的食品和能源部分,核心通胀率仅上升 3.0%,2020 年 4 月核心物价水平下降导致的“基数效应”推高了核心通胀,基数效应贡献了 0.6 个百分点,二手车价格上涨贡献了 0.6 个百分点。这使得潜在通货膨胀率保持在 1.8%,不是很高。

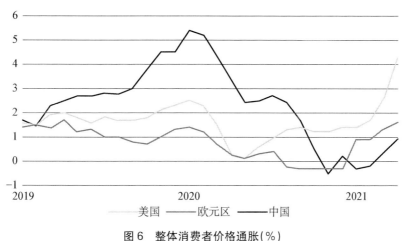

图 6　整体消费者价格通胀(%)

数据来源:万得资讯、第一财经

央行的计划很难做,因为它必须权衡经常指向不同方向的信息。此外,货币政策必须具有前瞻性,既要考虑通胀走向,也要考虑通胀的近期原因。制造业正在迅速复苏,部分供应链由于反应缓慢出现材料短缺,推动了物价上涨。在服务业依然疲弱的情况下,用货币政策给制造业降温似乎并不合适。尽管全球利率将随着时间的推移而上升,但对于央行而言,重要的是保持耐心,监控供应约束自行解决的过程,并与公众进行清晰的沟通。

Big Mac Prices — No Bull

March 1, 2021

Happy Year of the Ox! I want to take a moment, in my first Opinion Piece of this new lunar year, to wish you and your families health, prosperity and all good fortune.

In honor of this Chinese New Year's mascot, the Golden Bull, I wanted to explore a beefy dataset with you — *The Economist*'s Big Mac Index. *The Economist* has been collecting data on MacDonald's hamburger prices around the world for many years. In my opinion, these data provide an interesting perspective on the evolution of prices both in China and internationally.

A country's price level is central to assessing the size of its economy and the wealth of its citizens. So, economists have a strong interest in understanding how prices compare across countries.

To make cross-country comparisons, economists often rely on market exchange rates. However, market exchange rates can fluctuate wildly, they can be manipulated by central banks and they can diverge from economic fundamentals for long periods of time.

Purchasing power parity (PPP) exchange rates offer an appealing alternative. PPP exchange rates represent the rate at which the currency of one country would have to be converted into that of another to buy a common basket of goods and services. For example, if the basket costs $1,000 in the United States and 9,400 pesos in Mexico, then the dollar-peso PPP exchange rate is 1 to 9.4.

The task of defining this common basket and then pricing it around the world falls to the International Comparisons Program (ICP). The ICP is a statistical initiative under the auspices of the United Nations, which is coordinated by the World Bank.

The ICP calls itself "one of the largest statistical initiatives in the world" and it is easy to see why. In 2017, it collected the prices of close to 1,000 different goods and services in each of 176 countries. It took nearly three years to collate and release the results. And, the next update of this exacting process won't be conducted until 2021.

The ICP produces a useful trove of detailed cross-country price information, which data junkies like me really appreciate. But it seems to me that *The Economist* is able to do a very similar job at only a fraction of the cost. Indeed, *The Economist* updates its Big Mac Index twice a year, albeit for only 50-odd countries and regions, and can provide much more timely data than the ICP.

Let's take the bull by the horns and see how the two datasets compare.

The vertical axis in Figure 1 shows the January 2021 Big Mac exchange rate. That is the price of a Big Mac in a given country divided by the price in the US. The ICP's PPP exchange rate is plotted on the horizontal axis. Here too, the value of the common basket in a given country is expressed with respect to its price in the US. Both exchange rates are plotted in logs.

In many cases, the Big Mac and PPP exchange rates are quite close, suggesting that a simple hamburger is an excellent composite good. For example, in China, the Big Mac exchange rate is 4.0, while the ICP PPP exchange rate is 4.2.

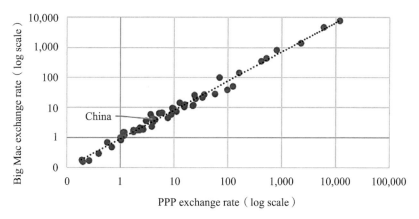

Figure 1   Big Mac and PPP Exchange Rates

Source: The Economist, IMF, Yicai

The Big Mac data provide useful information but they also have the potential to be misinterpreted.

For example, a Big Mac in the US cost $5.66, while the same burger went for CNY 22.40, or $3.46 at market exchange rates, in China. According to *The Economist*'s website, the Big Mac Index is based on the theory that "... in the long run exchange rates should move towards the rate that would equalise the prices of an identical basket of goods and services (in this case, a burger) in any two countries."

A simplistic application of the Index would imply that, since Big Macs are close to 40 percent cheaper in China than in the US, the renminbi must be significantly under-valued.

The Big Mac Index rests on one of economics' oldest theories: the Law of One price, which can be traced back to French economists in the mid-1700s. It states that the prices of tradable goods in different countries should be similar, differing only in the cost of transportation and taxes.

While one can send out for a hamburger, cross-border deliveries are uncommon and Big Macs really cannot be considered tradable goods. So, is there any value in comparing hamburger prices between countries?

I think there is. In fact, the hamburgers can be giving us important information about non-tradable prices, which are due to cross-country differences in incomes and wages.

According to *The Economist*'s January 2021 survey, the cheapest Big Macs could be found in Russia ($1.81), while those in Switzerland were the most expensive ($7.29). As Figure 2 shows, Big Macs tend to get more expensive as incomes rise. We use GDP per capita (at market exchange rates) as our measure of incomes.

This is not surprising and is in line with an empirical regularity called the "Balassa-Samuelson Effect" after the two economists that independently recognized it in the early 1960s. The idea is that countries with higher incomes per capita tend to be more productive and have a higher level of domestic prices.

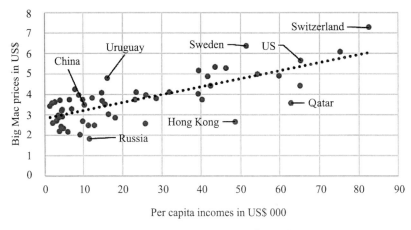

Figure 2   Big Mac Prices and per Capita Incomes

Source: The Economist, Yicai

But other factors play important rolls too. For example, Sweden and Hong Kong are fairly close in terms of per capita GDP, but Big Macs sell for $6.37 in the former and $2.64 in the latter. I suspect that taxes account for this large difference.

The price of Big Macs in China is just about where one would expect, given the country's per capita income, implying that the renminbi is fairly valued.

Over the last two decades, Chinese Big Mac prices have increased at an average annual rate of just over 4 percent. That's significantly faster than that of the general level of consumer prices (+ 2. 5 percent), as calculated by the National Bureau of Statistics.

No surprise here, as Chinese food products have accounted for much of the rise in consumer prices, rising at an average annual rate of over 5 percent. Non-food prices only increased by 1 percent annually. So, over time, Big Macs have become a relatively more affordable way to dine.

Figure 3 shows my estimates of the price level indices for the food and non-food components of the consumer price index (CPI), as well as for Chinese Big Macs.

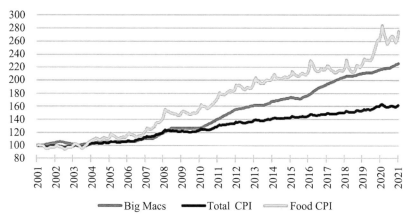

Figure 3   Chinese Price Indices (April 2001 = 100)

Source: The Economist, Wind, Yicai

The year-over-year price change data indicate that the Big Mac prices no longer simply reflect the costs of beef and buns. Figure 4 shows that there have been four major cycles in Chinese food prices since 2001. Big Mac prices responded to the first three but not the most recent one.

Considering that, this time last year, beef prices were rising by more than 20 percent, it is interesting that the prices of Big Macs were only up 3 precent. This disconnect likely reflects the efforts that firms like MacDonald's have been putting into improving their supply chains.

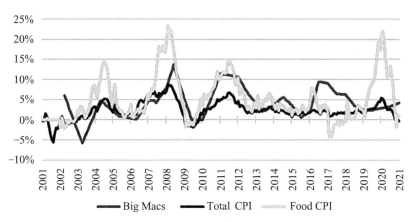

Figure 4   Year-Over-Year Price Changes

Source: The Economist, Wind, Yicai

While Big Mac prices have decoupled from those of food, they appear to be sensitive to labour costs. The spike in Big Mac prices in late 2016, when food prices were soft, corresponds to tightness in the Chinese labour market, as reflected in the employment component of the National Bureau of Statistics's purchasing managers' indices. Similarly, the low Big Mac inflation in early 2019 corresponds to weakness in those labour market indicators.

Regular readers of this column know that I can talk about data until the cows come home, but I really do believe that Big Mac prices contain much more information than the simple cost of a fast food burger.

巨无霸价格：牛年不吹牛

2021 年 3 月 1 日

牛年快乐！在这农历新年的第一篇评论文章中，我愿花一点时间，祝您和您的家人身体健康、万事如意。

为了纪念金牛这个中国新年吉祥物，我想和大家一起来探索一个强大的数据集：《经济学人》的"巨无霸指数"。多年来，《经济学人》一直在收集有关麦当劳汉堡在全球价格的数据。在我看来，这些数据为中国和国际价格的演变提供了一个有趣的视角。

一个国家的物价水平是评估其经济规模和国民财富的核心。因此，经济学家对了解各国的价格高低有着浓厚的兴趣。

经济学家通常依赖市场汇率来进行跨国比较。然而，市场汇率可能会剧烈波动，它们可能会受到中央银行的操纵，并且可能会在很长一段时间内偏离经济基本面。

购买力平价汇率提供了一个有吸引力的替代方案。购买力平价汇率是指一个国家的货币必须转换成另一个国家的货币才能购买一通用篮子商品和服务的汇率。例如，若这个篮子在美国的成本为 1,000 美元，在墨西哥的成本为 9,400 比索，则美元-比索的购买力平价汇率为 1 比 9.4。

定义这个通用篮子然后在世界范围内定价的任务落在了国际比较项目上。国际比较项目是一项由联合国发起，由世界银行负责执行的统计项目。

国际比较项目[①]自称为"世界上最大的统计项目之一"，原因很容易理解。2017 年，它收集了 176 个国家近 1,000 种不同商品和服务的价格，然后花了将近 3 年的时间整理和发布结果。而且，这个严格流程的下一次更新将在 2021 年。

[①] 国际比较项目（https://www.worldbank.org/en/programs/icp）。

　　国际比较项目生成了一个实用、详细的跨国价格信息宝库,像我这样的数据迷非常欣赏。但在我看来,《经济学人》能够以极少的成本完成非常类似的工作。事实上,尽管只针对 50 多个国家和地区,但《经济学人》每年更新两次巨无霸指数,可以提供比国际比较项目更及时的数据。

　　让我们直入正题,看看这两个数据集如何比较。

　　图 1 中的纵轴显示了 2021 年 1 月的巨无霸汇率,即某特定国家巨无霸的价格除以美国的价格。国际比较项目的购买力平价汇率绘制在横轴上。在这里,一个特定国家的通用篮子的价值也是根据其在美国的价格来表示的。两种汇率均以对数形式绘制。

　　很多情况下,巨无霸汇率和购买力平价汇率非常接近,这表明简单的汉堡是一种极好的复合商品。例如,在中国巨无霸汇率为 4.0,而国际比较项目的购买力平价汇率为 4.2。

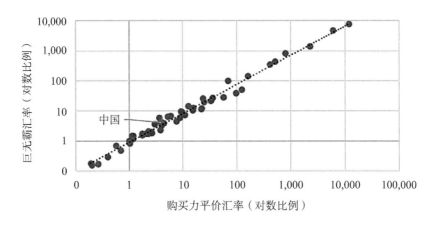

图 1　巨无霸汇率与购买力平价汇率

数据来源:《经济学人》、国际货币基金组织、第一财经

　　巨无霸数据提供了有用的信息,但也可能被误解。

　　例如,一个巨无霸在美国售价 5.66 美元,在中国售价为 22.40 元人民币,按市场汇率计算为 3.46 美元。根据《经济学人》的网站[①],巨无霸指数基于以下理论:"……从长远来看,汇率应当趋向于使在任何两个国家的一篮子商品和服务(在此情况下为汉堡)的价格相等。"

　　巨无霸指数的简单化应用意味着,由于巨无霸在中国比美国便宜近 40%,

①《经济学人》:巨无霸价格指数(https://www.economist.com/big-mac-index)。

人民币的价值应该被严重低估了。

巨无霸指数基于经济学最古老的理论之一：一价定律①，可以追溯到 18 世纪中叶的法国经济学家。它指出，不同国家的可交易商品的价格应该相似，仅在运输成本和税收方面有所不同。

虽然人们可以寄出一个汉堡，但跨境交付并不常见，巨无霸真的不能被视为可交易商品。那么，比较各国汉堡价格有价值吗？

我认为有。事实上，汉堡可以为我们提供关于不可交易商品价格的重要信息，而这是由各国收入和工资的差异造成的。

根据《经济学人》2021 年 1 月的调查，最便宜的巨无霸在俄罗斯（1.81 美元），而最贵的巨无霸在瑞士（7.29 美元）。如图 2 所示，随着收入的增加，巨无霸往往会变得更贵。我们使用人均 GDP（以市场汇率计算）作为收入的衡量标准。

这并不奇怪，符合由两位经济学家在 20 世纪 60 年代初期提出的经验规律，后来被称为"巴拉萨-萨缪尔森效应"。它提出，人均收入较高的国家往往生产率更高，国内价格水平也更高。

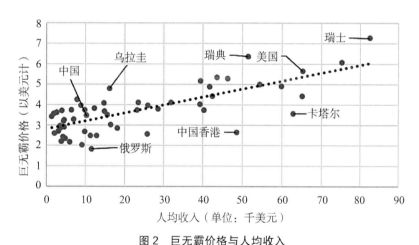

图 2　巨无霸价格与人均收入

数据来源：《经济学人》、第一财经

但是其他因素也很重要。例如，瑞典和中国香港的人均 GDP 相当接近，但瑞典的巨无霸售价为 6.37 美元，中国香港则为 2.64 美元。我怀疑税收是造成

---

① 一价定律（https://eh.net/encyclopedia/the-law-of-one-price/）。

这种巨大差异的原因。

考虑到中国的人均收入,巨无霸在中国的价格和人们预期的差不多,这意味着人民币的估值是合理的。

在过去20年里,中国巨无霸的价格以年均超过4%的速度提高。根据中国国家统计局的计算,这明显快于居民消费价格总水平的增长(2.5%)。

这并不奇怪,因为中国食品价格年均增长率超过5%,占消费价格上涨的很大一部分。非食品价格每年仅上涨1%。因此,随着时间的推移,巨无霸已经成为一种相对更实惠的用餐选择。

图3显示的是我对居民消费价格指数中食品和非食品成分以及中国巨无霸的价格水平指数的估计。

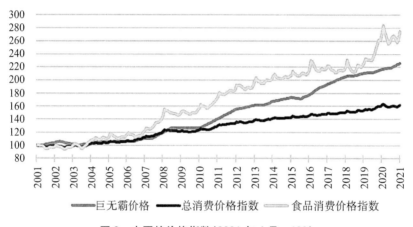

图3 中国的价格指数(2001年4月＝100)

数据来源:《经济学人》、万得资讯、第一财经

同比价格变化数据表明,巨无霸的价格不再仅仅反映牛肉和面包的成本。图4显示,自2001年以来,中国的食品价格经历了四个主要周期。巨无霸价格对应了前三个而不是最近一个周期。

考虑到2020年这个时候牛肉价格上涨了20%以上,而巨无霸的价格仅上涨了3%,这便显得有趣了。这种脱节可能反映了,像麦当劳这样的公司一直在努力改善其供应链[①]。

---

① 麦当劳计划在湖北建设价值2.293亿美元的工业园区,以加强中西部地区扩张(https://www.yicaiglobal.com/news/mcdonald-eyes-usd2293-million-industrial-park-in-hubei-to-bolster-midwest-out-reach)。

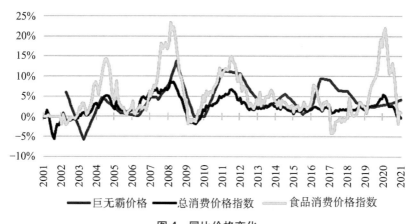

图4　同比价格变化

数据来源:《经济学人》、万得资讯、第一财经

虽然巨无霸价格已与食品价格脱钩,但它似乎对劳动力成本很敏感。2016年底食品价格疲软时巨无霸价格飙升,与中国劳动力市场吃紧相对应,这反映在国家统计局采购经理人指数①的就业情况中。同样,2019年初巨无霸通胀率较低,与劳动力市场指标的疲软相对应。

本专栏的老读者都知道,我谈论起数据来可能会没完没了,但我确实相信巨无霸价格包含的信息比汉堡的简单成本要多得多。

---

① 我们的目标是否已实现? 交通拥堵数据之再探究(https://www.yicaiglobal.com/opinion/mark.kruger/are-we-there-yet-another-look-at-the-traffic-congestion-data)。

Is the US Chip Export Ban Consistent With Its WTO Commitments?

November 11, 2022

These are tough times for those of us who believe in the value of the rules-based global trading system.

Seventy-five years ago, countries came together to sign the General Agreement on Tariffs and Trade (GATT). The GATT set out the key principles for open and fair trade: most-favoured-nation treatment (all of one's trading partners have equal standing) and national treatment (no discrimination against foreign products in favour of those produced domestically). In 1995, the GATT was incorporated into the World Trade Organization (WTO), which currently has 160 members representing 98 percent of world trade. The WTO's goal is to ensure that international trade flows as smoothly, predictably and freely as possible. The WTO has been an important component of the "global commons" — the institutional infrastructure that helps minimize international frictions. Indeed, the predictability offered by the WTO was instrumental in supporting the tremendous growth in international trade and the associated increase in global living standards.

Given these achievements, it is disturbing that the US believes that the WTO is no longer fit for purpose. The US contends that China routinely violates its WTO obligations and that the WTO can no longer police China's behaviour.

But was the rules-based trading system really so badly broken?

According to data collected by Shang-Jin Wei, a professor of finance and economics at Columbia University, China's record of compliance with WTO decisions is broadly comparable to those of other member countries (Figure 1).

Between 2001 and 2021, 47 complaints were lodged in the WTO against China's trading practices. The complaints filed against China accounted for 12 percent of all WTO dispute cases during those two decades.

Over the same period, there were 110 complaints lodged against the US — 28 percent of the total and more than twice as many complaints as against China. According to Professor Wei, China was regarded by the other WTO member-countries as only half as likely as the US to have violated its WTO commitments.

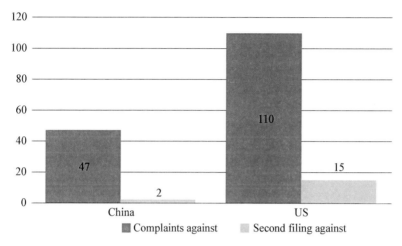

Figure 1   WTO Trade Dispute Indicators 2001 – 2021

Source: Shang-Jin Wei, Yicai

In addition, China had a reasonable record of modifying its policies when a WTO dispute settlement panel ruled against it. Professor Wei notes that one indication of non-compliance is the need for the original complainants to file a second WTO case against the country on the same, or a very similar, issue. Out of the 47 cases against China, only two required a second filing (4 percent). In contrast, there were 15 second-time filings against the US (14 percent).

These data do not support the contention that China was an egregious violator of its WTO commitments and that its trading practices were unchecked by the WTO's processes.

The WTO's dispute settlement mechanism was designed to allow for the appeal of unfavourable panel rulings. However, during the Trump Administration, the US refused to agree to the appointment of new members to the WTO's Appellate Body as existing members' terms expired.

This breakdown of the WTO's dispute settlement procedure has had adverse consequences for China. In September 2020, a WTO panel ruled that the tariffs the US imposed on Chinese imports in 2018 and 2019 were inconsistent with its WTO obligations. In October 2020, the US appealed the panel's decision. As the WTO's Appellate Body lacks a quorum of members — and therefore cannot hear appeals — there is no longer a way to resolve the dispute within the WTO. Thus, the US's decision to appeal was not designed to resolve this case. Rather it was a cynical move which put the status of its tariffs into legal limbo.

Even though the WTO's dispute settlement mechanism is in disarray, it still may be instructive to think through whether or not the US's recent ban on the export of high-performance computer chips to China is consistent with WTO principles.

On October 7, the US Commerce Department's Bureau of Industry and Security (BIS) announced new rules designed to restrict China's ability to obtain advanced computing chips, develop and maintain supercomputers and manufacture advanced semiconductors.

The BIS's rules prohibit companies anywhere in the world from selling high-performance chips to China if they were made using American tools or components. The rules also make it difficult for China to produce its own high-end chips. They prohibit the manufacture of Chinese-designed chips worldwide if the designers used American software. And they prohibit the sales of American-made chip-making equipment or components to China.

The BIS justified its rules by saying that they were necessary to protect the US's national security and foreign policy interests. No mention was made of any unfair Chinese trade practices.

In general, the GATT's Article 11, which was adopted by the WTO, prohibits the imposition of non-tariff export restrictions. There are, however, exceptions. One of these is the "national security exception" which is the subject of Article 21.

In particular, Article 21 permits countries to take actions which they consider necessary for the protection of their essential security interests with respect to (i) fissionable materials, (ii) traffic in arms, ammunition and implements of war and (iii) actions taken in time of war or other emergencies in international relations.

Chips are not fissionable material. While the BIS claims that high-performance chips can be used in advanced military systems, including weapons of mass destruction, they are a general-purpose technology rather than arms or ammunition. Indeed, according to the Boston Consulting Group, the US Department of Defense accounts for just 1 percent of the US chip industry's revenue.

Thus, for the US to justify its actions under WTO rules, it would have to argue that it was already at war with China. While this would be a bizarre line of reasoning, consider that the US's lawyers justified the 2018 – 19 tariffs by arguing that Chinese trading practices violated American public morals. Unsurprisingly, the WTO panel did not accept this line of reasoning.

Of course, China is unlikely to receive any meaningful satisfaction from a future WTO panel ruling that the US's chip export ban is inconsistent with its obligations. That's because the US can, once again, appeal an unfavourable ruling into oblivion.

US disdain for the WTO has undermined three-quarters of a century of rules-based trade policy. In addition, the chip export ban threatens to reduce the speed of global innovation and the improvement of living standards. The BIS's rules are designed to prevent China from reaching the technological frontier for chips, supercomputers and artificial intelligence. However, with the Chinese market closed, international firms will have less revenue to support research and development. Their ability to develop better technologies will suffer as a result of this lose-lose policy.

Industry experts argue that China may be able to manage the BIS's actions in the near term. Last year's chip shortage has turned into a surplus as the demand for personal computers has fallen.

Moreover, major international firms have received waivers that will allow them to continue operating their factories in China for the next year. Over the medium term, however, China and the global chip industry will need to find creative solutions to these trade restrictions.

美国芯片出口禁令符合其世界贸易组织承诺吗？

2022 年 11 月 11 日

对我们这些相信基于规则的全球贸易体系的人来说，时事艰难。

75 年前，各国走到一起签署了《关税及贸易总协定》（GATT）。该协定阐述了开放及公平贸易的关键准则：最惠国待遇（一方的所有贸易伙伴地位平等）和国民待遇（不歧视外国产品偏向本国产品）。① 该协定在 1995 年被吸收入世界贸易组织（WTO，以下简称"世贸组织"）。目前，世贸组织有 160 个成员，代表了全球贸易总量的 98%。② 世贸组织的目标是确保国际贸易尽可能平稳、可预测和自由地流动。③ 世贸组织始终是"全球共享物"的重要组成部分——帮助国际冲突最小化的基础设施机构。世贸组织提供的可预测性在支持国际贸易显著增长及相关联的生活水平提高方面起到了重要作用。

鉴于这些成就，美国认为世贸组织不再符合其宗旨令人不安。美国声称，中国惯于违反其世贸组织义务，世贸组织已无法再监督中国的行为。

但这个基于规则的贸易体系真的已经这么不堪了吗？

根据哥伦比亚大学财经和经济学教授魏尚进收集的数据，中国遵守世贸组织裁定的记录大体与其他成员国是有可比性的（图 1）。④

2001—2021 年间，世贸组织接到 47 起针对中国贸易行为的投诉，占到这 20 年中所有世贸组织争端案件总数的 12%。

同一时期，有 110 起投诉是针对美国发起的。这个数目占总数的 28%，是针对中国投诉的一倍还多。魏教授称，其他成员国认为中国违反世贸组织承诺

---

① 贸易体系准则（https://www.wto.org/english/thewto_e/whatis_e/tif_e/fact2_e.htm）。

② WTO 概况（https://www.wto.org/english/thewto_e/thewto_e.htm）。

③ WTO 概况（https://www.wto.org/english/thewto_e/thewto_e.htm）。

④ 误读中国的 WTO 记录伤害全球贸易（http://news.koreaherald.com/common/newsprint.php?ud = 20211212000043）。

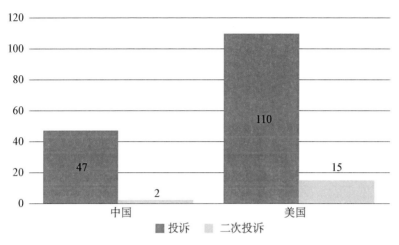

图 1　世界贸易组织贸易争端指标（2001—2021 年）

数据来源：魏尚进、第一财经

的可能性仅为美国的一半。

　　此外，在世贸组织争端解决小组做出不利于中国的裁决时，中国有合理的调整政策的记录。魏教授称，不遵守世贸组织判决的一个迹象是原告需要就相同或者非常相似的问题对同一个国家发起第二次投诉。在 47 起针对中国的投诉中，仅两起需要第二次提告（占 47 起的 4%）。相比之下，有 15 起针对美国的二次提告（占 110 起的 14%）。

　　没有数据支撑"中国是一个严重违反其入世承诺的国家，其贸易行为不受世贸组织程序制约"的观点。

　　世贸组织的争端解决机制旨在允许对不利的小组裁决进行上诉。然而，在特朗普政府期间，美国拒绝同意任命世贸组织上诉机构的新成员，而现有成员的任期已满。

　　这种世贸组织争端解决程序的崩溃对中国产生了不利影响。2020 年 9 月，世贸组织小组裁定，美国在 2018 年和 2019 年对中国进口产品征收的关税不符合其世贸组织义务。[①] 2020 年 10 月，美国对该小组的裁决提出上诉。由于世贸组织的上诉机构缺乏法定成员人数而无法审理上诉，所以在世贸组织内部无法解决该争端。因此，美国的上诉决定并不是为了解决此案件。相反，这是一个玩

---

① 世贸组织争端解决案 DS543：美国对来自中国的部分商品的关税措施（https://www.wto.org/english/tratop_e/dispu_e/cases_e/ds543_e.htm）。

世不恭的举动,将其对中国征收的关税争议置于法律的边缘。

即使世贸组织的争端解决机制处于混乱状态,但对美国最近禁止向中国出口高性能计算机芯片是否符合世贸组织原则的思考仍有启发。

2022年10月7日,美国商务部工业与安全局(以下简称"工业与安全局")宣布了新的规定,旨在限制中国获得先进计算芯片、开发和维护超级计算机以及制造先进半导体的能力。[①]

该规定禁止世界上任何地方的公司向中国出售使用美国工具或部件制造的高性能芯片。这些规定也使中国难以生产自己的高端芯片。如果中国设计者使用了美国软件,也不可以在全球范围内进行大规模生产。此外还禁止向中国销售美国制造的芯片制造设备或部件。[②]

工业与安全局辩称,这些规定对于保护美国的国家安全和外交政策利益是必要的,并没有提到任何不公平的中国贸易行为。

总的来说,由世贸组织继承和吸收的关贸总协定中的第11条规定,禁止非关税出口限制的实施。但是,也有例外的情况。其中之一便是"国家安全例外",这也是第21条的主题。

需特别指出的是,第21条允许各国采取它们认为必要的行动,以保护其在以下方面的基本安全利益:(1)可裂变材料;(2)武器、弹药和战争工具的贸易;(3)在战时或国际关系中的其他紧急情况下采取的行动。

芯片并非可裂变材料。尽管工业和安全局声称高性能芯片可用于先进的军事系统,包括大规模杀伤性武器,但芯片是一种通用技术,绝非武器或弹药专用。事实上,根据波士顿咨询集团的数据,美国国防部仅贡献了美国芯片行业收入的1%。[③]

因此,美国要根据世贸组织规则证明其行为的正当性,就必须辩称其已与中国开战。虽然这是一个奇怪的推论,但考虑到美国的律师通过辩称中国的贸易行为违反了美国的公共道德来证明其于2018—2019年间的加征关税是合理的

---

① 商务部对向中国出口先进计算和半导体制造产品实施新管制(https://www.bis.doc.gov/index.php/documents/about-bis/newsroom/press-releases/3158-2022-10-07-bis-press-release-advanced-computing-and-semiconductor-manufacturing-controls-final/file? utm_source = pocket_saves)。

② 掐断中国通往人工智能未来的通道(https://www.csis.org/analysis/choking-chinas-access-future-ai)。

③ 对于与中国贸易的限制如何终结美国在半导体行业的领导地位(https://www.bcg.com/publications/2020/restricting-trade-with-china-could-end-united-states-semiconductor-leadership)。

这一事实(也就不觉得奇怪了)。① 不出意料,世贸组织专家组并不接受这种推论。

　　当然,中国也不太可能从未来世贸组织专家组做出的"美国的芯片出口禁令与其义务不相符"这一裁决中获得任何有意义的补偿。这是因为美国可以再一次对不利裁决提出上诉,而使其不生效。

　　美国对世贸组织的蔑视破坏了长达75年的基于规则的贸易政策。此外,芯片进口禁令有可能放缓全球创新及生活水平提高的速度。工业和安全局的规定旨在阻止中国触及芯片、超级计算机和人工智能的技术前沿。然而,随着中国市场大门的"关闭",国际公司用于支持研发的收入将减少。而它们开发更先进技术的能力也将受到此种双输方针的影响。

　　业内专家认为中国或许能够在短期内设法应对工业和安全局所采取的行动。② 随着对个人电脑的需求的减少,2021年的芯片短缺已经转变为过剩。

　　此外,主要的跨国公司已经取得了能够令它们于2023年继续经营位于中国的工厂的豁免。然而,就中期而言,中国及全球芯片行业将需要为这些贸易限制寻得创造性的解决方案。

---

① 301条款 对来自中国的商品征收关税:国际和国内的法律挑战(https://crsreports. congress. gov/product/pdf/LSB/LSB10553? utm_source = pocket_saves)。

② 美国对中国的芯片制裁:影响分析(https://www. china-briefing. com/news/us-chip-sanctions-on-china-analysis-and-implications/? utm_source = pocket_saves)。

Can Robots Help Mitigate China's Demographic Decline?

March 3, 2023

With the recent census showing that China's population shrank last year, demographic pressures seem to be on everyone's mind.

A smaller population does not necessarily imply lower living standards. There are many ways to offset the effect of fewer workers on GDP per person.

First, people can be induced to work longer. Second, better education can make workers more productive. Third, "total factor productivity" can be raised by upgrading the country's product mix and by finding efficiencies in the production processes.

A fourth way to increase output in the face of a declining labour force is to give the remaining workers better tools. Raising "labour productivity" in this way seems to be the motivation behind China's "Robot + Application Action Plan". The Plan was jointly released earlier this year by the Ministry of Industry and Information Technology and 16 other ministries and departments.

The Plan aims to use robotics as a way to promote high-quality economic and social development. It targets ten industries in which it wants to increase the use of robots (Table 1).

Table 1　Industries Targeted Under the Robotics+ Application Action Plan

Manufacturing	Health
Agriculture	Elder services
Construction	Education
Energy	Commercial services
Commercial logistics	Safety & environmental emergency

Source: Ministry of Industry and Information Technology

The use of robots in industrial production processes is already widespread in China. According to the International Federation of Robotics (IFR), China has been the world's largest market for industrial robots since 2013.

In 2021, China installed close to 270,000 industrial robots, more than half of all those put into place worldwide (Figure 1). The rest of the world had installed 270,000 industrial robots in 2018, a peak that it has been unable to surmount in subsequent years. Despite the economic dislocation caused by the pandemic, China's installations continued to rise during 2020 and 2021. As a result, its share of global installations has increased sharply from the 38 percent it averaged between 2017 and 2019.

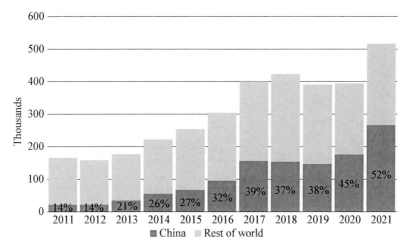

Figure 1   Installations of Industrial Robots

Source: IFR, Yicai

Since it has led the world in installations many years in a row, it is no surprise that the largest share of industrial robots can now be found in China. In fact, China's 1.2 million industrial robots account for 35 percent of the global total — more than those in Europe and the US combined (Figure 2).

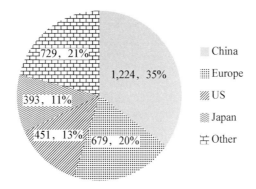

Figure 2   Stock of Industrial Robots in 000s (2021)

Source: IFR, Yicai

Data from the China Robot Industry Alliance (CRIA) show that China's manufacturing sector has used robots more intensively over time. Its "robot density" — measured as industrial robots per 10,000 employees in the manufacturing sector — more than doubled between 2018 and 2021 (Figure 3). The Robot + Application Action Plan envisages China's robot density doubling again between 2020 and 2025.

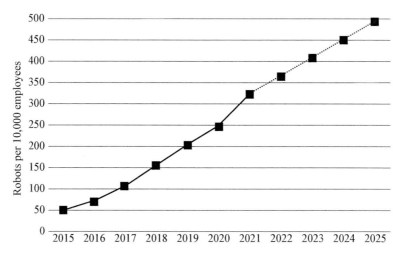

Figure 3　Robot Density: Manufacturing Industry

Source: CRIA, Yicai

In 2021, China's robot density (322) surpassed that of the US (274) for the first time (Figure 4). Likely, China will soon overtake Japan and Germany, which are just under 400. The use of robotics in manufacturing is highest in South Korea, which has a density of 1,000. This suggests that there is room to attain China's density target of 500 robots per 10,000 manufacturing sector employees.

Given its income level, China's intensive use of robotics in manufacturing seems to defy economic logic.

Robots are costly pieces of machinery. As traded goods, their prices should be similar across countries. We would expect a manufacturing firm to use robots to produce if so doing would increase its profits by more than the robots' purchase and installation costs. Looking around the world, the countries with the highest wages should be the ones that choose to substitute machines for people. But production workers' wages in China are only about half those in the US and average wages in South Korea and Japan are also well below American levels.

Demographics are likely driving the rapid adoption of robotics in Japan, South Korea and China. These countries are expected to experience much sharper

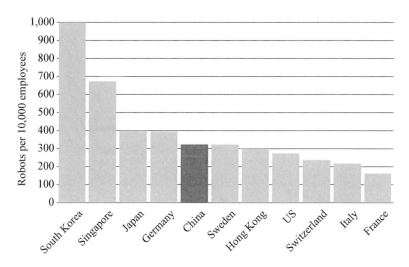

Figure 4   Robot Density: Manufacturing Industry (2021)

Source: IFR, Yicai

population declines than Germany, while the US's population is expected to continue growing over the next 40 years (Figure 5).

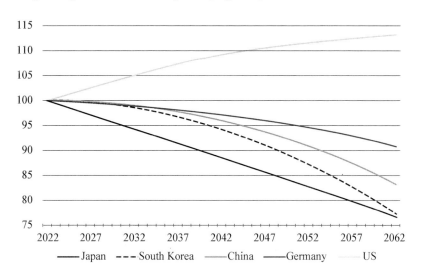

Figure 5   Population Indices (2022 = 100)

Source: UN, Yicai

Governments may be more sensitive to the impact of long-term demographic trends than businesses and China's plan to encourage the adoption of robotics resembles similar programs in Japan and South Korea.

In 2021, the distribution of the robots installed in China across the manufacturing industries was broadly similar to those of other countries (Figure 6). Somewhat more robots were installed in China's electrical/electronics industry, likely because it is relatively more important in the Chinese manufacturing sector. The automotive sector is a major user of robotics both in China and elsewhere.

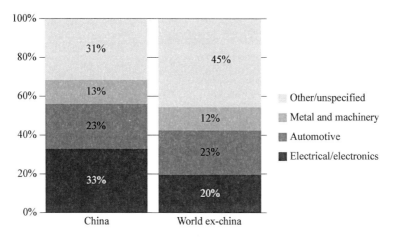

Figure 6   Industrial Robot Installation by Industry (2021)

Source: IFR, Yicai

Japan is the world's biggest producer of industrial robots but the Chinese industry is growing rapidly. In 2021, China installed close to 90,000 robots made under domestic brands, almost double the amount installed in 2018. Domestic brands accounted for close to one-third of all industrial robots China installed in 2021 (Figure 7).

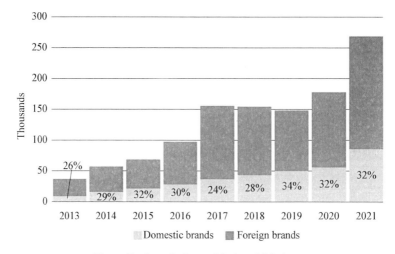

Figure 7   Installations of Industrial Robots

Source: IFR, CRIA, Yicai

China's domestic brands concentrate on producing robots for the plastics and chemicals and the metals and machinery industries where they accounted for three-quarters and two-thirds of the installations in 2021, respectively (Figure 8).

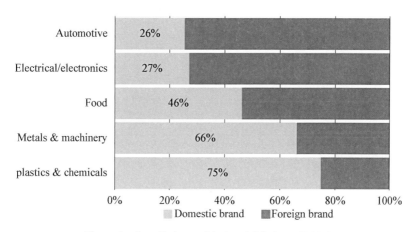

Figure 8　Installations of Industrial Robots (2021)

Source: CRIA, Yicai

China's robotics global leadership is also attracting new foreign investment.

ABB, a Swiss-Swedish multinational, recently opened a robotics mega factory in Shanghai. The CNY 1.1 billion ($150 million) production and research facility will manufacture next-generation robots. ABB predicts that the global robot market will grow from $80 billion today to $130 billion in 2025. The new Shanghai facility, one of three ABB Robotics factories worldwide, will support its customers in Asia.

The increased use of robotics may not offset the effects of demographic decline, but it should make the workforce more productive.

Cross-country research by economists at the Asian Development Bank shows that more intensive use of robotics leads to a fall in the demand for workers who perform routine manual tasks. However, automation also creates a demand for non-routine analytic jobs like programming, design and maintenance of high-tech equipment. The economists did not find a significant relation between robot adoption and overall employment growth. Nevertheless, moving workers from lower- to higher-value-added work is what ultimately increases living standards.

机器人能否帮助缓解中国人口下降的趋势？

2023 年 3 月 3 日

最近的统计数据显示中国人口去年出现负增长[1]，人口压力引发人们的担忧。

人口下降并不一定就意味着生活水平降低，有很多方法可以抵消劳动力减少对人均 GDP 的影响。

首先，可以劝导人们延长工作年限。其次，提高教育水平可以提高劳动力的生产力。再次，可以通过改善国家的产品结构以及生产效率来提高"全要素生产率"。[2]

还有一种方法可以在劳动力减少的情况下提高产出，那就是为现有的劳动力提供更好的工具。用这种方法提高"劳动生产率"似乎就是中国的《"机器人＋"应用行动实施方案》(以下简称"方案")的初衷。该方案由工业和信息化部等十七部门于今年初发布。[3]

该方案的目的是利用机器人促进高质量的经济社会发展，加快机器人技术在 10 个行业的应用(表 1)。

表 1　《"机器人＋"应用行动实施方案》的目标行业

制造业	医疗健康
农业	养老服务
建筑	教育
能源	商业社区服务
商贸物流	安全应急和极限环境应用

资料来源：中国工业和信息化部

---

[1] 正确看待中国人口下降（https://www.yicaiglobal.com/opinion/mark.kruger/putting-china-shrinking-population-in-perspective）。

[2] 改善法：理解日本的商业哲学（https://www.investopedia.com/terms/k/kaizen.asp）。

[3] 工业和信息化部等十七部门关于印发《"机器人＋"应用行动实施方案》的通知（https://www.miit.gov.cn/zwgk/zcwj/wjfb/tz/art/2023/art_c2a9bacca5114e42b5e16ed5277923a8.html）。

机器人已经普遍应用于中国工业生产过程中。据国际机器人联合会[①]数据,自 2013 年以来,中国已成为全球最大的工业机器人市场。

2021 年,中国工业机器人安装量达将近 270,000 台,占全球总量的一半以上(图 1)。除中国以外其他国家 2018 年工业机器人安装总量为 270,000 台,此后数年都没有超过这一记录。尽管新冠肺炎疫情对经济带来影响,但是中国的工业机器人安装量在 2020 年和 2021 年依然持续上升。因此,中国占全球安装量的份额较 2017 年至 2019 年平均 38% 的水平大幅提升。

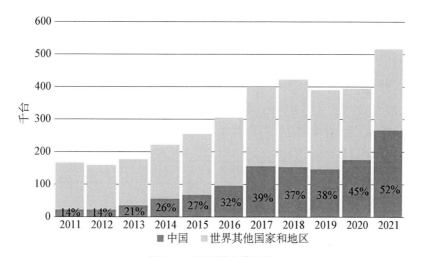

图 1　工业机器人装机量

数据来源:国际机器人联合会、第一财经

中国连续多年在装机量方面领先世界,因此,现在在中国工业机器人数量占比最高。中国有 120 万台工业机器人,占全球总数的 35%,超过了欧美工业机器人之和(图 2)。

中国机器人产业联盟(CRIA)的数据显示,中国制造业已经越来越密集地使用工业机器人。"机器人密度"代表制造业每万名工人所拥有的工业机器人数量,而这一数据在 2018 年到 2021 年间增长两倍以上(图 3)。[②] 按照方案的设想,中国的机器人密度将在 2020 年和 2025 年之间再翻一番。

---

① 国际机器人联合会官网(https://ifr.org/)。
② 2021 年中国市场工业机器人销售强劲增长(http://cria.mei.net.cn/news.asp? vid＝4004)。

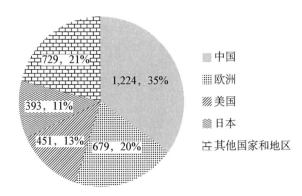

图 2　2021 年各国工业机器人保有量（千台）

数据来源：国际机器人联合会、第一财经

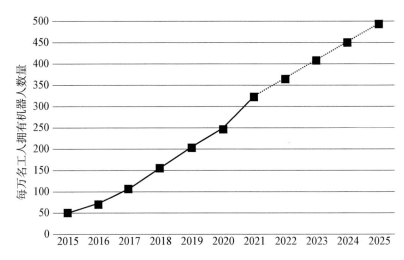

图 3　制造业机器人密度

数据来源：中国机器人产业联盟、第一财经

2021 年，中国的机器人密度（每万名工人 322 台）首次超过了美国（274 台）（图 4），不久将很可能超过日本和德国，这两个国家的机器人密度略少于 400 台。韩国制造业使用机器人最为广泛，其密度达到 1,000 台。这表明中国每万名制造业工人拥有 500 台机器人的密度目标还有待实现。

鉴于其收入水平，中国在制造业中大量使用机器人似乎违背了经济逻辑。

机器人是昂贵的机器。作为贸易商品，机器人的价格在各国之间应该是相似的。如果一个制造业公司使用机器人进行生产能使其利润的增加超过机器人的购买和安装成本，我们就会期望这样做。放眼世界，工资最高的国家应该是那些选择以机器代替人的国家。但中国生产工人的工资只有美国的一半

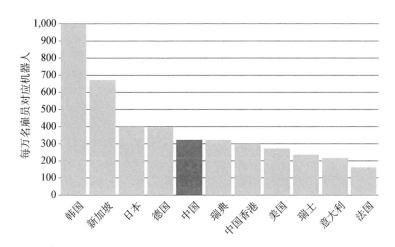

图4　制造业机器人密度（2021年）

数据来源：国际机器人联合会、第一财经

左右①，韩国和日本的平均工资也远远低于美国的水平②。

　　人口统计数据可能会推动机器人技术在日本、韩国和中国的迅速普及。这些国家预计将经历比德国更剧烈的人口下降，而美国的人口预计将在未来40年继续增长（图5）。

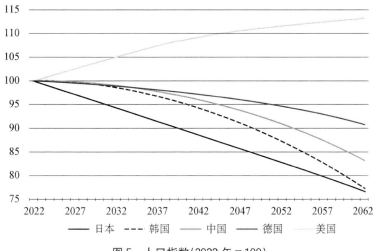

图5　人口指数（2022年＝100）

数据来源：联合国、第一财经

---

① 全球劳务费比较：对制造业选址决策和回流的影响（https://reshoringinstitute.org/wp-content/uploads/2022/09/GlobalLaborRateComparisons.pdf）。

② OECD数据：平均工资（https://data.oecd.org/earnwage/average-wages.htm）。

对长期人口趋势的影响,政府可能比企业更加敏感,中国鼓励采用机器人技术的计划与日本①和韩国②的相关方案很相似。

2021 年,安装在中国制造业的机器人的分布与其他国家大致相似(图 6)。从某种程度上而言,更多的机器人被布局于中国的电气、电子行业,也许是因为它(们)在中国的制造业中的地位相对更重要。而汽车行业则不论是对于中国还是世界其他地方来说,都是机器人的主要应用领域。

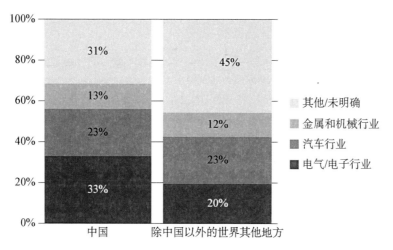

图 6　按行业划分的工业机器人布局(2021 年)

数据来源:国际机器人联合会、第一财经

日本是世界上最大的工业机器人制造国,但中国的这一产业也在迅速发展。2021 年,中国共安装了近 90,000 个国产品牌机器人,几乎是 2018 年相应安装量的 2 倍。而国产品牌占据了中国于 2021 年安装的工业机器人总数的近三分之一(图 7)。

中国本土品牌专注生产用于塑料和化学品以及金属和机械行业的机器人,2021 年它们分别占安装总量的四分之三和三分之二(图 8)。

中国机器人在全球的领导地位也在吸引新的外国投资。

瑞士-瑞典跨国公司 ABB 最近在上海开设了一家机器人大型工厂。③ 该

---

① 机器人技术(https://www.eubusinessinjapan.eu/sectors/electronics/robotics)。

② 韩国工业 4.0 框架下智能机器人产业发展战略(https://www.market-prospects.com/articles/smart-robot-industry-of-south-korea)。

③ ABB 在上海开设最先进的机器人大型工厂(https://new.abb.com/news/detail/97670/abb-opens-state-of-the-art-robotics-mega-factory-in-shanghai)。

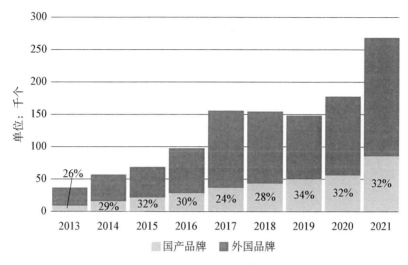

图7 工业机器人安装量

数据来源:国际机器人联合会、中国机器人产业联盟、第一财经

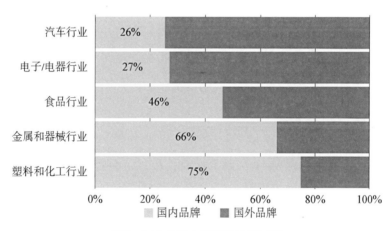

图8 工业机器人安装数(2021年)

数据来源:中国机器人产业联盟、第一财经

厂耗资11亿元人民币(1.5亿美元)的生产和研发设施将制造新一代机器人。ABB预测,全球机器人市场将从目前的800亿美元增长到2025年的1,300亿美元。新的上海工厂作为ABB机器人全球三家工厂之一将为亚洲客户提供支持。

更多机器人技术的使用可能无法抵消人口下降的影响,但应该会提高劳动力效率。

　　亚洲开发银行经济学家的跨国研究表明,更密集使用机器人技术导致对进行日常体力劳动的工人的需求下降。[①]　然而,自动化也创造了对非常规分析工作的需求,如高科技设备的编程、设计和维护。经济学家没有发现机器人的应用与整体就业增长之间存在明显关联。然而,将工人从低附加值工作转移到高附加值工作最终会提高生活水平。

[①] 机器人的兴起与流水线工作的衰落(https://www. adb. org/publications/rise-robots-fall-routine-jobs)。

The Demise of China's Private Sector: Greatly Exaggerated

July 5, 2022

Listening to the pundits, you could be excused for thinking that China's private sector is under mortal attack and is quickly losing ground to state-owned firms that benefit from extensive government support.

Three examples should suffice.

Late last autumn, Michael Pettis, a professor at Peking University's Guanghua School of Management, wrote that "Beijing has implemented a series of policies that have tightened control over the country's financial system, undermined private businesses and expanded the role of state-owned enterprises (SOEs) and public-sector investment".

Around the same time, Kevin Rudd, former Australian Prime Minister, in his speech to the Asia Society, said that the Chinese leadership has decided "to pivot toward the state" and away from the market.

And, this spring Scott Kennedy, a senior adviser at Center for Strategic and International Studies (CSIS), stated, "As everyone knows, over the last decade Chinese policies have given greater support to state-owned enterprises, giving rise to the idea of 'state ahead, private back'."

So, what do the data say?

According to China's State Administration for Market Regulation (SAMR), there were 45 million private enterprises active in China at the end of 2021. This represented a more than four-fold increase from 11 million in 2012. By comparison, Chinese real GDP only increased by 80 percent over the same period. Last year, private firms accounted for 92 percent of all Chinese enterprises, up from a 79 percent share in 2012.

The remarkable growth of the Chinese private sector was no accident. It was the result of a set of policies that supported firm creation by cutting red tape, reducing fees and increasing access to finance.

While the SAMR data show that private enterprises are thriving, many of the businesses in its database are likely to be very small. What do we know about the ability of private firms to grow and establish themselves in the upper ranks of the Chinese corporate sector?

Here we can rely on recent research conducted by Tianlei Huang and Nicolas Véron.

Huang and Véron sort Chinese firms into three categories based on the extent of the state's equity ownership. They consider those firms in which the state's ownership is 50 percent or more to be SOEs. Those in which the state owns 10 – 50 percent are called mixed-ownership enterprises (MOEs). And those in which the state has less than a 10 percent ownership share are classified as non-public enterprises (NPEs).

Huang and Véron painstakingly trace the state's ownership stake through an often opaque constellation of holding and investment entities to arrive at their assessment of beneficial ownership.

They then apply their ownership classification to the largest Chinese firms ranked by revenue as per *Fortune* magazine. This "Chinese Fortune 500" comprised 15 firms in 2005, 94 in 2015 and 130 in 2021. In 2021, the top firms in this list were the State Grid (ranked 2nd globally), China National Petroleum Corporation (ranked 4th), Sinopec (ranked 5th) and China State Construction Engineering Corporation (ranked 13th). All of these are SOEs. The largest NPE was Huawei (ranked 44th).

Huang and Véron find that the share of revenue earned by NPEs — essentially private firms — increased steadily, from under 5 percent in 2010 to just under 20 percent in 2020 (Figure 1). NPEs' share of other important business metrics — such as profits, assets and headcount — with respect to this set of the largest Chinese companies also rose steadily over time.

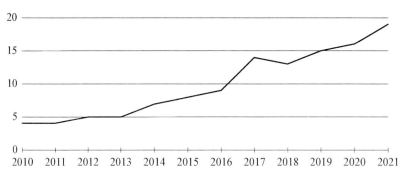

Figure 1　Revenue of Chinese Fortune 500: NPEs' Share (%)

Source: Huang & Véron, Bloomberg, Yicai

Huang and Véron conduct a second exercise in which they look at the ownership structure of China's 100 largest listed firms. Here they find that in 2010, NPEs' market cap was less than 10 percent of that of the 100 largest listed companies. But the NPEs' share rose to over 50 percent by 2020 (Figure 2). As at the end of 2021, the largest NPEs by market cap were Tencent (ranked 1st), Alibaba (ranked 3rd), CATL (ranked 5th) and Meituan (ranked 7th).

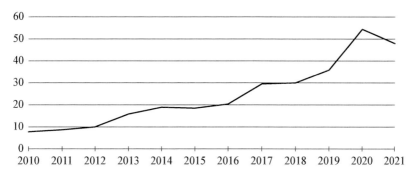

Figure 2　Chinese Top 100 Listed Companies' Market Cap: NPEs' Share (%)

Source: Huang & Véron, Bloomberg, Yicai

Huang and Véron conclude that the last decade has been one of "unprecedented displacement of state firms away from the top ranks of China's corporate world".

The Chinese leadership has consistently said that it wants a mixed economy in which both state-owned and private firms thrive. China's large state-owned sector makes it unique among major economies. Indeed, state-owned firms provide a useful complement to those that are market-driven.

To some extent, state-owned and private firms often operate in complementary spheres. SOEs typically operate upstream and provide basic materials, infrastructure and finance. Private firms typically operate downstream and produce consumer goods.

The functional differences between SOEs and private firms can be seen by looking at the distribution of assets across industrial sectors (here we use China's National Bureau of Statistics's definition of SOEs). SOEs own a very high share of the assets in the utilities sector. These are firms involved in the production and supply of electricity, thermal power, natural gas and water (Figure 3).

SOEs' assets only account for a quarter of those in the manufacturing sector and their share has declined in recent years. In contrast, SOEs' share in the mining sector has crept up and is approaching 50 percent.

Looking at the industrial sector as a whole, SOEs' asset share has declined marginally from just over 40 percent in 2012 to just under 40 percent in 2021.

We also see an apparent "division of labour" when we look at the distribution of assets across the largest manufacturing sub-sectors (Figure 4). SOEs dominate rail, ships and aerospace but account for a relatively small proportion of the assets

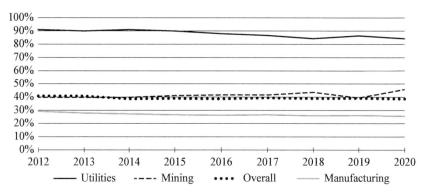

Figure 3　State Share of Assets by Industrial Sector

Source: Wind, Yicai

in computers and communication equipment and in electrical machinery and equipment. Autos is a sector in which both SOEs and private firms have major stakes, although the former's has fallen over time.

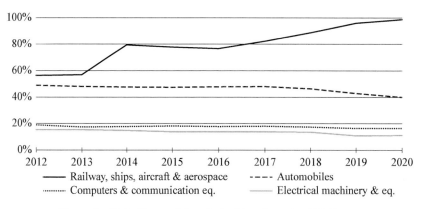

Figure 4　State Share of Assets by Manufacturing Sub-Sector

Source: Wind, Yicai

Domestic private firms have also increased their share of international trade (Figure 5). They account for close to 60 percent of all Chinese exports, compared to an 8 percent share for SOEs. Foreign firms (not shown) account for about one-third. Domestic private firms's hare of imports has almost doubled over the past decade, while that of SOEs has hovered around the 25 percent level.

While China's SOEs do not appear to dominate the economy, they are key vehicles for implementing economic policy.

The SOEs offer the leadership a useful tool for managing the business cycle. In the West, monetary policy has the primary responsibility for demand management.

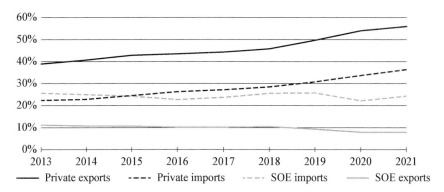

Figure 5   International Trade Shares

Source: CEIC, Yicai

However, as we have seen, in a downturn even a sizable interest rate reduction may be insufficient to induce private sector investment. Moreover, looser monetary policy could simply feed asset-price bubbles.

In 2009 and 2015 – 2016 and likely again this year, SOE investments provide an important offset to the weakness in private Chinese investment demand.

SOEs' investments can be very useful in situations where the social return exceeds that to private firms. This is often the case for large infrastructure projects. China's state-owned telecoms are currently constructing the infrastructure for 5G communication that will provide the basis for private firms to develop useful applications. Moreover, SOEs are at the forefront of installing the renewable power that will allow China to meet its carbon neutrality goals.

However, the use of SOEs to achieve goals other than profit maximization comes at a cost. In general, their profitability — in terms of return on assets — is lower than that of private firms (Figure 6).

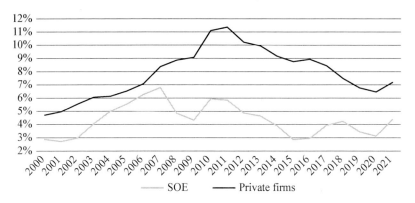

Figure 6   Industrial Firms: Return on Assets

Source: CEIC, Yicai

China is in the final year of a three-year action plan for SOE reform, which is designed to make state-owned firms more competitive, innovative and resilient to risks. One of its key initiatives is "mixed-ownership reform" which will allow SOEs to benefit from the private sector's capital and know-how.

If the data show that the Chinese private sector is thriving, how should we understand the recent regulatory crackdown?

For some time, China's regulatory environment had been somewhat opaque. Officials were given discretion to adapt rules to local conditions and see what arrangements worked best. While this "constructive ambiguity" probably did support rapid growth, it created other problems. For example, foreign firms have long complained that the regulatory environment was unpredictable and this lack of clarity prevented them from investing even more in China.

Under President Xi, China has increasingly stressed the rule of law over administrative discretion. Moreover, like other countries, China has become increasingly concerned about the platform companies' market power. Indeed, Chinese platform companies — in particular, Alibaba and Tencent — have become pervasive forces in the economy. They are much more powerful than Facebook, Google and Amazon in the West.

In recent years, the government issued a large number of new regulations, many of which caught the market by surprise. The goal here was not to crush this innovative segment of the private sector. Rather, the regulations provided more transparent guidelines on fair business operations, internet finance and practices that have the potential to endanger national security.

Late last month, the Standing Committee of the National People's Congress voted to pass a revised anti-monopoly law, which will come into effect on August 1. The revisions, which focus on the digital economy, are the first to be made to the law since its implementation in 2008. Clarifying the regulatory framework is welcome as it will further promote China's private sector's healthy development.

中国私营部门的败落：被过分夸大了

2022 年 7 月 5 日

只听专家言论的话，你可能会认为中国的私营部门正遭受到致命打击，迅速失去地盘，让位于政府大力支持的国有企业。

三个例子足矣。

2021 年秋天，北京大学光华管理学院教授迈克尔·佩蒂斯写道："中国政府采取了一系列措施收紧对国家金融体系的管控，削弱了私营企业，扩大了国有企业和公共部门投资的作用。"

大概在同一时间，澳大利亚前总理陆克文（Kevin Rudd）在亚洲协会的演讲中表示中国领导人决定要"转向政府"，远离市场。

美国战略与国际问题研究中心高级顾问甘思德（Scott Kennedy）则在 2022 年春天提到："众所周知，在过去 10 年间，中国政府加大了对国有企业的支持，因此产生了'国进民退'之说。"

那么，数据方面有什么体现呢？

据中国国家市场监督管理总局的数据，截至 2021 年底，中国共有 4,500 万活跃私营企业，是 2012 年的 1,100 万的 4 倍还多。[①] 相比之下，中国的实际 GDP 同期仅增长了 80%。2021 年，私营企业占中国企业总数的 92%，而 2012 年占比为 79%。

中国私营部门的大幅增长绝非偶然，而是简化一系列涉及企业创办手续、降低费用、增加金融市场准入政策的结果。

虽然国家市场监督管理总局数据显示私营企业蓬勃发展，但是很多企业规模都很小。我们对私营企业发展壮大并跻身中国企业前列的能力了解多少？

[①] 从 2012 年 1,085.7 万户增长到 2021 年 4,457.5 万户 民营企业数量 10 年翻两番（https://www.samr.gov.cn/xw/mtjj/202203/t20220323_340715.html）。

我们来看一下黄天磊和尼古拉斯·贝隆(Nicolas Véron)最近的研究。[①]

二人将中国公司根据国有股权比例分为三类。国有股权占比达50%及以上的为国有企业,10%至50%之间的为混合所有制企业,10%以下的为非公有制企业。

二人努力通过一组通常不透明的控股和投资实体信息追踪到国有股权比例,以得出他们对实益所有权的评估结果。

之后他们将该企业分类方法用在了《财富》杂志按收入排名收入最多的那些中国公司上。这些公司被称为"中国财富500强",包括2005年的15家公司,2015年的94家,以及2021年的130家。2021年,排名前列的公司为国家电网(全球排名第2)、中国石油天然气集团有限公司(排名第4)、中国石化(排名第5)、中国建筑集团有限公司(排名第13)。它们全部都是国有企业,最大的非公有制企业是华为(排名第44)。

黄天磊和贝隆发现非公有制企业(基本上都是私有企业)的收入在中国财富500强中的比例稳定增长,从2010年的5%上升到2020年的略低于20%(图1)。在其他重要业务指标(如利润、资产和员工人数)方面,非公有制企业在中国财富500强中所占的份额也随着时间的推移稳步上升。

图1　中国财富500强收入:非公有制企业占比(%)

数据来源:黄天磊和贝隆、彭博社、第一财经

黄天磊和贝隆进行了第二次研究,他们研究了中国前100名上市公司的所有制结构。他们发现,2010年非公有制企业的市值在前100名上市公司中占比低于10%,但是到2020年这一份额超过了50%(图2)。截至2021年末,市值最

① 私营企业在中国的发展(https://www.piie.com/sites/default/files/documents/wp22-3.pdf)。

大的非公有制企业为腾讯,第 3 名为阿里巴巴,宁德时代排第 5,美团第 7。

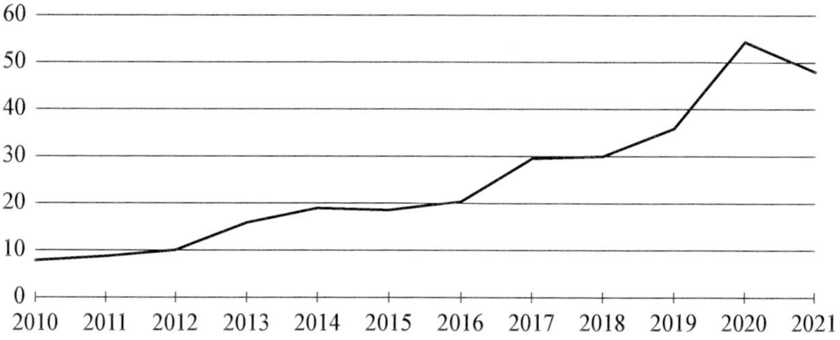

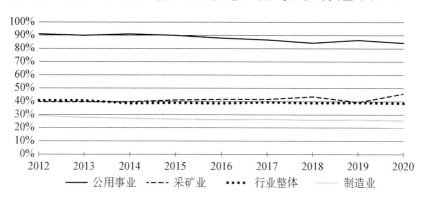

图 2　中国前 100 名上市公司的市值:非公有制企业占比(%)

数据来源:黄天磊和贝隆、彭博社、第一财经

黄天磊和贝隆的结论是,过去 10 年间,"国有企业渐渐从中国企业界前列的位置上下滑,这是前所未见的"。

中国政府一直坚持混合经济,使国有企业和私营企业都能蓬勃发展。中国国有部门之庞大,在主要经济体中独一无二。应该看到,国有企业确实是以市场为导向的私营企业的有益补充。

在某种程度上,国有企业和私营企业往往互补。国有企业通常在上游经营,提供原材料、基础设施和资金,而私营企业通常在下游经营,生产消费品。

通过观察各产业部门的资产分布,可以看出国有企业和私营企业之间的功能差异(这里使用中国国家统计局对国有企业的定义)。在公用事业部门,国有企业资产占比很高,主要涉及电力、火力发电、天然气和水的供应(图 3)。

图 3　不同行业国有资产占比

数据来源:万得资讯、第一财经

在制造业中,国有企业资产占比仅为四分之一,最近几年还有下降。相反,国有企业在采矿业的份额正悄然增加,接近 50%。

从整个工业部门来看,国有企业资产份额已经从 2012 年的略高于 40% 小幅下降到 2021 年的略低于 40%。

在最大的制造业子行业资产分布中,也可以看出明显的"分工"(图 4)。国有企业在铁路、船舶和航空航天领域占主导地位,但在计算机、通信设备以及电气机械和设备领域资产占比较小。汽车行业中,国有企业和私营企业平分秋色,但国有企业份额已经开始下降。

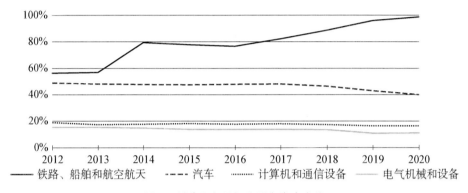

图 4　制造业各子行业国有资产占比

数据来源:万得资讯、第一财经

本土私营企业在国际贸易中的份额也有所增加(图 5),占到了中国总出口的 60%,而国有企业只占 8%,外国公司(未显示)约占三分之一。过去 10 年,国内私营企业的进口份额几乎翻了一番,而国有企业的进口份额一直徘徊在 25% 左右。

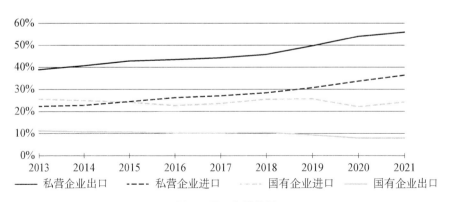

图 5　国际贸易份额

数据来源:环亚经济数据、第一财经

虽然中国的国有企业看似并不主导经济,但它们是实施经济政策的关键工具。

国有企业为领导层提供了管理商业周期的有用工具。在西方,货币政策主要负责需求管理。然而,正如我们所看到的,在经济低迷时期,即使是大幅降息也可能不足以吸引民营企业投资。此外,更宽松的货币政策只会助长资产价格泡沫。

在 2009 年、2015—2016 年,国有企业投资抵消了疲软的中国私有投资需求,今年可能再次出现这样的情况。

国有企业投资在以社会回报为主要诉求的情况下十分有效。大型基础设施项目往往如此。中国国有电信企业目前正在建设 5G 通信基础设施,这会为民营企业开发有用的应用提供基础。此外,国有企业处于使用可再生能源的最前沿,这将促使中国实现其碳中和目标。

然而,利用国有企业来实现利润最大化以外的目标是有代价的。总的来说,它们的盈利能力——就资产回报率而言——低于民营企业(图 6)。

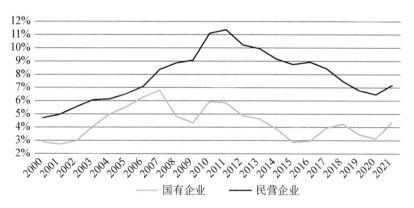

图 6　工业企业——资产回报率

数据来源:环亚经济数据、第一财经

中国正处于国有企业改革三年行动①的最后一年,该计划旨在使国有企业更具竞争力、创新性和抗风险能力。其主要举措之一是“混合所有制改革”,这将使国有企业能够从民营企业的资本和专有技术中受益。

如果数据显示中国民营企业正在蓬勃发展,我们应该如何理解最近的监管

① 中国国有企业如何进行三年改革行动(http://www.xinhuanet.com/english/2021-01/29/c_139707120.htm)?

打击^①?

一段时间以来,中国的监管环境有些不透明。官员们被赋予了自由裁量权,可以因地制宜。虽然这种"建设性的模糊性"可能确实支持了快速增长,但也带来了其他问题。例如,外资企业长期以来一直抱怨监管环境不可预测,这种不明确性使它们无法在中国投资更多。

在习近平主席的领导下,中国越来越强调法治而不是行政自由裁量权。此外,与其他国家一样,中国越来越关注平台公司的市场力量。事实上,中国平台公司——尤其是阿里巴巴和腾讯——已经成为经济中无处不在的力量。它们比西方的脸谱网、谷歌和亚马逊强大得多。

近年来,中国政府发布了大量新法规,其中许多法规令市场措手不及。其目标不是粉碎民营企业的这一创新部分。相反,这些规定为公平的商业运作、互联网金融和可能危害国家安全的行为提供了更透明的指导方针。

上月底,全国人民代表大会常务委员会投票通过了修订后的反垄断法^②,该法将于8月1日生效。此次修订以数字经济为重点,是自2008年实施以来首次对该法进行修订。明确监管框架广受好评,因为它将进一步促进中国民营企业的健康发展。

---

① 中国的监管打击如何重塑技术和房产企业(https://www.reuters.com/world/china/education-bitcoin-chinas-season-regulatory-crackdown-2021-07-27/)?

② 中国反垄断法修订,加强监管平台经济(https://www.yicaiglobal.com/opinion/mark.kruger/restrictions-are-lifted-let-go-shopping)。

Part III

China and the Rest of the World

第三部分

中国与世界

US Companies: In China for the Long Haul

March 20, 2020

Last week, the American Chamber of Commerce in the People's Republic of China (AmCham) released its 2020 China Business Climate Survey Report. The AmCham is a non-profit, non-governmental organization, whose membership includes the major US businesses operating in China, such as Apple, Cisco and JPMorgan. I am an avid reader of these Reports, which give us American companies' on-the-ground perspective.

Survey respondents appear to be looking through the headlines, soundbites and tweets and remain committed to China. They say China's investment environment has gotten better, intellectual property rights (IPR) protection is improving and that they are feeling more and more welcome here.

This is my summary of the Report's highlights. For those of you who want to read the Report and enjoy its rich detail, I refer you to the AmCham website, where you can download it for free.

Last year was a challenging one for AmCham members. Only 46 percent of survey respondents reported a year-over-year increase in revenue, down from an average of 60 percent in recent years (Figure 1). Those firms which produce for the US market had the toughest time. Only 26 percent of them reported higher revenues.

While 61 percent of the respondents reported that they were either "profitable" or "very profitable" last year, this is down from close to 70 percent, on average, over 2014 – 18. Indeed, AmCham reports that, in 2019, profitability dropped to its lowest level since it began asking the question 18 years ago.

Despite the challenges of operating in China, 72 percent of the respondents said that their profit margins were higher than, or comparable to, those of their global operations. This suggests that times are tough everywhere.

Respondents continue to see an improvement in the business environment (Figure 2). In 2016, more than half said that foreign companies were treated unfairly, relative to local ones. By 2019, that share had dropped to just over a third.

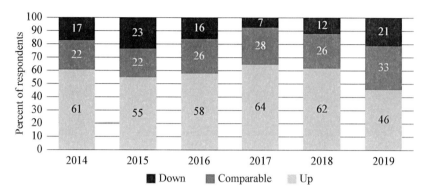

Figure 1　How Does the Revenue of Your China Operations Compare With the Previous Year?

Source: AmCham 2020 Survey (2017 adds to 99), Yicai

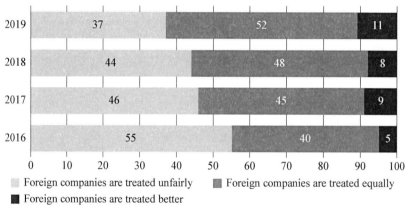

Figure 2　How Are Foreign Companies Treated Relative to Local Companies?

Source: AmCham 2020 Survey, 2019 Survey, Yicai

Unequal market access remains the principal concern. Indeed, more than a quarter of the respondents said that lack of market access "significantly" inhibited their China operations. This was a particularly sore point for firms in the Consumer sector.

China's investment environment looked a lot better in 2019. Half of the respondents saw the quality of China's investment environment improving, up from one-third over 2013 – 18 (Figure 3). The Report noted that concrete actions taken in 2019 — the Foreign Investment Law, the Regulations on Optimizing the Business Environment, and the reforms in the financial services sector — were important confidence boosters.

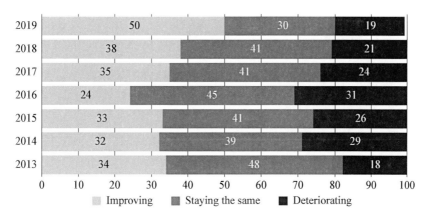

Figure 3   The Quality of China's Investment Environment Is

Source: AmCham 2020 Survey (2019 responses add to 99), 2019 Survey, Yicai

Close to 70 percent of the respondents said that China's enforcement of IPR has improved in the last five years (Figure 4). This is up 10 percentage points from last year's survey.

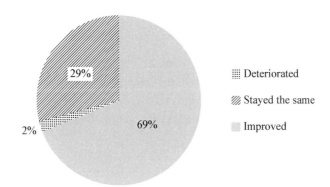

Figure 4   In the Last Five Years, China's Enforcement of IPR Has

Source: AmCham 2020 Survey, Yicai

Despite the news reports about the trade tensions leading firms to relocate their supply chains, respondents show an increasing commitment to China. Figure 5 illustrates that fewer firms were relocating, or considering doing so, in 2019 than in previous years. This increased commitment to China is consistent with the steady improvement in the business environment.

While US firms may be here to stay, a growing share of respondents will not expand, or may actually decrease, their investments in the near term. Uncertainty over US-China relations and the tariffs are weighing on investment plans as is the

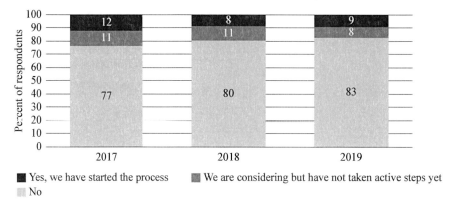

Figure 5 Is Your Company Considering Relocating Manufacturing or Sourcing Outside of China?

Source: AmCham 2020 Survey (2019 adds to 99), Yicai

expectation of slower growth in China.

Policies that increase the transparency, predictability and fairness of the regulatory environment would boost investment. More than 40 percent of the firms surveyed said such measures would have a "very significant" or "extremely significant" impact on their investment levels.

All local governments are not created equal when it comes to offering foreign investors a welcoming investment environment. The respondents overwhelmingly chose Shanghai, among the mainland provincial and municipal governments, as being most effective in attracting and working with foreign investors. Figure 6 shows how Shanghai's rating compares with the four next-best ranked provincial governments.

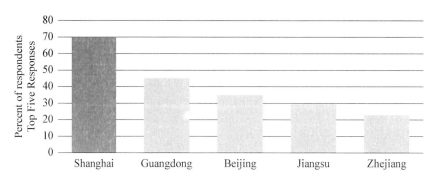

Figure 6 Which Provincial Governments Are Most Effective in Working With and Attracting Foreign Investors?

Source: AmCham 2020 Survey, Yicai

AmCham's 2020 survey was conducted between October 24 and November 25, 2019. This was prior to the signing of the Phase One trade deal and the COVID－19 outbreak. While these are certainly significant events, I do not expect they will alter these companies' long-term commitment to China.

美国公司：在中国作长远打算

2020 年 3 月 20 日

2020 年 3 月，中国美国商会（AmCham）发布了《2020 年中国商业环境调查报告》。美国商会是一个非营利性的非政府组织，成员包括苹果、思科和摩根大通等在华经营的美国大公司。我是这些报告的热心读者，这些报告为我们提供了美国公司的实地视角。

受访企业似乎在浏览新闻头条、言论和推文，仍然致力于中国。它们认为中国的投资环境越来越好，知识产权（IPR）保护正在改进，它们觉得在中国越来越受欢迎。

以下是我对报告要点的总结。如果你想阅读这份报告，享受其中丰富的细节，我建议你去中国美国商会的网站，在那里你可以免费下载报告①。

对商会成员来说，2019 年是充满挑战的一年。只有 46% 的受访企业报告它们在华业务收入高于 2018 年，低于近年来 60% 的平均值（图 1）。那些为美国市场生产产品的公司经历了最艰难的时期。只有 26% 的公司报告收入增长。

虽然有 61% 的受访企业表示，它们去年"盈利"或"收获颇丰"，但这一比例低于 2014—2018 年近 70% 的平均值。事实上，中国美国商会表示，2019 年美国企业在华盈利水平降至其 18 年前开始提出这个问题以来的最低水平。

尽管在中国运营面临挑战，但 72% 的受访企业表示，它们在华业务的利润率高于或与全球业务相当。这说明世界各地的情况都很艰难。

受访企业继续看到商业环境的改善（图 2）。2016 年，超过一半的受访企业表示，相对于本土公司，外国公司受到了不公平待遇。到 2019 年，这一比例降至略高于三分之一。

---

① 2020 年中国商业环境调查报告（https://www.amchamchina.org/about/press-center/amcham-statement/2020-business-climate-survey-released）。

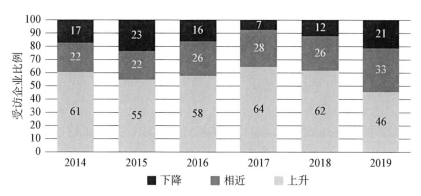

图1　当年在华业务收入与上一年相比不同情况的比例

注：2017年总比例为99%。

数据来源：中国美国商会、第一财经

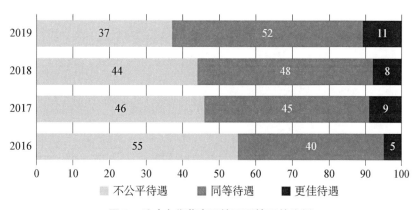

图2　反映在华营商环境不同情况的比例

数据来源：中国美国商会、第一财经

市场准入不平等仍然是主要问题。事实上，超过四分之一的受访企业表示，缺乏市场准入"严重"阻碍了它们在中国的业务。这对于消费领域的公司来说尤其是个痛点。

2019年，中国投资环境明显改善。半数受访企业认为中国的投资环境质量在改善，高于2013—2018年的三分之一（图3）。报告指出，2019年采取的具体行动，如《中华人民共和国外商投资法》《优化营商环境条例》和金融服务业改革是重要的信心助推器。

近70%的受访者表示，中国知识产权执法在过去5年有所改善（图4），比2019年的调查高出10个百分点。

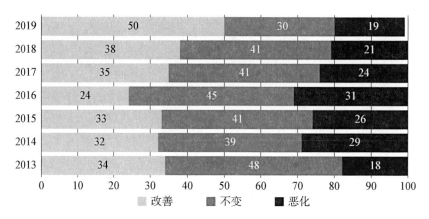

图 3　反映中国投资环境质量不同情况的比例

注：2019 年总比例为 99%。

数据来源：中国美国商会、第一财经

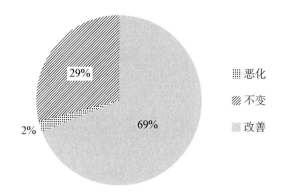

图 4　反映过去 5 年中国知识产权执法不同情况的比例

数据来源：中国美国商会、第一财经

　　尽管有新闻报道称贸易紧张导致企业转移供应链，但受访企业实际上越来越专注于中国市场。图 5 显示，2019 年搬迁或考虑搬迁的受访企业少于前几年。在华投资的增加与营商环境的稳步改善是一致的。

　　虽然美国公司可能会留下来，但表示近期不会扩大投资，甚至可能减少投资的受访企业比例在提高。中美关系和关税的不确定性，以及对中国经济增长放缓的预期，正在给投资计划带来压力。

　　提高监管环境透明度、可预测性和公平性的政策将促进投资。超过 40% 的受访企业表示，这些措施将对其投资水平产生"非常显著"或"极其显著"的影响。

　　在为外国投资者提供良好的投资环境方面，地方政府的表现不尽相同。在

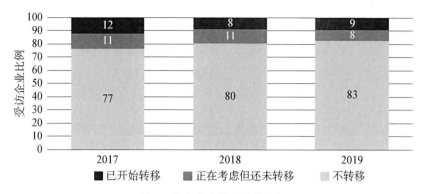

图5　考虑转移供应链的比例

注：2018 年总比例为 99%。

数据来源：中国美国商会、第一财经

省级政府中，绝大多数受访企业认为上海在吸引和与外国投资者合作方面效率最高。图 6 比较了上海与其他四个次好的省市在这方面的表现。

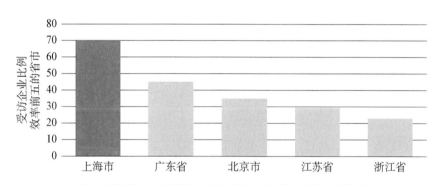

图6　不同省市在吸引和与外国投资者合作方面的效率比较

数据来源：中国美国商会、第一财经

　　中国美国商会 2020 年调查于 2019 年 10 月 24 日至 11 月 25 日进行，早于中美签署第一阶段贸易协定和新冠肺炎疫情暴发。虽然这些都是重大事件，但我不认为它们会改变这些公司对中国的长期承诺。

Will Japanese Firms Desert China?

April 28, 2020

The Abe government is encouraging Japanese firms to leave China and return home.

As part of its massive supplementary budget, the Japanese government is providing 220 billion yen (US $2 billion) in loans to support firms in relocating their operations from China to Japan. It is offering an additional 23.5 billion yen in loans to help those companies that might wish to move their operations from China to third countries.

Why is the Japanese government doing this? According to the *Japan Times*, it is worried about the impact that supply chain disruptions in China can have on Japanese manufacturers. It wants Japanese firms to broaden their sources of inputs — by buying more from Southeast Asia — and to return the production of high value-added products to Japan.

Apparently, the exodus is already beginning. The Nikkei Asian Review reports that Iris Ohyama will likely be the first Japanese company to take advantage of the relocation support program. Iris Ohyama makes a range of household products and it currently produces face masks at its Chinese plants in Dalian and Suzhou. These plants procure non-woven and other materials from Chinese suppliers. In June, Iris Ohyama will begin producing face masks for non-medical uses in Kakuda, Miyagi prefecture, with Japanese-sourced materials. Nevertheless, it plans to continue making masks at its two Chinese factories.

Is Iris Ohyama's move an anomaly or does it indicate that a significant amount of Japanese capital is likely to return to Japan from China?

Japan's stock of foreign direct investment (FDI) abroad totalled US $1,645 billion as at the end of 2018. Figure 1 shows how evenly distributed these investments were: 32 percent in North America, 28 percent in Asia, 27 percent in Europe and 13 percent in other countries. Japan's investments in China totalled US $124 billion or close to 8 percent of the total.

Two points emerge from this graph.

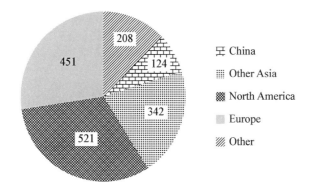

Figure 1   Distribution of Japanese FDI Stock 2018 (US $ bn)

Source: JETRO, Yicai

First, Japan's Chinese investments are small compared to China's economic importance. The IMF expects China to account for 17 percent of global GDP this year (at market exchange rates), second only to the US's 25 percent. Moreover, China is Japan's number one trading partner. In 2019, trade with China accounted for more than a fifth of total Japanese goods trade. By comparison, trade with all of Europe only amounted to 13 percent of the total. From a strategic perspective, Japan does not appear to be excessively reliant on its Chinese investments.

Second, the Japanese government's relocation support program is equal to less than 2 percent of Japan's stock of investments in China. So, even if the program were fully utilized, we should not expect that more than a very small portion of Japan's China-based capital stock would return home.

Notwithstanding rising trade tensions, Japanese firms have continued to increase their investments in China. Figure 2 shows that the stock of Japanese FDI in China grew by US $5 billion per year, on average, between 2013 and 2018.

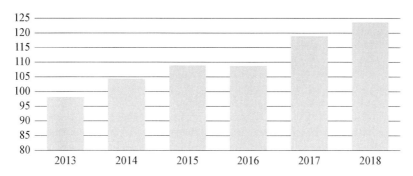

Figure 2   Japanese Direct Investment in China (US $ bn)

Source: JETRO, Yicai

While the data on Japan's FDI stocks are not yet available for 2019, the flows numbers suggest growth of a similar magnitude last year. This means that new annual Japanese investments in China have been more than double the size of the Japanese government's relocation support program.

In recent years, most of Japan's investments in China have been in the manufacture of transportation equipment and in the wholesale and retail trades. Japanese companies in these sectors are unlikely to go anywhere because their success depends on being close to the Chinese consumers.

Japanese auto manufacturers in China have been doing well in a very challenging market. In 2019, Japanese auto brands increased sales by 3 percent, while those of European brands fell by 2 percent, South Korean brands by 18 percent and US brands by 23 percent. Sales by domestic Chinese brands fell by 15 percent last year. Honda and Toyota achieved record sales last year and Japanese brands attained their highest market share since 2011.

In addition to being the world's factory, China is also the world's shopping mall and Japanese firms have been successful in cashing in on China's growing consumer demand. Some companies, like Uniclo, Muji and Casio are taking advantage of China's vibrant online retail culture to market their products. Moreover, Aeon, Japan's largest retailer, is planning to invest US $4.6 billion through 2021 in its Chinese digital business. Other companies, like Asics and Shiseido have levered their extensive bricks and mortar presence in China into sales growth well surpassing that of other markets.

On the one hand, favourable Chinese demand is likely to continue to act as a magnet for Japanese firms. On the other, unfavourable demographics make it challenging for Japanese firms to return home.

Japan's society is aging rapidly and, despite the rising participation of women in the workforce, its labour market is incredibly tight. Figure 3 shows the Japanese

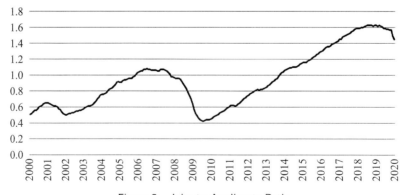

Figure 3　Jobs-to-Applicants Ratio

Source: CEIC, Yicai

job-to-applicants ratio, a key labour market indicator. Even after a virus-related dip, there are still close to 1. 4 jobs per applicant. This suggests that it will be difficult for Japan to find the workers needed to re-absorb a significant amount of its Chinese investment stock.

The foregoing analysis suggests that the Japanese government's relocation support program will only facilitate the return of niche production to Japan.

Even so, no place on earth is immune from an "act of God" that could potentially undermine supply chains. Indeed, Miyagi prefecture itself was hard hit by the 2011 earthquake and tsunami. Ultimately, open boarders and a nimble global supply response may be the best disaster management plan.

日本企业会离开中国吗？

2020 年 4 月 28 日

　　日本政府正鼓励日本企业离开中国，回到日本。

　　作为巨额补充预算的一部分，日本政府将提供 2,200 亿日元（20 亿美元）贷款，支持企业将业务从中国转移到日本。日本政府还将提供 235 亿日元的贷款，帮助那些可能希望将业务从中国转移到第三国的公司。

　　日本政府为什么要这么做？据《日本时报》报道，政府担心中国供应链中断会对日本制造商造成影响。它希望日本公司通过从东南亚购买更多的产品来扩大投入品的来源，并将高附加值产品的生产转移回日本[1]。

　　显然，大迁徙已经开始了。据《日经亚洲评论》报道，爱丽思集团（Iris Ohyama）可能会成为第一家使用搬迁支持项目的日本公司[2]。爱丽思集团生产一系列家用产品，公司目前在位于大连和苏州的中国工厂生产口罩。这些工厂从中国供应商那里采购非织造布和其他材料。2020 年 6 月起，爱丽思集团将开始在宫城县角田市使用日本原料生产非医用口罩。尽管如此，该公司仍计划继续在中国的两家工厂生产口罩。

　　爱丽思集团的行为是反常现象，还是意味着大量日资可能会从中国回流日本？

　　截至 2018 年底，日本对外直接投资存量总计 1.645 万亿美元。图 1 显示了这些投资在各大洲的分布十分均匀：北美占 32%，亚洲占 28%，欧洲占 27%，其他地区占 13%。日本对华投资为 1,240 亿美元，占其对外投资总额的 8% 左右。

　　从这张图中我们可以看出两点。

---

① 鉴于新冠疫情　日本打算切断对中国的供应链依赖（https://www.japantimes.co.jp/news/2020/03/06/business/japan-aims-break-supply-chain-dependence-china/#.XqJHTGgzZPY）。

② 日本为将生产移出中国的公司准备第一笔补贴（https://asia.nikkei.com/Spotlight/Coronavirus/Japan-preps-first-subsidy-to-company-moving-production-out-of-China）。

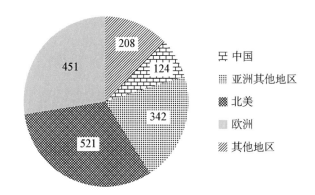

图1　2018年日本对外直接投资存量分布情况（单位：十亿美元）

数据来源：日本贸易振兴机构、第一财经

首先，与中国的经济重要性相比，日本在中国的投资规模很小。国际货币基金组织预计，2020年中国将占全球GDP的17%（按市场汇率计算），仅次于美国的25%。此外，中国是日本的第一大贸易伙伴。2019年，对华贸易占日本商品贸易总额的五分之一以上。相比之下，与整个欧洲的贸易仅占日本商品贸易总额的13%。从战略角度来看，日本似乎并没有过度依赖对中国的投资。

其次，日本政府的搬迁支持项目规模不到日本在华投资存量的2%。因此，即使该计划得到充分实施，我们也不应该期望会有相当一部分的日本在华资本存量回流日本。

尽管贸易紧张局势升级，但日本公司仍在继续增加在中国的投资。从图2可以看出，2013—2018年，日本对华直接投资存量平均每年增长50亿美元。虽然2019年日本对外投资存量数据尚未公布，但流量数据显示，2019年的增长幅度与此前类似。这意味着日本每年在华新增投资是日本政府搬迁支持项目规模的两倍多。

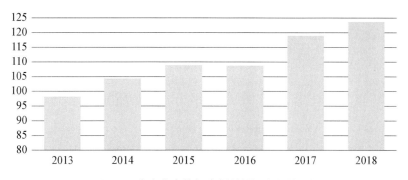

图2　日本在华直接投资额（单位：十亿美元）

数据来源：日本贸易振兴机构、第一财经

近年来,日本在华投资集中在交通运输设备制造和批发零售行业。这些领域的日本企业不太可能转移到其他地方,因为它们的成功取决于与中国消费者的密切关系。

在充满挑战的中国市场上,日本汽车制造商一直表现出色。2019 年,日本汽车品牌的销量增长了 3%,同一时期欧洲品牌销量下降了 2%,韩国品牌销量下降了 18%,美国品牌销量下降了 23%。2019 年,中国国产品牌的销量下降了 15%。本田(Honda)和丰田(Toyota)的销量则创下纪录,日本品牌的市场份额达到 2011 年以来的最高水平[1]。

除了世界工厂,中国也是世界购物中心,日本公司在从中国不断增长的消费需求中获利这方面一直很成功。优衣库(Uniqlo)、无印良品(Muji)和卡西欧(Casio)等公司正利用中国充满活力的在线零售来营销自己的产品。此外,日本最大的零售商永旺(Aeon)计划在 2021 年向中国的数字业务投资 46 亿美元。亚瑟士(Asics)和资生堂(Shiseido)等其他公司则利用它们在中国广泛的实体店网络实现了远超其他市场的销售增长。

一方面,有利的中国需求可能会继续吸引日本公司。另一方面,不利的人口结构使日本企业回国后面临挑战。

日本社会正在迅速老龄化,尽管女性的劳动力市场参与度越来越高,但日本的劳动力市场仍非常紧张。图 3 显示了日本的职位空缺与申请人数比,这是一个关键的劳动力市场指标。即使在新冠病毒导致的相关下降之后,每个申请人仍然有接近 1.4 个职位可选。这表明,日本很难找到重新吸收大量中国投资存量所需的工人。

图 3　职位空缺与申请人数比

数据来源:环亚经济数据、第一财经

① 2019 年各大汽车品牌在华销量分析(https://carsalesbase.com/china-car-sales-analysis-2019-brands/)。

　　以上分析表明,日本政府的搬迁支持计划只会促进利基生产回归日本。

　　即便如此,地球上没有任何地方可以免受可能破坏供应链的"天灾"的影响。宫城县自身也在 2011 年的地震和海啸中遭受了重创。说到底,开放边界和灵活的全球供应反应可能是最好的灾难管理计划。

Shall the Twain Never Meet?

August 2, 2021

If you follow the news like I do, you could be forgiven for thinking that China and the West are drifting ever further apart. The headlines evoke Rudyard Kipling's 1889 poem, which begins "Oh, East is East, and West is West, and never the twain shall meet, Till Earth and Sky stand presently at God's great Judgment Seat".

But there is another perspective — an important one, I think. It comes from the American and European companies that are here, on the ground, doing business in China. We are lucky that local American and European business associations have, for many years, surveyed these firms. These indispensable surveys provide a snapshot of how their members actually feel about China's current business environment. Moreover, they give a sense of how that sentiment has evolved over time.

The American Chamber of Commerce in the People's Republic of China (AmCham) traces its roots back to 1919. Its membership includes representatives from 900 companies. It has been publishing surveys of its members for 23 years. You can find its 2021 China Business Climate Survey Report here. Similarly, the European Union Chamber of Commerce in China (European Chamber) was founded in 2000 and now has more than 1,700 member companies. It has published its surveys since 2004 and you can find the Business Confidence Survey 2021 here. These documents provide a wealth of information on foreign firms' successes and challenges in navigating the China market. I commend both of them to you.

In combing through these surveys, four points stood out. First, rather than decoupling, American and European firms are increasingly committed to China. Second, these firms' China operations are becoming relatively more profitable. Third, the business environment for foreign firms is improving. Fourth, notwithstanding these positive developments, foreign firms would make even greater investments if they had the same opportunities as their domestic Chinese competitors.

I found it striking that, notwithstanding high-profile political frictions, there is little sign that American and European firms are deserting China. European firms were asked if they were considering shifting current or planned China investments to other markets. Ninety-one percent of the respondents said they were not — the highest share recorded over the past decade (Figure 1). According to the European Chamber, its business community "... has steadily come to the conclusion that a company cannot be globally competitive without a strong presence in China". In the same vein, American firms were asked if they were considering, or had already begun, the process of relocating manufacturing or sourcing outside of China. Eighty-five percent of the respondents said that their manufacturing and sourcing were staying put. This share has steadily risen from 77 percent in the 2018 survey (Figure 1). According to the AmCham, its commitment to the China market has increased "despite widespread reports of pandemic-fueled supply chain disruptions and bilateral trade tension-inspired reviews of risks and vulnerabilities ...".

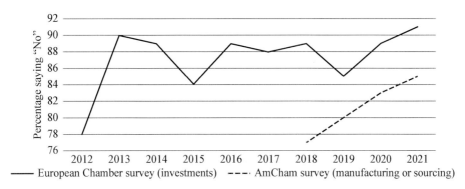

Figure 1   Is Your Firm Reducing Its China Presence?

Source: AmCham, European Chamber, Yicai

European firms are not simply staying put. The share of companies that intends to invest more in China reached 59 percent in the most recent survey, the highest ratio in the last eight years (Figure 2). Last year, a quarter of the European firms which have joint ventures increased their ownership shares, with many obtaining control. It is likely that this trend will persist in 2021.

In general, American firms have been more eager to increase their investments in China than their European counterparts (Figure 2). Investment intentions rebounded for 2021 but remain somewhat below those of previous years. Firms in the consumer sector are planning to invest less than in 2020, perhaps reflecting ongoing COVID-related challenges. Firms in all other sectors are planning to invest more than last year.

It will come as no surprise that 2020 was a difficult year for foreign firms'

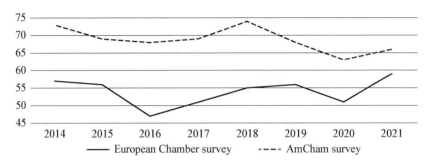

Figure 2   Percentage of Companies Planning to Increase Investment in China

Source: AmCham, European Chamber, Yicai

China operations. Indeed, a greater share of companies reported falling revenues and losses than in past years. However, it was a tough year everywhere. In relative terms, profitability in China fell by less than in other countries. Fewer American and European firms reported that their earnings before interest and tax (EBIT) margins were lower in China than in other countries (Figure 3). In fact, the surveys show that, in relative terms, China appears to be an increasingly profitable market in which to operate.

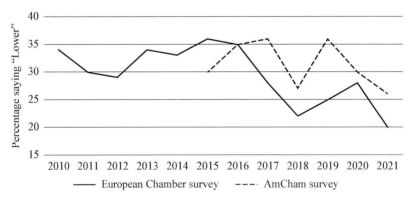

Figure 3   EBIT Margins in China Compared to Other Countries

Source: AmCham, European Chamber, Yicai

The business environment for foreign firms is improving. Just over a third of American and European firms say that they are treated less favourably than their Chinese counterparts, down from 55 percent only four years ago (Figure 4). While this improvement is welcome, it suggests that there is still work to be done before full national treatment is achieved.

The difficulty of protecting intellectual property (IP) in China is an issue that

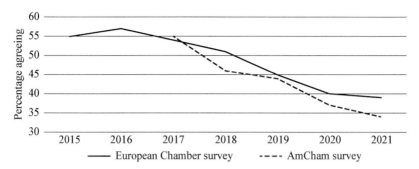

Figure 4   Foreign-Invested Enterprises Are Treated Unfavourably Compared to Chinese Companies

Source: AmCham, European Chamber, Yicai

receives a lot of press. However, American firms see IP leakage and data security risks in China increasingly becoming comparable with what they experience in other countries (Figure 5). The AmCham survey indicates improved IP protection is one of the key areas in which the Foreign Investment Law, which took effect on January 1, 2020, is having a positive impact.

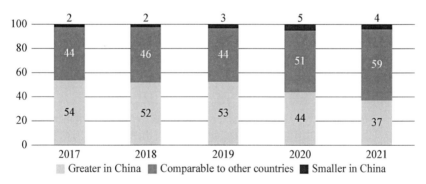

Figure 5   IP Leakage and Data Security Risks Are (%)

Source: AmCham, Yicai

European firms see the quality of IP law enforcement slowly getting better over time (Figure 6). However, with half the firms still characterizing enforcement as "Inadequate", there is still room for further improvement.

Forced technology transfer is another hot-button issue for foreign firms and the surveys highlight the scope of this problem. According to AmCham, two-thirds of US firms shared proprietary knowledge voluntarily. An additional 16 percent did so to improve their market access. A further 15 percent did so either because of joint venture regulations or because of informal pressure (Figure 7).

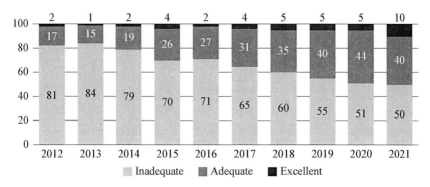

Figure 6   How Do You Rate the Enforcement of China's IP Laws? (%)

Source: European Chamber, Yicai

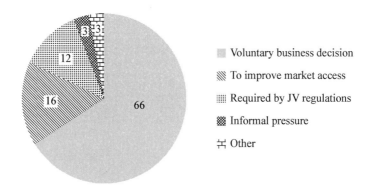

Figure 7   Reason for Sharing Proprietary Knowledge (%)

Source: AmCham, Yicai

The European Chamber's survey shows that a similar share of firms was compelled to transfer technology in order to maintain market access (Figure 8). While this share is falling slowly over time, European firms would have hoped for even greater progress given that the Foreign Investment Law expressly prohibits unfair technology transfers.

Foreign firms are clearly in China for the long haul. Nevertheless, the surveys indicate that further reform would lead to even deeper levels of engagement.

For American firms, the priority reforms are (i) increasing the transparency, predictability and fairness of the regulatory environment; (ii) greater IP protection; (iii) limiting the use of industrial policies that create barriers and (iv) opening business or product segments that are currently restricted.

European firms emphasize the importance of increasing market access, with only one-third of survey respondents saying that their industry is fully open to

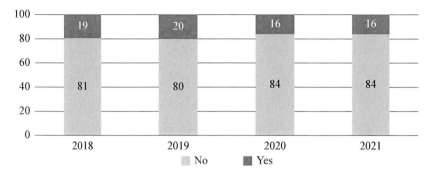

Figure 8   Has Your Company Been Compelled to Transfer Technology in Order to Maintain Market Access? (%)

Source: European Chamber, Yicai

foreign participation. Forty-five percent say that market access restrictions or regulatory barriers resulted in their missing out on business opportunities. This share has been fairly stable over time. Almost two-thirds of respondents say that they would increase their investments if market access barriers were to be removed.

Rudyard Kipling's famous poem goes on to say, "But there is neither East nor West, Border, nor Breed, nor Birth, When two strong men stand face to face, though they come from the ends of the earth!" Indeed, beneath the surface, East and West are more similar than they first appear. In recognizing these similarities and building trust, East and West can increase opportunities for mutually-beneficial enterprises.

无问西东，相向而行

2021 年 8 月 21 日

　　如果你像我一样关注新闻，你可能会认为中国和西方越来越疏远，这是可以原谅的。许多新闻标题让人想起拉迪亚德·吉卜林（Rudyard Kipling）1889 年的诗，诗的开头写道："哦，东是东，西是西，东西永古不相期，直至天地跪在神前受审。"

　　但我认为还有另一个重要的视角。它来自在中国做生意的美国和欧洲公司。幸运的是，美国和欧洲的地方商业协会多年来一直在调查这些公司在中国的经营状况。这些不可或缺的调查反映了协会成员对中国当前商业环境的真实感受。此外，它们还让我们知道这种感受是如何随着时间的推移而演变的。

　　中国美国商会成立于 1919 年，其成员包括来自 900 家公司的代表。23 年来，它一直在发布对其成员的调查，最新报告为《2021 中国商务环境调查报告》。中国欧盟商会（European Chamber）成立于 2000 年，目前拥有 1,700 多家会员公司。它从 2004 年开始发布调查，最新报告为《商业信心调查 2021》。这些报告提供了大量关于外国公司在中国市场获得成功和遭遇挑战的信息。两份报告都值得一读。

　　通过梳理这些调查，将会有四个显著的发现。首先，欧美企业并没有和中国脱钩，而是在中国投入了更多精力。其次，这些企业在中国的利润在增加。第三，外资企业的营商环境正在不断改善。第四，尽管有这些积极的发展，如果外资企业有与中国竞争对手同样的机会，它们会进行更多的投资。

　　令人震惊的是，尽管存在明显的政治摩擦，但几乎没有迹象表明美国和欧洲企业正在放弃中国。当欧洲公司被问及是否考虑将目前或计划在中国的投资转移到其他市场时，91%的受访者表示不会这样做——这是过去 10 年记录的最高比例（图 1）。根据中国欧盟商会的说法，其商业团体"已经坚定地得出结论，如果一家公司在中国没有强烈的存在感，就不可能有全球竞争力"。同样，美国公司被问及是否正在考虑或已经开始将制造或采购环节转移到中国以外。85%的受访者表示保持不变。这一比例从 2018 年调查的 77% 稳步上升（图 1）。据中国美国商会称，其在中国市场的投资有所增加，"尽管有关新冠肺炎疫情导致供应链中断以及双边贸易形势紧张带来对风险和脆弱性的反思的报道被广泛传播"。

图 1 贵公司是否会消减在中国市场的业务规模(%)

数据来源：中国美国商会、中国欧盟商会、第一财经

欧洲公司并非没有行动。在最近的调查中，计划在中国增加投资的公司比例达到 59%，是过去 8 年来的最高比例（图 2）。去年，拥有合资企业的欧洲公司中有四分之一增持了持股，其中许多公司获得了控制权。这一趋势可能会持续到 2021 年结束。

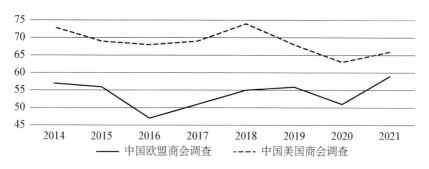

图 2 拟在中国增加投资的公司占比(%)

数据来源：中国美国商会、中国欧盟商会、第一财经

总体而言，美国公司比欧洲公司更渴望增加在中国的投资（图 2）。2021 年整体投资意向有所回升，但仍略低于前几年。可能受当前新冠肺炎疫情带来的

相关挑战影响,消费行业公司计划投资低于 2020 年,而其他所有行业的公司都准备加大投资规模。

2020 年是外国企业在中国经营艰难的一年,这一点不足为奇。事实上,与过去几年相比,收入下降和亏损的公司所占比例更大。然而,无论在哪里,去年都是艰难的一年。相对而言,在中国市场的盈利下降幅度要小于其他国家。只有少数美国公司和欧洲公司声称它们在中国的息税前利润率(EBIT)低了其他国家(图 3)。事实上,调查显示,中国似乎比其他国家更有利可图。

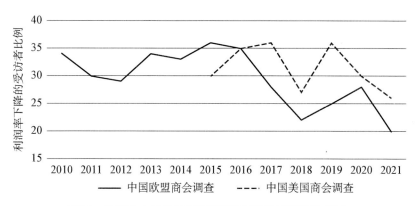

图 3　公司在中国的息税前利润率与其他国家相比(%)

数据来源:中国美国商会、中国欧盟商会、第一财经

在华经营的外国企业营商环境不断改善。只有略多于三分之一的美国和欧洲公司表示,它们受到的待遇不如中国同行,这一比例低于 4 年前的 55%(图4)。虽然这一改善值得欢迎,但也表明要实现全面国民待遇仍有许多工作要做。

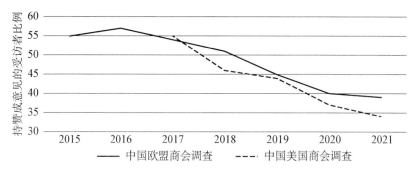

图 4　外国企业在中国的待遇不如中国企业优厚(%)

数据来源:中国美国商会、中国欧盟商会、第一财经

在中国,知识产权保护问题曾受到媒体广泛关注。然而,美国公司认为,中国的知识产权泄露和数据安全风险与其他国家越来越具有可比性(图5)。根据中国美国商会的调查,加强知识产权保护是 2020 年 1 月 1 日生效的《中华人民共和国外商投资法》产生积极影响的关键领域之一。

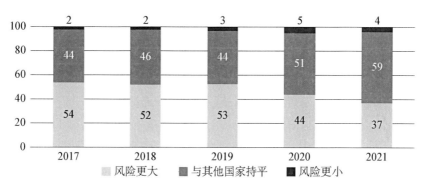

图 5　美国公司对中国知识产权泄露和数据安全风险与其他国家对比的态度(持不同态度的企业占比,%)

数据来源:中国美国商会、第一财经

欧洲企业认为,中国对知识产权的执法力度正在逐步加强(图 6)。但仍有一半的公司认为力度"不足",需要不断提高。

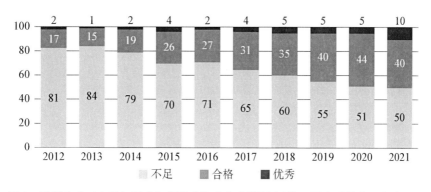

图 6　欧洲企业对中国知识产权保护法执法力度的看法(持不同意见的企业占比,%)

数据来源:中国欧盟商会、第一财经

强制技术转让是外国公司关注的另一个热点问题,此次调查凸显了这一点。根据中国美国商会的数据,三分之二的美国公司自愿分享专有技术。另有 16%的企业这样做是为了提高其市场准入机会。另有 15%的公司这样做是因为合资企业规定或非正式的压力(图7)。

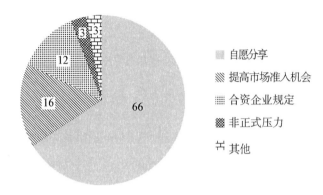

图7　美国公司分享专有技术的原因(%)

数据来源:中国美国商会、第一财经

中国欧盟商会的调查显示,与美国几乎相同比例的欧盟公司被迫转让技术以获得市场准入(图8)。虽然这一份额随着时间的推移在慢慢下降,但由于《中华人民共和国外商投资法》明确禁止不公平的技术转让,欧洲企业本希望能取得更大的进步。

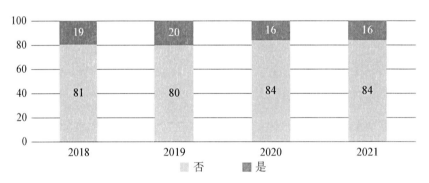

图8　贵公司是否被迫转让技术以维持市场准入?(%)

数据来源:中国欧盟商会、第一财经

外国企业在中国的发展显然是长期的。不过,调查显示,进一步改革将带来更深层次的参与。

对美国公司来说,改革的重点是:(1)提高监管环境的透明度、可预测性和公平性;(2)加强知识产权保护;(3)限制使用造成壁垒的产业政策;(4)开放目前受限的业务或产品领域。

欧洲公司强调增加市场准入的重要性,只有三分之一的受访者表示,他们的行业对外国参与者完全开放。45%的受访者表示,市场准入限制或监管壁垒导致他们错失商机。这个比例在一段时间内相当稳定。近三分之二的受访者表示,如果消除市场准入壁垒,他们将增加投资。

　　拉迪亚德·吉卜林的那首著名的诗接着写道:"即使来自海角天涯,当两位强者对面而立,则不分东与西,亦无论疆界族群和出身!"事实上,在表面之下,东方和西方比它们最初看起来要相似得多。通过认识到这些相似性并建立信任,东西方可以为互利企业提供更多机会。

The High Cost of US-China Decoupling

April 2, 2021

Many of us had hoped that last month's meeting between the US and Chinese delegations in the Alaskan city of Anchorage would open a new phase of dialogue after the Trump-era freeze in bilateral relations.

While no specific next steps were announced after the meeting's conclusion, Xinhua reported that the Americans and Chinese would continue talking about climate change, reopening diplomatic missions and increasing cross-border media representation. But the risk is that the two sides will move even further apart.

The potential cost of a growing rift between the world's two largest economies is the subject of Understanding Decoupling: Macro Trends and Industry Impacts, a recent report by the Rhodium Group. This exhaustive, well-researched text looks at the intricate ways in which the US and Chinese economies are intertwined and tries to quantify the cost of tearing them apart.

The Report attributes "decoupling" to the US's use of policies designed to reduce economic interactions, which are seen as either posing a security threat or based on unfair practices. This suite of policies includes: (i) the extraordinary imposition of tariffs; (ii) the expanded use of export controls; (iii) a more restrictive approach to Chinese acquisitions of US firms; (iv) the expulsion of students and researchers suspected of being affiliated with the Chinese military; (v) the closure of consulates and (vi) the deportation of journalists. China's retaliation further exacerbates the decoupling.

By implementing the above-mentioned policies, the US intends to punish and deter China. However, the Report points out that these policies actually impose significant costs on American firms and consumers. Ironically, while the US is looking to diminish China's importance as a "strategic competitor", these policies could, over time, actually reduce American firms' competitive advantage. The implementation of the above-mentioned policies has already led to a certain degree of decoupling. Yet the Report ominously warns that a "comprehensive decoupling" is possible and that a "complete rupture" is the most likely outcome of the current policy trajectory.

The Report assesses the impact, on the US, of a full loss of trade and investment relations with China. It examines this scenario both via a top-down, macroeconomic analysis and bottom-up, in-depth studies of the aviation, semiconductor, chemical and medical device industries. The industry-level investigations provide detailed illustrations of how decoupling could ripple through supply chains and final good markets.

The Report emphasizes five channels through which decoupling comes back to bite Americans.

First, in many industries, there is a high cost to being cut out of China's growing markets.

For example, China's market for medical devices is expected to grow by 15 percent annually for the next 10 years. US firms would forego $48 billion annually, should they not be able to service this demand. Similarly, China's fleet of airplanes is expected to increase by close to 8 percent annually to the end of the decade. If China stopped buying US planes and using their repair and maintenance services, US firms would be $36 billion per year poorer. The global market for semiconductors is expected to grow at an annual average rate of 5 percent. The Report estimates that US firms would forgo revenues of between $83 and $95 billion, if they lost access to the Chinese market.

Second, decoupling raises costs in the US, reducing both firms' competitiveness and consumers' real incomes.

American companies import chemicals from China as inputs into their production of a host of products. Tariffs raise these firms' costs of doing business. The American Chemistry Council notes that US manufacturers have no choice but to pass the higher costs they face on to their customers. This diminishes the competitiveness of firms that use chemicals as an input. The tariffs on Chinese imports hit US consumers as well as producers. For example, they raise the cost of imported parts and components for US medical device manufacturers. These increased costs are passed down to hospitals and then to patients.

Third, decoupling will lower the amount of R&D undertaken by US firms, reducing their ability to innovate.

Firms typically scale the amount of R&D they undertake by the size of their global market. That is because it is easier to spread the costs of R&D over a large customer base. Producing leading-edge semiconductors is a complex and costly undertaking. The industry is highly concentrated and dominated by a small number of players. Currently, US firms are world leaders in terms of sales, profits, and innovation. But it takes significant investment in R&D to stay at the top. In the semiconductor industry, investment in R&D is typically 30 percent of sales. The

Report estimates a reduction in R&D spending of $12 billion per year should US semiconductor firms lose access to the Chinese market. In an industry that requires constant upgrading of designs and processes, it predicts that a fall of R&D of this magnitude would severely diminish US innovation leadership. It increases the likelihood that American firms will fall behind their global competitors.

Fourth, decoupling will block cross-border flows of people.

The exclusion of Chinese students from high tech and advanced science courses in US universities will not only reduce the incomes of these institutions, but it will also shrink the talent pool from which US firms can draw. The 370,000 students from China represent a third of all international students studying in the US. The Report estimates they contribute $14 billion annually in tuition and living expenses.

Fifth, policy uncertainty will reduce third-country investment in the US.

The Report suggests that firms from third countries will withdraw from the US, if their American operations serve Chinese clients. This is to mitigate the risk of running afoul of American laws. In fact, both BMW and Daimler, which export a significant number of US-made cars to China, are now thinking twice about using the US as a global production platform.

The five channels outlined by the Report provide American policymakers, who are in the process of reassessing the US-China relationship, with important food for thought. Moreover, the Report is posted on the website of the US Chamber of Commerce, suggesting the US business community is squarely behind its analysis. But US business interests are not stopping at promoting rigorous analysis. In March, the National Foreign Trade Council announced the re-launch of the Tariff Reform Coalition, a broad alliance of business and agriculture groups, which is looking to have the tariffs imposed by the Trump Administration repealed.

Given the analysis that the tariffs hurt rather than help the US and the stance of the American business community, it is surprising that Katherine Tai, the new Trade Representative, is reluctant to have them removed. In her view, actors in the US economy need time to prepare for the tariffs' removal. And, she says, the tariffs provide leverage in the US's negotiations with China. This position is unfortunate. Last September, a World Trade Organization panel ruled that the tariffs were inconsistent with the US's WTO obligations. One expects that the Biden Administration would — after the unilateralism of its predecessor — uphold the importance of the rules-based, multilateral trading system. It ought to comply with the WTO's ruling and remove the tariffs. We can only hope that reasoned analysis, like the report authored by the Rhodium Group, and pressure from US businesses will have an impact on policymakers' thinking, which will, ultimately, prevent a costly decoupling.

中美"脱钩"的高昂代价

2021 年 4 月 2 日

我们许多人希望,2021 年 3 月在美国阿拉斯加安克雷奇举行的中美高层战略对话,将在特朗普时代双边关系冻结后,为双方对话开启一个新阶段。

虽然会后双方没有宣布下一步的具体措施,但新华社报道称,中美将继续讨论气候变化,重开外交使团,增加跨境媒体报道。但危险在于,双方的分歧将进一步扩大。

世界上最大的两个经济体之间日益扩大的鸿沟的潜在成本,是美国荣鼎咨询公司(Rhodium Group)最近发布的一篇报告的主题——"理解脱钩:宏观趋势和行业影响"。这篇详尽的报告着眼于中美经济相互交织的现状,试图量化将两者拆散的成本。

报告将"脱钩"归因于美国使用旨在减少中美经济互动的政策(被视为针对安全威胁或不公平的做法),这一系列政策包括:(1)加征关税;(2)扩大出口管制;(3)对中国企业收购美国企业采取更严格的限制;(4)驱逐涉嫌与中国军方有关联的学生和研究人员;(5)关闭领事馆;(6)遣送中国记者回国。中国的反应则进一步加剧了"脱钩"。

美国想通过实施上述政策来惩罚和威慑中国。然而,报告指出,这些政策实际上给美国企业和消费者带来了沉重的成本。具有讽刺意味的是,美国正试图削弱中国作为"战略竞争对手"的重要性,但随着时间的推移,这些政策实际上可能会降低美国企业的竞争优势。上述政策的实施导致了一定程度的"脱钩"。该报告警告称,全面"脱钩"是可能的,"完全破裂"是当前政策轨迹最有可能的结果。报告评估了中美贸易和投资关系完全丧失对美国的影响,通过自上而下的宏观经济分析和自下而上深入研究航空、半导体、化工和医疗器械行业,探讨了这种情况。行业层面的调查详细展示了"脱钩"将如何在供应链和终端产品市场引起连锁反应。

该报告强调,"脱钩"将对美国产生五个方面的影响。

第一,对于许多行业来说,退出不断增长的中国市场的成本非常高。

比如,未来 10 年,中国医疗器械市场预计每年增长 15%,按此计算,如果美国企业放弃中国市场,每年将损失 480 亿美元。同样,未来 10 年,中国民航机队有望以每年近 8% 的速度增长。如果中国停止购买美国飞机,停止使用其维修和维护服务,美国企业每年将损失 360 亿美元。全球半导体市场预计年均增长5%。报告估计,如果美国企业失去中国市场,每年将损失 830 亿至 950 亿美元的收入。

第二,"脱钩"会增加美国的成本,从而降低美国企业的竞争力和消费者的实际收入。

美国企业从中国进口化学品作为它们生产大量产品的投入,关税提高了这些企业的经营成本。美国化学理事会指出,美国制造商别无选择,只能将它们面临的更高成本转移给客户,这降低了使用化学品作为投入的企业的竞争力。对从中国进口的商品征收关税打击了美国消费者和生产商,例如,美国医疗设备制造商的进口零件成本增加了。这些增加的费用将被转移到医院,然后转移到病人身上。

第三,"脱钩"会减少美国企业的研发投入,从而降低其创新能力。

企业通常会根据其全球市场的规模来衡量其研发规模,这是因为将研发成本分散到更大的客户群更容易。生产尖端半导体是一项复杂和高成本的工作,该行业高度集中,由少数参与者主导。目前,美国企业在销售、利润和创新方面处于世界领先地位。然而,如果你想保持领先,就需要在研发上投入大量资金。在半导体行业,研发投入通常占销售额的 30%。报告估计,如果美国半导体企业失去进入中国市场的机会,它们每年将减少 120 亿美元的研发支出。在一个需要不断升级设计和流程的行业中,如此巨额的研发下降将严重削弱美国创新的领先地位,这使美国企业落后于全球竞争对手的可能性增加了。

第四,"脱钩"会阻碍人员跨境流动。

将中国学生排除在美国大学的高科技和高级科学课程之外,不仅会降低这些机构的收入,还会缩小美国企业的人才库。37 万中国留学生占美国留学生总数的三分之一。报告估计,这些中国学生每年将为美国贡献高达 140 亿美元的学费和生活费。

第五,政策的不确定性会减少第三国在美国的投资。

报告指出,如果第三国企业在美国的业务是为中国客户服务的,它们就会从美国撤出,这是为了降低违反美国法律的风险。事实上,向中国出口大量美国制造汽车的宝马(BMW)和戴姆勒(Daimler)现在正在重新考虑是否将美国作为其全球生产平台。

报告中概述的五点为正在重新评估美中关系的美国决策者提供了重要的参考。此外,该报告在美国商会网站上发布,表明美国商界完全支持其分析。美国企业并未止步于提倡严谨的分析。2021年3月,美国对外贸易委员会宣布重新启动"关税改革联盟",这是一个由商业和农业团体组成的广泛联盟,它希望废除特朗普政府征收的关税。

鉴于上述分析,即这些关税对美国有害无益,以及美国商界的立场,令人惊讶的是,新任美国贸易代表戴琪(Katherine Tai)不愿意取消加征的关税。在她看来,美国需要时间来为关税取消做准备,她还表示,关税为美国与中国的谈判提供了筹码。这种情况令人遗憾。2020年9月,世贸组织专家组裁定,美方涉案征税措施违反其世贸组织义务。在特朗普政府的单边主义之后,人们期待拜登政府重视基于规则的多边贸易机制。美国应该遵守世贸组织的裁决,取消关税。目前,我们只能希望像荣鼎咨询公司的报告那样的理性分析和美国企业的压力能够影响决策者的思维,最终阻止代价高昂的"脱钩"。

China's Balance of Payments Show the Dual Circulation Strategy at Work

April 13, 2021

A strong undercurrent of self-reliance runs through China's 14th Five-Year Plan.

On the supply side, the Plan emphasizes innovation-driven development. It sets ambitious targets for R&D, the creation of patents and the value added of core digital technologies. Self-reliance also motivates the push to raise the quality, efficiency and competitiveness of China's agricultural sector. The Plan raised the target for domestic grain production by 18 percent to 650 million tons. The 13th Five-Year Plan had only targeted a 10 percent increase, to 550 million tons. It is easy to see why China is looking to safeguard the supply of key inputs — from chips to wheat — given the backlash against globalization and the loss of respect for the rules-based multilateral trading system.

On the demand side, the 14th Five-Year Plan calls for enhancing the "fundamental role" of consumption in China's economic development. The rationale for relying on domestic demand is also straightforward. Until recently, Chinese consumers have not been rich enough to fuel demand for quality products. But that is changing. Not only have Chinese households become much wealthier, but their income growth is also impressive, compared to what we see elsewhere in the world. Figure 1 shows that the level of Chinese personal disposable incomes, in US dollars, grew by close to a third between 2015 and 2020. In contrast, global GDP ex-China only grew by 9 percent over the same period. So, it appears as if a tipping point may have been crossed and China can now increasingly rely on domestic consumption as a source of demand for high-end goods and services.

Does increased self-reliance mean that China is turning its back on the rest of the world?

With China's productivity still lagging the global leaders', that would be foolhardy. China needs to learn from the rest of the world in order to keep moving toward the technological frontier.

In return, China can offer the rest of the world a growing market in which it

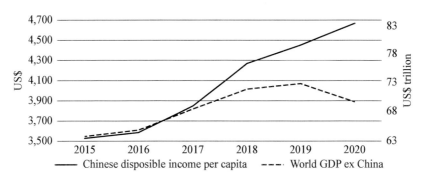

Figure 1   Income Measures

Source: Wind, Yicai

can scale up new products and processes. China's market is likely to be most attractive to innovators in smaller countries that do not have a strong sales base over which they can spread R&D costs.

It is this bargain that lies at the heart of the "Dual Circulation Strategy", the development paradigm first proposed by President Xi last May. According to the 14th Five-Year Plan, China must strengthen the leading role of domestic circulation, use international circulation to improve domestic circulation's efficiency and achieve mutual benefit. As a matter of policy, then, China will continue to deepen its engagement with the rest of the world.

China's balance of payment accounts provide the most extensive record of its international transactions. The most recent data show that, despite the dislocation caused by the pandemic, China and the rest of the global economy have never been so tightly interlinked. The current account records payments and receipts for goods, services and income earned abroad. International trade in goods and services collapsed last year. Nevertheless, China's current transactions ticked up to $5.7 trillion, the second highest amount on record (Figure 2). China's success, in an otherwise dismal market, was due to its ability to control the spread of the virus and get its supply chains in shape to benefit from a surge in foreign demand for durable goods.

Payments for goods dominate China's current transactions with the rest of the world, accounting for close to four-fifths of the total last year. Both exports and imports of goods grew modestly, which was no mean feat all things considered.

The pandemic did have a strong impact on China's service trade. In particular, there was a sharp decline in cross-border travel. With its growing middle class increasingly fond of international tourism, China has imported a significant amount of travel services in recent years. Its payments for travel services in 2019 were close

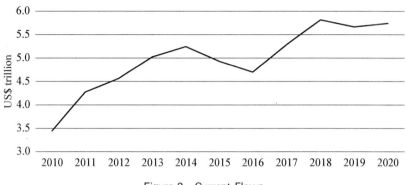

Figure 2　Current Flows

Source: Wind, Yicai

to six times as high as in 2009. While travel suffered a pandemic-related decline, other elements of the service account reveal China's growing interconnection with the rest of the world.

Figure 3 shows the tremendous growth of the trade in information and communication technology (ITC) services and for two-way payments for intellectual property (IP). China's payments for IP essentially tripled between 2010 and 2020, while its IP receipts have grown ten-fold (from a much lower base).

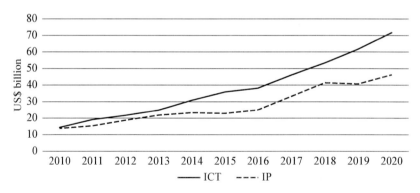

Figure 3　Selected Two-Way Trade in Services

Source: Wind, Yicai

The financial account of China's balance of payments tracks transactions in assets and liabilities. Figure 4 shows that these two-way investment flows hit a record high in 2020.

Three types of investment flows are recorded in the financial account. The first is direct investment: the construction of new facilities in a foreign country and cross-border mergers and acquisitions. These are typically long-term investments,

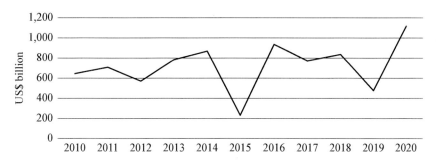

Figure 4   Two-Way Investment Flows

Source: Wind, Yicai

which are not easily liquidated. Last year, global foreign direct investment flows dropped by more than 40 percent, falling to their lowest level since 2004. In this context, both Chinese direct investment abroad and direct investment in China held up very well, with flows in both directions increasing. Indeed, despite the uncertainty caused by the Trump Administration's trade policy, inflows were surprisingly strong and China surpassed the US to become the world's largest recipient of foreign direct investment (Figure 5).

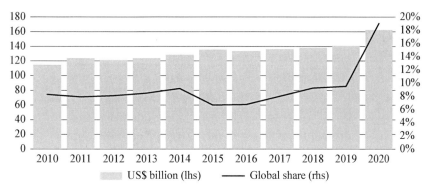

US$ billion (lhs)　━━━　Global share (rhs)

Figure 5   Direct Investment Inflows

Source: UNCTAD, Yicai

Cross-border investments in financial assets, like stocks and bonds, represent the second type of financial flow. These "portfolio" flows tend to be shorter term than direct investments and are easily liquidated in deep markets. China's inward and outward portfolio flows both spiked last year.

Foreigners, attracted by the relatively high yields on Chinese bonds and their inclusion in global indices, made record investments in Chinese debt markets. Meanwhile, Chinese investors bought more foreign equities in 2020 than in the previous four years combined. Many of these purchases were made in Hong Kong, where initial public offerings were up sharply. Chinese investors were eager to purchase stakes in familiar names such as JD. com, JD Health International and NetEase.

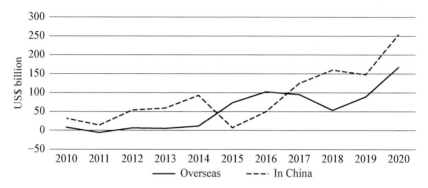

Figure 6　Portfolio Investment Flows

Source: Wind, Yicai

The remaining items on the financial account are called "other" investment flows. They essentially reflect changes in bank-related assets and liabilities (cross-border loans and deposits). Chinese lenders were very active last year. Their international loans rose by a record amount. Moreover, Chinese residents also increased their deposits abroad by the most since 2014. Unlike the elements of the balance of payments discussed above, which are seen as desired or "autonomous", other investment flows are seen as financing items and are characterized as "induced". A country needs to pay for its balance of payments deficit and other flows are a key channel through which this financing happens. Figure 7 shows that

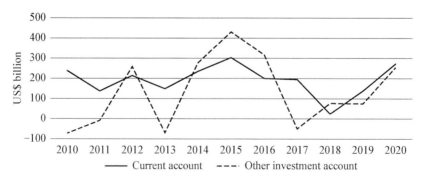

Figure 7　Current and Other Investment Account Balances

Source: Wind, Yicai

the other investment account tracks the broad movements in the current account. China's current account surplus rose last year. The increase in loans by Chinese banks and deposits by Chinese residents helped provide foreigners the funds required to purchase Chinese goods and services.

In sum, the picture painted by the balance of payments accounts is one of China ever more intimately engaged with the rest of the world. The resilience of China's goods and services trade, the robustness of direct investment inflows and the sharp growth in two-way portfolio flows are evidence of the Dual Circulation Strategy at work.

中国的国际收支表明"双循环"战略正在奏效

2021 年 4 月 13 日

"自力更生"的意识贯穿中国"十四五"规划。

在供给侧,"十四五"规划强调创新驱动发展,并为研究与开发支出、专利创造和数字经济核心产业增加值设定了宏伟目标。"自力更生"也促进中国农业部门努力提高质量、效率和竞争力。"十四五"规划提出国内粮食增产 18% 达到 6.5 亿吨的目标,而"十三五"规划的目标只是增产 10% 达到 5.5 亿吨。考虑到近年来逆全球化趋势和基于规则的多边贸易体系的丧失,很容易理解中国为什么寻求保证关键投入(从芯片到小麦)的供应。

在需求侧,"十四五"规划提出要增强消费在中国经济发展中的"基础性作用"。依赖内需的理由也很简单,虽然目前中国消费者还没有足够的财富来满足对高质量产品的需求,但这种情况正在发生改变。与我们在世界其他地方看到的相比,中国家庭变得越来越富裕,收入增长令人印象深刻。图 1 显示,2015 年至 2020 年间,中国人均可支配收入(以美元计)增长了近三分之一。相比之下,同期全球 GDP(不包括中国)仅增长 9%。因此,中国似乎已经越过了一个临界点,现在可以越来越依赖国内消费作为高端商品和服务的需求来源。

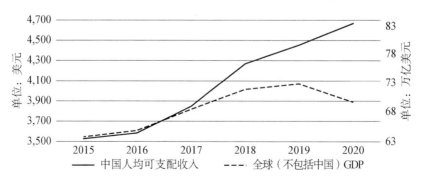

图 1　中国人均可支配收入和全球(不包括中国)GDP 走势

数据来源:万得资讯、第一财经

"自力更生"能力的提高是否意味着中国正在偏离世界其他国家？如果在中国的生产力仍落后于全球领先者的情况下，那将是鲁莽之举。中国需要向世界其他国家学习，以便不断走向技术前沿。作为回报，中国可以为世界其他地区提供一个不断增长的市场，在这个市场中，中国可以扩大新产品和新工艺的规模。中国市场可能对小国的创新者最具吸引力，因为这些国家没有强大的销售基础来分担研发成本。

2020 年 5 月，习近平主席首次提出了"双循环"新发展格局，其核心是"互通有无"。根据"十四五"规划，中国必须强化国内大循环的主导作用，以国际循环提升国内大循环效率和水平，实现国内国际双循环互促共进。那么，作为一项政策，中国将继续深化与世界其他地区的合作。

中国的国际收支账户提供了最广泛的国际交易记录。最新数据显示，尽管疫情造成了混乱，但中国从未与世界其他经济体如此紧密地联系在一起。经常账户记录的是货物、服务和海外收入的收支情况。2020 年，国际商品和服务贸易崩溃，然而，中国的经常项目交易额却上升到 5.7 万亿美元，为历史第二高水平(图 2)。中国之所以能够在原本惨淡的市场上取得成功，是因为它有效地控制了病毒的传播，并保持供应链良好运行，从而受益于国外对耐用品需求的激增。

图 2　中国经常项目交易额

数据来源：万得资讯、第一财经

目前，商品贸易在中国国际贸易中占主导地位，占 2020 年贸易总额的近五分之四，商品出口和进口都有适度增长，从各方面来看都不是一件容易的事情。

疫情对中国的服务贸易产生了强烈影响，尤其是跨境旅游大幅减少。随着中国日益壮大的中产阶级对国际旅游越来越感兴趣，中国近年来进口了大量的旅游服务。2019年,中国旅游服务支出是2009年的近6倍。虽然旅游业受到疫情的影响,但服务账户的其他要素显示,中国与世界其他地区的联系越来越紧密。

图3显示了信息和通信技术(ITC)服务贸易和知识产权(IP)双向支付的巨大增长。2010—2020年期间,中国的知识产权支付增长了两倍,而其知识产权收入增长了十倍(基数低得多)。

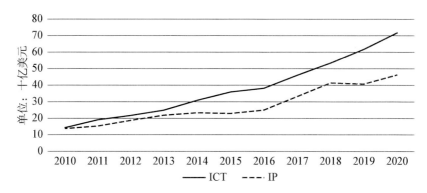

图3　ITC和IP双向服务贸易额走势

数据来源:万得资讯、第一财经

中国国际收支的金融账户跟踪资产和负债的交易。图4显示,这两种双向投资流量在2020年创下历史新高。

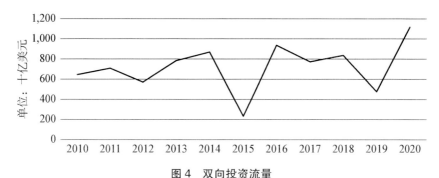

图4　双向投资流量

数据来源:万得资讯、第一财经

金融账户中记录了以下三种类型的投资。第一种是直接投资,涉及海外新设施建设和跨国并购。这些都是典型的长期投资,不容易变现。2020年,全球对外直接投资下降了40%以上,降至2004年以来的最低水平。在这种情况下,中国的对外直接投资和外国对华直接投资都保持增长。虽然特朗普政府的贸易政策带来了不确定性,但中国的资金流入却出人意料地强劲,中国已经超越美国,成为全球最大的外国直接投资接受国(图5)。

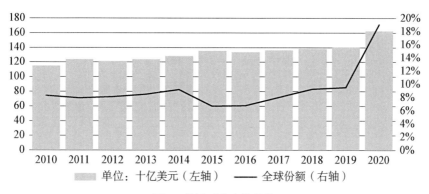

图 5　外国对华直接投资

数据来源:联合国贸易与发展会议、第一财经

第二种是跨境证券投资,比如股票、债券。与直接投资相比,证券投资往往是短期投资,在流动性好的市场中很容易变现。去年,流入和流出中国的此类投资激增。中国债券收益率相对较高,且被纳入全球指数,因此吸引了许多外国投资者,他们在中国债券市场进行了创纪录的投资。与此同时,2020 年中国投资者购买的外国股票数量是前 4 年的总和,其中许多是在首次公开发行飙升的中国香港市场购买的。中国投资者愿意购买他们熟悉的股票,比如京东、京东健康和网易。

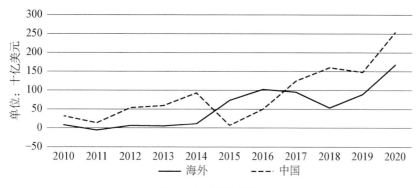

图 6　证券投资流量

数据来源:万得资讯、第一财经

第三种被称为其他投资,它基本上反映了与银行相关的资产和负债(跨境贷款和存款)的变化。2020年,中国的银行非常活跃,它们的国际贷款创纪录地增长。此外,中国居民海外存款也创下2014年以来的最大增幅。与上述"自主"的国际收支要素不同,其他投资被视为融资项目,并具有"被动"特征。一个国家需要支付其国际收支赤字,其他投资是这种融资发生的一个关键渠道。图7显示,其他投资账户与经常账户具有较高的相关性,2020年中国的经常账户有所增加,中国的银行的贷款和存款的增加为外国人提供了购买中国商品和服务所需的资金。

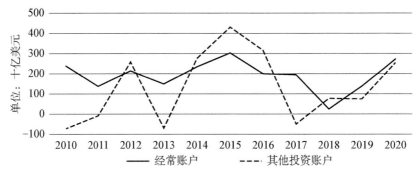

图7　其他投资账户和经常账户余额变化

数据来源:万得资讯、第一财经

综上所述,国际收支账户描绘的图景是,中国与世界其他国家的关系越来越密切。中国商品和服务贸易的恢复力、直接投资流入的强劲势头以及双向证券流动的大幅增长,都证明了"双循环"战略正在奏效。

How Long Will Foreign Investors' Love Affair With Chinese Bonds Last?

December 10, 2020

Foreign inflows into the Chinese onshore bond market continued to grow rapidly in November. Foreigners now hold more than CNY 3 trillion ($460 billion) in Chinese bonds, triple the amount they held only three years ago. While macroeconomic and institutional factors account for foreign investors' recent infatuation with Chinese bonds, the benefits of portfolio diversification and the creation of an international financial center in Shanghai will underpin a steady long-term relationship.

Despite foreign investors strong interest in Chinese bonds, their holdings comprise less than 3 percent of the entire onshore bond market. Nevertheless, since foreign investors are focused on buying the bonds sold by the highest quality issuers, they are becoming key players in specific markets.

Figure 1 shows that 90 percent of foreign holdings are in bonds issued by the Government of China or one of the three policy banks, which are essentially seen as sovereign risk. Corporate bonds and those issued by local governments only account for 9 percent of foreigners' holdings, while investment in the small Panda market accounts for 1 percent.

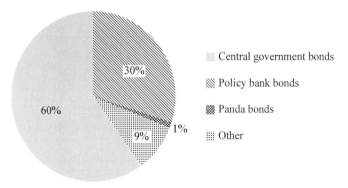

Figure 1   Composition of Foreign Onshore Bond Holdings

Source: Wind, Yicai

Three factors explain foreigners' preferences for high-quality bonds.

First, many of the foreign investors in the Chinese market are public institutions — central banks and international financial institutions — whose mandates are limited to holding sovereign or quasi-sovereign debt.

Second, the international indices into which Chinese bonds are being included generally only consider government debt. This leads asset managers who follow these indices to buy sovereign or quasi-sovereign issues.

Third, tax uncertainty related to investment in Chinese corporate bonds has largely kept foreigners away from this asset class.

Given their focused preferences, foreign investors now hold close to 10 percent of the bonds issued by the Government of China and 5 percent of those issued by the three policy banks. They also hold about a sixth of the bonds issued in the Panda market, which is designed to allow foreigners the opportunity of raising onshore RMB funding for their China operations.

In the current macroeconomic environment, Chinese bonds are benefitting from foreign investors' search for yield. Central banks outside of China are running very accommodative monetary policy to limit the economic fallout from COVID – 19. This has led to a precipitous decline in North American and European bond yields.

Figure 2 shows that the yield on US 10-year bonds dropped sharply at the beginning of the year and has remained low since. In contrast, that of Chinese 10-year bonds dipped temporarily but returned to its late-2019 level. As a result, the 10-year yield differential has widened to just under 2.5 percentage points, compared to a 1 percentage point differential, on average, over 2017 – 2019.

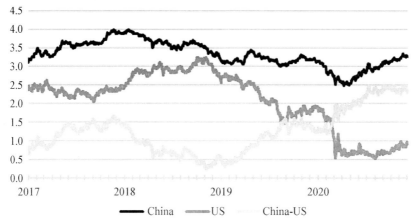

Figure 2　10-Year Government Bond Yields (%)

Source: Wind, Yicai

High interest rates, by themselves, are not a sufficient inducement to buy Chinese bonds. Investors make their decisions based on their assessments of both reward and risk. Given the risks of investing in Chinese government bonds, these securities appear to be very attractively priced.

S&P gives China's sovereign bonds an A + credit rating. Figure 3 compares the yields on Chinese bonds to those of other sovereigns with broadly similar credit ratings. Not only are Chinese bonds the highest yielding of those rated A + , their yield also exceeds those rated A and A − .

Some of the recent foreign appetite for Chinese bonds can be explained by their being good value for money. Moreover, the reforms undertaken in recent years have improved foreign investors' access to the onshore bond market. In addition, China's ability to control the virus and support what appears to be a full recovery suggest that the renminbi is unlikely to depreciate in the near future.

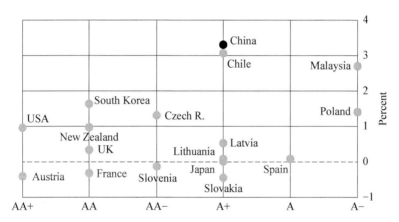

Figure 3   10-Year Bond Yields and S & P Credit Ratings

Source: Trading Economics, Yicai

Foreign investment in Chinese bonds is also being supported by their inclusion in major global bond indices. Trillions of dollars track these indices and many investment managers need to purchase Chinese bonds in order to align their portfolios with the benchmarks.

JPMorgan chose to add Chinese bonds to their Emerging Market Government Bond Index in February. Along with those of Brazil, they will be the most heavily weighted, with each country accounting for 10 percent of the benchmark.

More importantly, Bloomberg/Barclays and FTSE/Russell are adding Chinese bonds to their global indices. The former began in April 2019 and the latter will begin in October 2021. The weight of Chinese bonds in these indices will only be between 5 − 6 percent. But there is a lot more money tracking global bonds than emerging market debt. So, the impact on the Chinese market will be greater.

The three indices are only gradually increasing China's share towards its target weight. Ultimately, including Chinese bonds in these three indices could mean that foreign investors will need to purchase some $300 billion in Chinese debt. So, asset managers' positioning could also explain some of the interest we have been seeing.

Looking beyond the shorter-term macroeconomic and institutional factors, it is reasonable to believe that foreign investors will increase their holdings of Chinese bonds over time.

Chinese policy makers have long sought to enhance the role of capital markets. Increased foreign participation could raise the sophistication of the bond market and create more high-value added jobs in China's financial sector. This is consistent with the government's objective of boosting the share of services in GDP as well as transforming Shanghai into an international financial center.

For foreign investors, the Chinese bond market offers not only high returns at low risk, but also the benefit of diversification. Chinese bonds have low correlations with financial assets in overseas markets. This is due to the tendency of Chinese commercial banks to hold their bonds to maturity and China's monetary policy being independent from those of the US and Europe.

It is important to note that, in some sense, the world is under-invested in Chinese debt. Figure 4 presents the IMF's data on foreign holdings of debt securities. This measure would include debt held offshore as well as onshore. The data show that at 3 percent of GDP, foreign holdings of Chinese bonds is the smallest of all G20 countries.

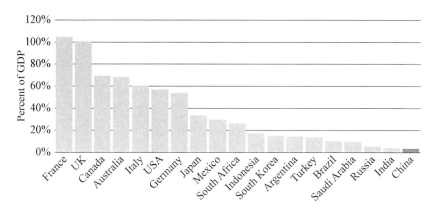

Figure 4　Liabilities to Foreigners: Debt Securities

Source: IMF, Yicai

So, how long might foreigners' love affair with Chinese bonds last?

Let's assume that foreigners' holdings of Chinese bonds reach the median of the G20 countries, which is 26 percent of GDP. This is where South Africa is in Figure 4. That would imply additional foreign investment of $3.3 trillion — seven times what foreigners hold today!

Given the benefits to both sides from further capital market integration, it does, indeed, sound like a match made in heaven.

外国投资者和中国债券的"恋情"会持续多久？

2020 年 12 月 10 日

2020 年 11 月，流入中国在岸债券市场的外资继续快速增长。外国人现在持有超过 3 万亿元(4,600 亿美元)的中国债券，是 3 年前的 3 倍。虽然宏观经济和制度因素是最近外国投资者迷恋中国债券的原因，但投资组合多元化和上海国际金融中心建设带来的好处将支持稳定的长期关系。

尽管外国投资者对中国债券兴趣浓厚，但他们持有的中国债券在整个在岸债券市场中所占的比例不到 3%。然而，由于外国投资者专注于购买由最优质发行人发行的债券，他们正在成为特定市场的关键参与者。

从图 1 可以看出，外国投资者持有的债券 90% 是中国政府或三家政策性银行之一发行的债券，本质上被视为主权风险。公司债券和地方政府发行的债券仅占其持有量的 9%，而在规模较小的熊猫债市场的投资则仅占持有总量的 1%。

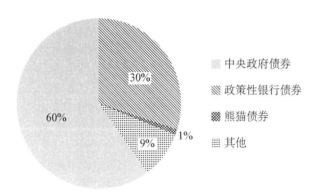

图例：
中央政府债券
政策性银行债券
熊猫债
其他

图 1　外国投资者在岸债券持有构成情况

数据来源：万得资讯、第一财经

三个因素可以解释外国投资者对高质量债券的偏好。

首先,中国市场上的很多外国投资者是公共机构,如央行和国际金融机构,它们的授权仅限于持有主权或准主权债务。

其次,国际指数在纳入中国债券时一般只考虑政府债务。这导致跟踪这些指数的资产管理公司购买主权或准主权债券。

第三,与投资中国公司债券相关的税收不确定性①,在很大程度上让外国投资者远离这一资产类别。

鉴于他们的偏好,外国投资者目前持有中国政府发行的近 10% 的债券,以及三家政策性银行发行的 5% 的债券。他们还持有熊猫债市场发行的约六分之一的债券。熊猫债市场旨在让外国人有机会为其中国业务筹集在岸人民币资金。

在当前宏观经济环境下,中国债券正受益于外国投资者对收益率的追求。中国以外的央行正在实施非常宽松的货币政策,以限制新冠肺炎疫情对经济的影响。这导致北美和欧洲的债券收益率大幅下降。

图 2 显示,2020 年初,美国 10 年期国债收益率大幅下降,此后一直处于低位。相比之下,中国 10 年期国债收益率只是暂时下降,随后又回到了 2019 年底的水平。因此,中美 10 年期国债收益率差扩大至略低于 2.5 个百分点,而2017—2019 年的平均收益率差为 1 个百分点。

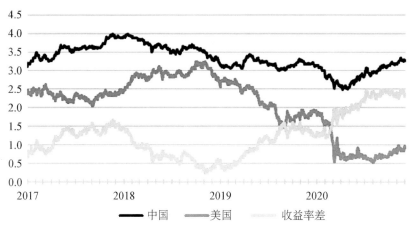

图 2　中美 10 年期国债收益率和利差变化情况(%)

数据来源:万得资讯、第一财经

---

① 中国债券市场的未来(https://www.elibrary.imf.org/view/books/071/25402-9781484372142-en/25402-9781484372142-en-book.xml? language = en&redirect = true)。

高利率本身并不是购买中国债券的充分诱因。投资者根据对回报和风险的评估做出决策。考虑到投资中国政府债券的风险,这些证券的定价似乎很有吸引力。

标普给予中国主权债券 A+ 信用评级。图 3 比较了中国债券与其他主权国家债券的收益率,这些主权国家的信用评级大致相似。中国债券不仅是 A+ 级债券中收益率最高的,其收益率也超过了评级为 A 和 A- 的债券。

最近,外国投资者对中国债券的兴趣在一定程度上可以解释为它们物有所值。此外,近年来实施的改革也改善了外国投资者进入国内债券市场的渠道。此外,中国控制病毒和支持经济全面复苏①的能力,表明人民币在近期不太可能贬值。

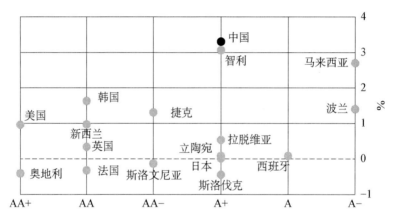

图 3　各国 10 年期国债收益率和标普信用评级

数据来源:全球经济指标、第一财经

中国债券被纳入全球主要债券指数,这也为外资投资中国债券提供了支持。数万亿美元的资金追踪这些指数,许多投资经理需要购买中国债券,以便使自己的投资组合与基准保持一致。

2020 年 2 月,摩根大通(JPMorgan)选择将中国债券纳入其新兴市场政府债券指数(Emerging Market Government Bond Index)。中国和巴西债券将是该指数中权重最大的,各占基准的 10%。

更重要的是,彭博/巴克莱(Bloomberg/Barclays)和富时/罗素(FTSE/Russell)正将中国债券纳入其全球指数。前者于 2019 年 4 月开始,后者将于

---

① 10 月份数据显示中国经济复苏是完全的(https://www.yicaiglobal.com/opinion/mark.kruger/october-data-indicates-china-recovery-is-complete)。

2021年10月开始。中国债券在这些指数中的权重将仅为5%—6%。但追踪全球债券的资金要比追踪新兴市场债券的资金多很多。因此,对中国市场的影响将会更大。

这三个指数只是逐渐将中国所占比重向目标权重靠拢。最终,将中国债券纳入这三个指数可能意味着外国投资者需要购买大约3,000亿美元①的中国债券。因此,资产管理公司的持仓也可以在一定程度上解释我们所看到的兴趣。

超越短期的宏观经济和制度因素,我们有理由相信,随着时间的推移,外国投资者将增持中国债券。

长期以来,中国政策制定者一直在寻求增强资本市场的作用。更多的外资参与可能会增加债券市场的复杂性,并为中国金融业创造更多高附加值的就业机会。这符合政府提高服务业在GDP中所占比重和把上海打造成国际金融中心的目标。

对于外国投资者来说,中国债券市场不仅提供了低风险和高回报,还具有多元化的好处。中国债券与海外市场金融资产的相关性较低②。这是因为中国商业银行倾向于持有债券至到期,而且中国的货币政策独立于美国和欧洲。

值得注意的是,从某种意义上来说,世界对中国债务的投资不足。图4显示

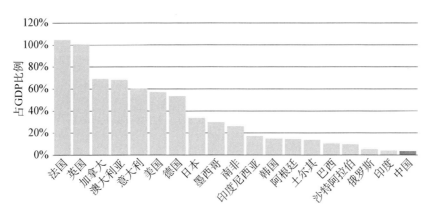

图4　外资所持债务证券占各国GDP比例

数据来源:国际货币基金组织、第一财经

---

① 中国加入基准指数　深化全球金融联系(https://blogs.imf.org/2019/06/19/china-deepens-global-finance-links-as-it-joins-benchmark-indexes/)。

② 中国固定收益:低相关性——为什么以及持续多久?(https://www.ubs.com/global/en/assetmanagement/insights/thematic-viewpoints/apac-and-emerging/articles/china-fixed-income-low-correlation.html)。

了国际货币基金组织关于外资持有的债务证券的数据。这些数据包括在岸和离岸持有的债务。数据显示,外国持有的中国债券仅占 GDP 的 3%,在 G20 成员国中比重最低。

那么,外资与中国债券的"恋情"还能持续多久?

假设外国投资者持有的中国债券达到 G20 成员国的中位数,即占 GDP 的26%。这是图 4 中南非所在的位置。这意味着新增外资高达 3.3 万亿美元,是目前外资所持中国债券的 7 倍!

考虑到资本市场的进一步整合对双方都有利,外资和中国债券真像是天造地设的一对。

Can China and the US Cooperate and Reform the WTO?

May 19, 2021

The World Trade Organization (WTO) is in crisis.

The WTO was designed to be the forum in which the rules for international trade are negotiated, administered and reviewed. Moreover, its dispute settlement mechanism had come to be seen as the "crown jewel" of the international system.

The WTO's 164 country-members are treated equally, regardless of their economic size. Decisions are made by consensus. While this governance structure is equitable, it tends to sap the WTO's dynamism and leave it out of step with changing times.

There is widespread agreement that industrial subsidies are the most contentious set of issues. But there is no consensus on how reform should proceed.

Members disagree on the scope of the subsidies that should be prohibited. The WTO forbids subsidizing exports. It also bans subsidies that favour the use of domestic goods instead of imports. The US, the EU and Japan find this definition too narrow. They want to broaden the definition of subsidy to include other "market-distorting" behaviour, such as keeping insolvent firms afloat (in the absence of a restructuring plan).

Subsidies are provided by the government and members disagree about the extent to which state-owned enterprises act as agents of the government. In particular, China does not want WTO reform to be used as a vehicle for special and discriminatory disciplines against its state-owned firms.

Members disagree on how the amount of a subsidy should be calculated. The US, the EU and Japan argue that if the subsidizing member's domestic market is "distorted", then prices from third countries ought to be used to establish the benchmark for the unsubsidized price. However, China rejects the use of this "surrogate country" methodology in anti-dumping investigations.

In its report on foreign trade barriers, the US Trade Representative enumerates a long list of China's trade-distorting non-tariff measures. At the top of the list are China's industrial policies. It singles out Made in China 2025, a ten-year plan that is designed to raise industrial productivity, noting that financial support could amount to $500 billion. While this only works out to 0.3 percent of GDP annually, the report warns that Made in China 2025 is likely to "create or exacerbate market distortions and create severe excess capacity in many of the targeted sectors".

The US has clearly lost patience with the WTO and it has acted unilaterally. In its 2020 Report to Congress on China's WTO compliance, the US Trade Representative argued that it "identified the critical need for new and more effective strategies — including taking actions outside the WTO where necessary — to address the challenges presented by China's state-led, mercantilist approach to the economy and trade."

Thus, the US circumvented international rules by levying tariffs on China — an action which a WTO panel determined was inconsistent with the US's obligations.

The US's frustration with the WTO is not limited to its perception that the multilateral system is unable to constrain China's behaviour. It has long felt that its Appellate Body — the WTO's appeal court — oversteps its mandate. Here too, it has taken matters into its own hands and blocked the appointment of members to the WTO's Appellate Body, effectively undermining the dispute settlement mechanism.

The WTO's dispute settlement mechanism does not appear to have treated the US unfairly. Indeed, no country used it more often than the US. It was the "complainant" in 114 of 522 cases, more than any other WTO member. Moreover, it prevailed on 91 percent of adjudicated issues. On the flip side, it lost 89 percent of adjudicated issues when it was the "respondent" (129 cases).

Countries generally believe that a functioning dispute settlement mechanism is an indispensable public good. Thus, China and the Ottawa Group of 13 like-minded WTO members have stressed the urgent need to unblock the Appellate Body appointments. Moreover, the EU, China and 15 other countries have pursued a workaround. They agreed to develop a multi-party interim appeal arrangement that will allow participating WTO members to settle disputes.

It is clear that to resolve the WTO crisis, some compromise needs to be found on industrial subsidies. Chad Brown and Jennifer Hillman have an interesting proposal, which could offer a way forward.

They recall that agriculture was a highly protected sector that, until the mid-1990s, was poorly covered by the global trading rules. However, methods were developed to assess the scale of agricultural support and the extent to which it distorted global markets. Brown and Hillman suggest a similar approach could be used in the case of industrial subsidies, not just for China but for all countries.

As was done for agriculture, members could create three categories of industrial subsidies. Permitted or "green light" subsidies would be those that promote the public good, such as addressing climate change. Members would commit to limit their spending on "amber light" subsidies, those which likely distort production and trade. Prohibited or "red light" subsidies would be those which directly promote exports or favour domestic products over imported ones.

Clearly, the project that Brown and Hillman propose cannot be accomplished overnight. It will take considerable time and resources to examine country policies and will require extensive negotiations to iron out differences. Should their solution test the US's patience, the eminent Canadian trade economist Dan Ciuriak offers a quick-fix alternative.

In a recent paper, Ciuriak argues that whatever export subsidies China may have "work as much to the advantage of third country exporters to China as they help China's own exporters". The counter-intuitive implication is that the US should embrace rather than worry about China's subsidies!

In making his argument, Ciuriak draws on the work of the great economist Abba Lerner, in particular the "Lerner Symmetry", originally articulated in a 1936 paper. Lerner explained that a tariff on one's trading partner's imports is equivalent to a tax on one's own exports. The logic is as follows. An import tax reduces imports. This causes a real appreciation of the exchange rate, as demand for domestic substitutes increases and wages rise. This appreciation ultimately reduces exports.

Ciuriak says that if China subsidizes its exports, it is simply imposing a negative tax. By the logic of the Lerner Symmetry, it is simultaneously providing a subsidy on imports from the rest of the world.

To support Lerner's theory, Ciuriak presents the results of two modelling exercises, one for Canada and one for the UK. These exercises show that unilateral trade liberalization — dropping one's own import barriers — leads to a fairly symmetric increase in both imports and exports.

Despite the elegance of Ciuriak's reasoning, I fear that the likelihood of the Lerner Symmetry informing US trade policy is small.

Since decisions at the WTO are made by consensus, progress can be glacial. A China-US compromise on subsidies would be a good way to bring the membership together to resolve this difficult issue.

The US could begin by unblocking the appointment of Appellate Body members and restoring this important public good. It could also recognize that China's domestic prices are not particularly distorted and can be used as benchmarks for subsidy investigations.

In his 2019 Report on the Work of the Government, Premier Li Keqiang committed to following the principle of "competitive neutrality". This means that private and state-owned enterprises will be treated equally when it comes to accessing factors of production, markets, licenses, government procurement contracts and so on.

If Chinese state-owned companies' do not have favourable access to resources, then the same principle of competitive neutrality should ensure that they do not provide resources at a subsidized rate.

China has every incentive to keep state-owned companies from providing subsidized inputs. Its development model has evolved and now emphasizes the quality rather than the quantity of growth. It wants to improve the management of state-owned assets. And its carbon neutrality targets imply one more constraint that the economy needs to respect.

Where does that leave us? Brown and Hillman provide a framework for re-thinking the scope of industrial subsidies. Perhaps the time is right for China and the US to find compromises on the definition of "government" and the appropriate benchmark for the subsidies calculation. Taken together, these steps can help resolve the WTO's crisis.

中美可以合作并改革世界贸易组织吗？

2021 年 5 月 19 日

世贸组织正处于危机之中。

世贸组织旨在成为谈判、管理和审查国际贸易规则的国际组织。此外，其争端解决机制被视为国际体系"皇冠上的宝石"①。

世贸组织的 164 个成员无论经济规模大小，都受到了平等对待。决策是通过协商一致做出的。虽然这种治理结构是公平的，但它往往会削弱世贸组织的活力，使其与时代的变化脱节。

人们普遍认为，产业补贴是最具争议的一系列问题。但是对于改革应该如何进行尚未达成共识。

各成员对应禁止补贴的范围存在分歧。世贸组织禁止补贴出口。它还禁止偏向使用国内产品而非进口产品的补贴。美国、欧盟和日本②认为这个定义太窄了。它们希望扩大补贴的定义，将其他"扭曲市场"的行为也包括在内，比如在没有重组计划的情况下让破产的公司继续运营。

补贴由政府提供，各成员对国有企业在多大程度上充当政府的代理人存在分歧。中国③尤其不希望世贸组织改革成为针对中国国有企业的实施特殊和歧视性纪律的工具。

各成员在如何计算补贴的数额方面同样存在分歧。美国、欧盟和日本认为，如果提供补贴的成员的市场被"扭曲"，那么来自第三方的价格就应该被用来确立无补贴价格的基准。然而，中国拒绝在反倾销调查中使用这种"替代方"方法。

---

① WTO 前总干事帕斯卡尔·拉米（Pascal Lamy）在土耳其获颁荣誉博士学位后的演讲中警示"远程全球治理"（https://www.wto.org/english/news_e/sppl_e/sppl272_e.htm）。

② 日本、美国和欧盟三方贸易部长会议的联合声明（https://trade.ec.europa.eu/doclib/docs/2020/january/tradoc_158567.pdf）。

③ 中国关于世贸组织改革的立场文件（https://www.mfa.gov.cn/ce/cerw//eng/xwdt/t1617375.htm）。

在有关贸易壁垒的报告①中,美国贸易代表办公室列举了一长串中国扭曲贸易的非关税措施。首当其冲的是中国的产业政策。报告特别提到了"中国制造2025",这是一个为期10年,旨在提高工业生产率的计划。报告指出,对该计划的财政支持可能达到5,000亿美元。虽然这仅相当于全年GDP的0.3%,但报告警告称,"中国制造2025"可能"造成或加剧市场扭曲,并导致许多目标行业产能严重过剩"。

美国显然对世贸组织失去了耐心,采取了单边行动。美国贸易代表办公室在2020年向国会提交的关于中国履行入世承诺的报告②中表示,"确定迫切需要新的更有效的战略,包括在必要时在世贸组织之外采取行动,以应对中国由国家主导的重商主义经济和贸易方式带来的挑战"。

因此,美国通过对中国征收关税来规避国际规则。对此,世贸组织的一个小组认定这一行动不符合美国的义务。③

美国对世贸组织的失望不仅在于它认为世贸组织的多边体系无法约束中国的行为,美国还认为世贸组织的上诉法庭超越了它们的权限④。在这方面,美国同样自行其是,通过阻止世贸组织上诉机构成员的任命,有效地破坏了争端解决机制。

世贸组织的争端解决机制似乎并未不公平地对待美国。事实上,没有哪个成员比美国更频繁地使用它。在522起案件中,美国是114起案件的"申诉人",比任何其他世贸组织成员都多⑤。此外,它赢得了91%的起诉。另一方面,当它是"被告"时,它输掉了89%的判决(129起案件)。

各成员普遍认为,有效的争端解决机制是不可或缺的公共产品。因此,中国和由13个想法类似的世贸组织成员组成的渥太华小组⑥强调,迫切需要消除对

---

① 2021年关于外贸壁垒的全国贸易报告(https://ustr. gov/sites/default/files/files/reports/2021/2021NTE. pdf)。

② 中国遵守入世承诺情况的报告(https://ustr. gov/sites/default/files/files/reports/2020/2020USTRReportCongressChinaWTOCompliance. pdf)。

③ 世贸组织专家组裁定美国对中国进口产品征收301关税不符合世贸组织义务(https://www. asil. org/insights/volume/24/issue/26/no-unilateral-action% E2% 80% 94wto-panel-ruled-us-section-301-tariffs-chinese)。

④ 关于世界贸易组织上诉机构的报告(https://ustr. gov/sites/default/files/Report_on_the_Appellate_Body_of_the_World_Trade_Organization. pdf)。

⑤ 特朗普有关美国输掉绝大多数WTO诉讼的说法不完全正确(https://www. factcheck. org/2017/10/trump-wrong-wto-record/)。

⑥ 渥太华部长会议关于WTO改革的联合声明(https://www. canada. ca/en/global-affairs/news/2018/10/joint-communique-of-the-ottawa-ministerial-on-wto-reform. html)。

上诉机构成员任命的阻碍。此外,欧盟、中国和其他 15 个国家都在寻求一种变通的办法。它们同意①制定一项多方临时申诉安排,使参与其中的世贸组织成员能够解决争端。

显然,要解决世贸组织危机,需要在产业补贴方面找到一些解决办法。查德・布朗(Chad Brown)和詹妮弗・希尔曼(Jennifer Hillman)提出了一个有趣的建议②,可能能够提供一条出路。

他们回顾,农业一直是一个受到高度保护的产业,在 20 世纪 90 年代中期之前,全球贸易规则对农业的覆盖十分薄弱。然而,人们开发了一些方法来评估农业支持的规模及其对全球市场的扭曲。布朗和希尔曼建议,类似的方法可以用于工业补贴,不仅仅适用于中国,也适用于所有国家。

正如在农业方面所做的那样,成员可以设立三类工业补贴。允许的或"绿灯"补贴是那些促进公共利益的补贴,比如应对气候变化。成员将承诺限制在"琥珀色"补贴上,这些补贴可能扭曲生产和贸易。被禁止的或"红灯"补贴是那些直接促进出口或偏向国内产品而非进口产品的补贴。

显然,布朗和希尔曼提出的项目不可能一蹴而就。审查国家政策将需要相当多的时间和资源,并需要进行广泛的谈判来消除分歧。如果说他们的解决方案考验了美国的耐心,那么加拿大著名贸易经济学家丹・丘里亚克(Dan Ciuriak)③提供了一个速战速决的替代方案。

在最近的一篇论文④中,丘里亚克认为,无论中国的出口补贴是什么,"对中国的第三国出口商都是有利的,因为它们帮助了中国自己的出口商。"这一反直觉的暗示是,美国应该接受而不是担心中国的补贴!

在阐述他的论点时,丘里亚克借鉴了伟大的经济学家阿巴・勒纳(Abba Lerner)⑤的著作,特别是最早在 1936 年的一篇论文⑥中论述的"勒纳对称"(Lerner Symmetry)。勒纳解释说,对贸易伙伴的进口产品征收关税相当于对

---

① 瑞士达沃斯会议部长声明(https://trade.ec.europa.eu/doclib/docs/2020/january/tradoc_158596.pdf)。

② 中国补贴问题的 WTO 式解决方案(https://www.piie.com/sites/default/files/documents/wp19-17.pdf)。

③ 丹・丘里亚克简介(https://www.cigionline.org/people/dan-ciuriak/)。

④ 我们时代的贸易政策碰撞:中国的补贴邂逅阿巴・勒纳和大卫・里卡多(https://papers.ssrn.com/sol3/papers.cfm?abstract_id=3789391)。

⑤ 阿巴・勒纳生平(https://www.hetwebsite.net/het/profiles/lerner.htm)。

⑥ 进出口税的对称性(https://www.jstor.org/stable/2549223?seq=1)。

自己的出口产品征收关税。其逻辑如下：进口税减少进口。这导致汇率实际升值，因为对国内替代品的需求增加，工资上涨。这种升值最终会减少出口。

丘里亚克说，如果中国对其出口进行补贴，其实是在征收负赋税。根据"勒纳对称"的逻辑，中国同时也在为来自世界其他地区的进口产品提供补贴。

为了支持勒纳的理论，丘里亚克展示了两个建模的结果，一个是加拿大的，另一个是英国的。这些实践表明，单边贸易自由化，即消除本国的进口壁垒，会导致进口和出口相当对称的增长。

虽然丘里亚克的推理很巧妙，但我担心，"勒纳对称"不太可能影响美国的贸易政策。

由于世贸组织的决定是通过协商做出的，因此进展可能非常缓慢。中美在补贴问题上达成妥协，将是促使成员团结起来解决这一棘手问题的好办法。

美国可以首先解除对上诉机构成员任命的阻碍，恢复这一重要的公共产品。美国还可以承认，中国国内价格并没有被特别扭曲①，并基于这一认识进行补贴调查。

李克强总理在 2019 年政府工作报告②中承诺坚持"竞争中立"原则。这意味着民营企业和国有企业在获取生产要素、市场、许可证、政府采购合同等方面将得到平等对待。

如果中国国有企业并未在资源获取方面受到优待，那么同样的竞争中立原则应能确保它们不会以补贴价格提供资源。

中国有充分的动机阻止国有企业提供补贴投入。中国的发展模式发生了变化，从注重数量转向注重质量。中国希望改善国有资产的管理。中国的碳中和目标意味着经济多了一个需要遵守的约束。

我们该怎么办呢？布朗和希尔曼为重新思考工业补贴的范围提供了一个框架。或许现在是中美两国就"政府"的定义和补贴计算的合适基准达成妥协的时候了。同时，采取这些措施有助于解决世贸组织的危机。

---

① 专家：反倾销调查中的"替代国"做法对中国不公平（http://www.chinadaily.com.cn/a/201712/13/WS5a3097f5a3108bc8c672cfc5.html）。

② 2019 年政府工作报告（http://english.www.gov.cn/premier/speeches/2019/03/16/content_281476565265580.htm）。

Are the Worst in US-China Relations Behind Us?

June 9, 2021

I want to go out on a limb and make a prediction. I think that US-China relations have hit bottom and that we will see a modest improvement from here on in.

I am basing my forecast on the recent video call between Vice Premier Liu He and Treasury Secretary Janet Yellen and the phone call between Liu and Trade Representative Katherine Tai. Apparently, the calls were cordial and both Ms Yellen and Ms Tai looked forward to further discussions with Mr Liu.

There have always been cycles in the US-China relationship. I attribute this, on the American side, to an ongoing tug-of-war between two factions: the security establishment and the broader business community.

In the US, the security establishment has traditionally played an outsized role in formulating foreign policy. Sixty years ago, in his farewell address, President Eisenhower admonished Americans to "... guard against the acquisition of unwarranted influence, whether sought or unsought, by the military-industrial complex. The potential for the disastrous rise of misplaced power exists and will persist".

How powerful is this military-industrial complex? One way to gauge its influence is arms sales. US firms accounted for more than half of the world's sales of arms and military services in 2019 (Figure 1). This was more than twice the US's share of global GDP.

Since the US government is its major client, the American arms industry has a clear incentive to promote the view that the US's security is at risk. For thirty years following President Eisenhower's speech, that threat came from the Soviet Union. Then it came from Iran. Then from Iraq. Then from al-Qaida. With the Trump Administration, the focus shifted to China.

In its most recent Annual Threat Assessment, the US Intelligence Community said, "China increasingly is a near-peer competitor, challenging the United States in multiple arenas — especially economically, militarily, and technologically — and

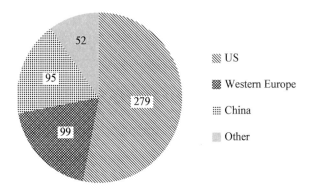

Figure 1   Sales of Top 100 Arms Producing and Military
Service Companies in 2019 (US $ billion)

Source: Defence News, Yicai

is pushing to change global norms. "

What kind of military threat does China really pose to the US?

Looking at the numbers, it is hard to see China challenging the US's supremacy. Figure 2 shows that the US spends three times more on its military than China does. Even after adjusting for lower prices in China, Chinese military expenditures are only 53 percent of what they are in the US.

Figure 2   Military Spending in 2020 (US $ billion)

Source: SIPRI, Yicai

Over the years, the US has built up an overwhelming advantage in military hardware.

In its report on China's military, the US Defense Department stated that China plans to double its nuclear warhead stockpile — "currently estimated to be in the low-200s" — over the next decade. The US's own nuclear stockpile is estimated to be around 3,800 warheads, or 9.5 times what China might achieve by the decade's end.

The US has 11 aircraft carriers, while China only has two. The US has four times as many military aircraft as China. And so on.

Not only is China far behind the US in current military capability, but the profile of Chinese government spending does not suggest that it is in the midst of an arms race. Figure 3 shows that military spending, as a share of general government spending, has fallen from over 10 percent in the early 2000s to under 5 percent last year. Military spending accounted for just under 8 percent of US government spending in 2020.

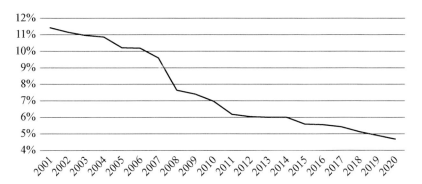

Figure 3   China's Military Spending (Share of General Government Expenditure)

Source: SIPRI, Yicai

Does China pose an economic and technological threat to the US?

It is true that China's economy is poised to overtake the US's as the world's largest sometime toward the end of the decade. Moreover, innovation will play a greater role in China's economic development.

Nevertheless, US per capita incomes are four times higher than those in China (in purchasing power parity terms) and the productivity of China's manufacturing sector is only about half as high. So, even if China is developing quickly, it will take generations before it catches up with the US.

The more important point is that China's development is not a "zero sum game". China is deeply embedded in the global economy. Notwithstanding the political frictions, Nike, Disney, Starbucks and the NBA remain extremely popular here, illustrating how the US benefits from China's rise.

This is what the broader US business community sees. It understands the high cost of being cut out of China's growing markets — both in terms of lost sales and the inability to spread the costs of R&D over a larger customer base. The ongoing opportunities in China is what drove BlackRock and Goldman Sachs to announce new wealth management joint ventures and JPMorgan to take full control of its securities JV.

The broader US business community also knows that import barriers raise costs and reduce their competitiveness. This is why 3,700 US companies, including Ford, Tesla, Walmart, and Coca-Cola have challenged the legality of the tariffs imposed by the Trump Administration on China.

I believe that we are at a turning point. President Biden's new budget reflects the priorities of a less hawkish administration, suggesting the influence of the security establishment is waning. By investing heavily in infrastructure, education and R&D, it represents a sharp change from the concerns of the Trump Administration.

In part, because of this reorientation of priorities, military spending is being squeezed out. Following many years of decline during the Obama Presidency, defence spending grew by 5 percent per year under the Trump Administration. President Biden is budgeting for defence spending to only grow by 1.3 percent per year over the next four years (Figure 4).

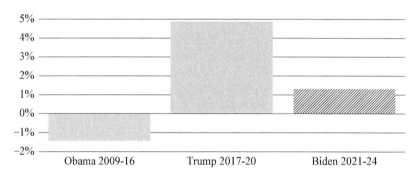

Figure 4   Average Annual Change in Defence Spending

Source: CBO, White House, Yicai

President Biden's emphasis on repairing domestic deficiencies, while keeping military spending below the rate of inflation bodes well for US-China relations.

While I expect the two countries to become more cooperative, it may take some time for the rhetoric to cool off. Neither side will want to be seen as soft on the other.

For example, President Biden's recent executive order prevents Americans from investing in 59 Chinese companies which "undermine the security or values" of the US and its allies. This is clearly a rhetorical rather than a material development.

Given China's huge pool of domestic savings, the ban will have no effect on these firms' cost of capital. Moreover, for Americans who want to invest in China's development, it clarifies that owning shares in the remaining pool of Chinese listed companies is not unpatriotic.

While President Biden's executive order may make headlines, I believe the recent calls between top American and Chinese officials will actually bring us one step closer to President Eisenhower's vision "... that this world of ours, ever growing smaller, must avoid becoming a community of dreadful fear and hate, and be instead, a proud confederation of mutual trust and respect".

中美关系触底了吗？

2021 年 6 月 9 日

我想冒险做个预测。我认为中美关系已经触底，从现在开始，我们将看到适度的改善。

我的预测基于近期中国国务院副总理刘鹤与美国财政部长珍妮特·耶伦(Janet Yellen)的视频通话以及刘鹤与美国贸易代表戴琪的语音通话。显然，这些通话是热情友好的，耶伦和戴琪都期待与刘鹤进一步讨论有关问题。

中美关系总是存在周期。我认为，在美国方面，这是由安全建制派和更广泛的商界两派之间持续不断的拉锯战造成的。

在美国，安全机构传统上在制定外交政策方面发挥了过大的作用。60 年前，艾森豪威尔总统在他的告别演说[1]中告诫美国人"要警惕军事工业联合体有意无意地获得不适当的影响。不适当的权力恶性增长的可能性已经存在并将继续存在下去"。

美国的军工复合体有多强大？衡量其影响力的一个方法是武器销售额。2019 年美国公司占世界武器和军事服务销售的一半以上（图 1），这一比例是美国占全球 GDP 份额的两倍多。

由于美国政府是其主要客户，美国军工行业显然有动机宣扬美国安全面临危险的观点。在艾森豪威尔总统演讲之后的 30 年里，这种威胁先后来自前苏联、伊朗、伊拉克和基地组织。随着特朗普政府的上台，焦点转向了中国。

在最近的年度威胁评估[2]中，美国情报界称："中国日益成为一个与美国不相上下的竞争对手，在多个领域挑战美国，尤其是经济、军事和技术，并正在推动

---

[1] 艾森豪威尔总统在白宫办公室所作演讲（https://www. eisenhowerlibrary. gov/sites/default/files/research/online-documents/farewell-address/1961-01-17-press-release. pdf）。

[2] 美国情报界年度威胁评估（https://www. dni. gov/files/ODNI/documents/assessments/ATA-2021-Unclassified-Report. pdf）。

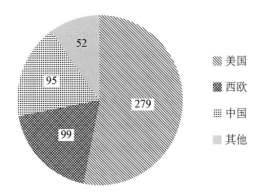

图 1　全球百大军火生产和军事服务企业 2019 年销售额(单位:十亿美元)

数据来源:美国《国防新闻周刊》、第一财经

改变全球规范。"

中国究竟对美国构成了什么样的军事威胁?

从数据中很难看出中国在挑战美国的霸权。图 2 显示,美国的军事开支是中国的三倍。即使在调整中国较低的价格后,中国的军费开支也只有美国的 53%。

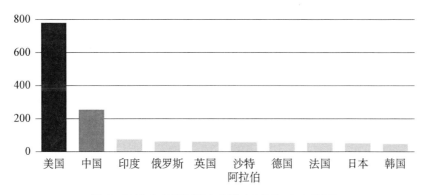

图 2　2020 年各国军事支出排名(单位:十亿美元)

数据来源:斯德哥尔摩国际和平研究所、第一财经

多年来,美国在军事装备方面建立了压倒性优势。

美国国防部在其关于中国军事的报告[①]中表示,中国计划在未来 10 年将核弹头储备增加一倍,"目前估计在 200 枚以下"。据估计,美国自己的核武库中大

————————

[①] 2020 年涉及中华人民共和国的军事和安全发展:向国会提交的年度报告(https://media. defense. gov/2020/Sep/01/2002488689/-1/-1/1/2020-DOD-CHINA-MILITARY-POWER-REPORT-FINAL. PDF)。

约有 3,800 枚核弹头,是中国到 2020 年可能达到的核弹头数量的 9.5 倍。[①]

美国有 11 艘航母,而中国只有 2 艘。[②] 美国的军用飞机数量是中国的 4 倍。[③] 诸如此类数据还有很多,就不一一列举了。

中国目前的军事能力不仅远远落后于美国,而且从中国政府支出来看,也没有陷入军备竞赛。图 3 显示,军费开支占政府总开支的比例从 21 世纪初的 10%以上降至 2020 年的 5%以下。2020 年,军事开支占美国政府开支的比例略低于 8%。

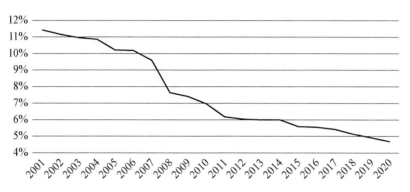

图 3 中国军事开支占政府支出的比重变化情况

数据来源:斯德哥尔摩国际和平研究所、第一财经

中国对美国构成经济和技术威胁吗?

事实上,中国经济有望在近 10 年的某个时候超过美国[④],成为世界上最大的经济体。创新将在中国经济发展中发挥更大作用。

然而,美国的人均收入(按购买力平价计算)是中国的 4 倍,而中国制造业的生产率仅为美国的一半左右[⑤]。因此,即使中国发展迅速,也需要几代人的时间才能赶上美国。

更重要的是,中国的发展不是"零和游戏"。中国已经深深融入全球经济。

[①] 美国军事力量评估(https://www.heritage.org/sites/default/files/2020-11/2021_IndexOfUSMilitary-Strength_ASSESSMENT_POWER_ALL.pdf)。

[②] 2021 年各国航母数量(https://worldpopulationreview.com/country-rankings/aircraft-carriers-by-country)。

[③] 2021 年世界空军报告(https://www.flightglobal.com/defence/world-air-forces-2021)。

[④] 新冠疫情加速缩小中美经济规模的差距(https://www.yicaiglobal.com/news/covid-19-is-accelerating-china-us-convergence)。

[⑤] 中国能成为下一个韩国吗(https://www.yicaiglobal.com/opinion/mark.kruger/can-china-be-the-next-korea)?

尽管存在政治摩擦,耐克、迪士尼、星巴克和 NBA 在中国仍然非常受欢迎,这说明美国是如何从中国的崛起中获益的。

这是更广泛的美国商界所看到的。它明白被排除在中国不断增长的市场之外的高昂成本,无论是损失的销售额,还是无法将研发成本分摊到更大的客户基础上。正是由于中国持续存在的机遇,贝莱德[①]和高盛[②]宣布成立新的财富管理合资企业,摩根大通[③]则宣布全资控制其合资证券公司。

更广泛的美国商界也知道,进口壁垒会增加成本,降低竞争力。这就是为什么包括福特、特斯拉、沃尔玛和可口可乐在内的 3,700 家美国公司[④]对特朗普政府对中国征收关税的合法性提出质疑。

我相信我们正处于一个转折点。拜登总统的新预算反映了一个不那么强硬的政府的优先事项,表明安全部门的影响力正在减弱。大举投资基础设施、教育和研发,表明拜登政府与特朗普政府的担忧截然不同。

在某种程度上,由于优先事项的重新定位,军费开支被挤出。在奥巴马总统任期内,国防开支连续多年下降,在特朗普政府执政期间,国防开支每年增长5%。拜登总统预计,未来 4 年的国防开支每年仅增长 1.3%(图 4)。

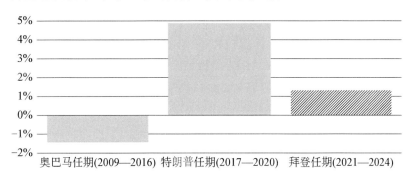

图 4　美国国防开支的平均年度变化

数据来源:美国国会预算办公室、白官、第一财经

---

① 贝莱德获准在中国经营财富业务(https://www.ft.com/content/3fd79007-e556-4f04-aa6e-43557652890f)。

② 高盛在华财富管理交易获批(https://www.ft.com/content/263c5b4a-8c29-485a-8b25-20f74c04ae7d)。

③ 摩根大通申请完全控制中国证券合资企业(https://www.ft.com/content/3bd19ceb-50ed-4555-a3e3-e06401b77879)。

④ 拜登政府在法律摊牌中为特朗普的中国关税辩护(https://news.bloombergtax.com/international-trade/biden-white-house-defends-trump-china-tariffs-in-legal-showdown)。

拜登总统强调弥补国内不足,同时将军费开支增速保持在通货膨胀率以下,这对美中关系来说是个好兆头。

虽然我预计两国之间会有更多合作,但要让"口水战"冷却下来可能还需要一段时间。双方都不希望被视为对对方软弱。

例如,拜登总统最近的行政命令禁止美国人投资 59 家"破坏美国及其盟友的安全或价值观"的中国公司。这显然是有名无实的举措。

考虑到中国庞大的国内储蓄,这项禁令不会对这些公司的资本成本产生影响。此外,对于希望投资中国的美国人来说,它表明"持有其他中国上市公司的股票并非不爱国"。

虽然拜登总统的行政命令可能会成为头条新闻,但我相信,最近美国和中国高级官员之间的通话会让我们离艾森豪威尔总统的愿景更近一步:"我们的这个世界变得越来越小,必须避免成为一个充满恐惧和仇恨的可怕社会,应该是一个相互信任和尊重的自豪联盟。"

China and American Foreign Policy for the Middle Class

August 25, 2021

A few weeks ago, we looked at the attitudes expressed by American and European firms operating here in China. Surveys show that they are increasingly committed to this market, which is becoming relatively more profitable. While the business environment is improving, these foreign firms would invest even more in China, if they had the same opportunities as their domestic competitors.

This week, we turn our attention to the views of firms in the US that import from or export to China.

On August 5, thirty-four American business organizations sent letters to Treasury Secretary Janet Yellen and Trade Representative Katherine Tai. These organizations — as disparate as the Idaho Potato Commission, the Securities Industry and Financial Markets Association (SIFMA), the Semiconductor Industry Association and the American Apparel and Footwear Association — asked the US government to deepen its engagement with China on trade and economic issues.

The groups have three specific requests.

First, they urge the Administration to work with the Chinese government to increase purchases of US goods and implement all structural commitments under the Phase One US-China Economic and Trade Agreement. Second, they ask the Administration to re-instate tariff exemptions for those products whose exemptions expired in 2020. Moreover, they request a "new, fair, and transparent" process to determine which products can be exempted from the tariffs. Third, they propose that the Administration negotiate with China so as to remove " both nations' counterproductive tariffs as soon as possible".

While it is difficult to say how the US Administration will respond to the letters, we continue to see encouraging signs of an incipient warming in Sino-US relations. In late July, Deputy Secretary of State Wendy Sherman met with State Councillor and Foreign Minister Wang Yi in Tianjin. Sherman emphasized that while the US "welcomes the stiff competition" with China, it does "not seek conflict with the PRC". Moreover, she underlined how important it is for the US to cooperate with China on such issues as the climate crisis, counternarcotics, non-proliferation, and various regional concerns. In another positive development, shortly before Sherman's visit, the US dropped charges against five Chinese scholars who were accused of hiding their military affiliations in their visa applications.

Of course, these are only baby steps toward confidence-building and greater cooperation. And the road ahead is bound to be a bumpy one. Ultimately, the way the Administration responds to the business organizations' requests will be informed by strategic considerations. But, here too, there are reasons to be optimistic.

In pursuing his foreign policy for the middle class, President Biden says, "Every action we take in our conduct abroad, we must take with American working families in mind."

"Trade policy," he says, "must grow the American middle class, create new and better jobs, raise wages, and strengthen communities."

In my view, the Administration's positive response to the business organizations' requests would go a long way toward achieving these objectives.

According to the thirty-four groups, the Chinese government has met important benchmarks and commitments made in the Phase One Agreement. They say that this has resulted in benefits for "American businesses, farmers, ranchers, and workers". The letter specifically mentions the importance of having followed through on opening up the financial sector and addressing most long-standing agricultural market access barriers.

In contrast, the organizations emphasize the harm the tariffs are causing to American consumers, manufacturers, service providers and businesses. They cite analysis by Moody's that shows the burden of the tariffs has disproportionally fallen on Americans — US importers are paying around 18.5 percent more for the affected Chinese products, while Chinese exporters receive just 1.5 percent less. They also refer to estimates by the Congressional Budget Office (CBO) that the tariffs cost the average American household close to $1,300 in 2020 alone.

In the same report, the CBO estimates that the trade barriers reduce the level of US real GDP by 0.5 percent in 2020. The negative effect of the trade barriers is projected to linger for as much as ten years, with the level of GDP in 2030 still 0.1 percent below that of the "no trade barrier" scenario. With potential GDP growth estimated at 1.7 percent, these are very significant output losses. And they most certainly depress middle-class incomes and employment.

The business groups stress how the tariffs have increased their costs of manufacturing and providing services. The tariffs raise product prices domestically and reduce the attractiveness of US exports abroad. Indeed, US firms face international competitors who do not pay the tariffs on their inputs from China and those whose goods enter China tariff-free. As long as the tariffs remain in place, the organizations request that the Administration "mitigate the damage to US workers and other stakeholders" by resuming a process of exempting particular goods from the tariff.

While it appears that engaging China, along the lines proposed in the letters, may indeed be middle-class friendly trade policy, it is clear that the two countries have many unresolved differences. For example, the business organizations mention subsidies, government procurement, digital trade, data governance, market access barriers for US-manufactured goods and many other issues as long-standing and unaddressed. Given the US and China's global importance, these issues need to be addressed, preferably in a transparent and even-handed manner and via multilateral fora, where appropriate.

Take subsidies for example. Every major economy, from time to time, appears to have engaged in some sort of subsidy. It is instructive that the Americans and the Europeans only recently called a truce in the 17-year, Airbus-Boeing subsidy war. Some subsidies may be beneficial. For example, subsidizing the production of solar panels might correct for the severe negative externalities associated with burning fossil fuels and spur the transition to a low-carbon economy. Some subsidies may promote research and development with large social benefits.

Addressing subsidies requires creative thinking along the lines of the proposal made by Chad Brown and Jennifer Hillman. Their idea is to classify subsidies into three groups. Permitted or "green light" subsidies would be those that promote the public good, such as addressing climate change. Countries would commit to limit their spending on "amber light" subsidies, those which likely distort production and trade. Prohibited or "red light" subsidies would be those which directly promote exports or favour domestic products over imported ones.

Reaching international agreement on such a framework would take time — perhaps as much as 17 years! But the type of deepened engagement proposed by the 34 American business organizations appears to be the right place to start for resolving such long-standing differences.

中国与美国对中产阶级的外交政策

2021 年 8 月 25 日

几周前,我们观察了在中国运营的美国和欧洲公司表达的态度。调查显示,它们对利润空间正变得相对更大的中国市场的态度越来越坚定。虽然营商环境正在改善,但如果这些外国公司拥有与国内竞争对手相同的机会,它们将增加在中国市场的投资。

本周,我们将关注经营对中国进出口生意的美国公司的观点。

2021 年 8 月 5 日,包括爱达荷州马铃薯委员会（Idaho Potato Commission）、证券和金融市场协会（Securities Industry and Financial Markets Association,SIFMA）、半导体行业协会（Semiconductor Industry Association）以及美国服装和鞋类协会（American Apparel and Footwear Association）在内的 34 个美国商业组织致信美国财政部长珍妮特·耶伦和贸易代表戴琪,要求美国政府深化与中国的经贸往来。

具体要求包括以下三个方面。

首先,它们敦促美国政府与中国政府合作,增加对中国的出口,履行中美第一阶段经贸协议下的所有结构性承诺。其次,它们要求美国政府恢复对 2020 年免税到期的产品的关税豁免。此外,它们要求建立一个"新的、公平的、透明的"程序来确定哪些产品可以免除关税。第三,它们建议美国政府与中国进行谈判,尽快取消"两国间的那些适得其反的关税"。

虽然很难说美国政府会如何回应这些信件,但我们仍然看到中美关系开始升温的令人鼓舞的迹象。2021 年 7 月下旬,美国副国务卿温迪·谢尔曼（Wendy Sherman）在天津会见了中国国务委员兼外长王毅。谢尔曼强调,尽管美国"欢迎与中国的激烈竞争",但并"不想与中国发生冲突"。此外,她强调了中美在气候危机、毒品管制、防止核扩散和其他区域性问题上开展合作的重要性。另一个积极的进展是,在谢尔曼访问前不久,美国撤销了对五名中国学者在签证申请过程中隐瞒其军事背景的诉讼。

当然,这些只是两国建立互信、加强合作进程中的一小步。前路注定坎坷。最终,美国政府将基于战略考虑对商业组织信函中的请求做出回应。但在这方面,也有理由乐观。

美国总统拜登在推进为中产阶级服务的外交政策时说:"我们在国外采取的每一项行动都必须考虑到美国的工薪家庭。"他表示:"贸易政策必须壮大美国中产阶级,创造新的更好的就业机会,提高工资,并加强社区的凝聚力。"

我认为,政府积极回应商业组织的要求对实现这些目标大有帮助。

据 34 家商业组织介绍,中国政府已经达到了第一阶段经贸协议中的重要基准并兑现了承诺。它们认为,这给"美国企业、农民、牧场主和工人"带来了好处。信中特别提到了落实金融市场开放和解决大多数长期存在的农产品市场准入壁垒的重要性。

相反,这些组织强调关税对美国消费者、制造商、服务提供商和企业造成的伤害。它们引用了穆迪的分析,该分析显示,关税负担不成比例地落在美国人身上——美国进口商为受影响的中国产品多支付了约 18.5%,而中国出口商多支付了不到 1.5%。它们还提到了美国国会预算办公室(CBO)的估计,即仅在 2020 年,关税令美国普通家庭的开支增加近 1,300 美元。

在同一份报告中,国会预算办公室估计,贸易壁垒使美国 2020 年的实际 GDP 降低了 0.5%。其负面影响预计将持续长达 10 年,到 2030 年,美国的 GDP 水平仍将比"没有贸易壁垒"的情形下低 0.1%。在 GDP 潜在增长率预估为 1.7% 的情况下,产出损失明显。这些必然会减少中产阶级的收入和就业。

这些商业组织强调关税如何增加它们制造商品和提供服务的成本。关税推高了国内产品的价格,降低了美国出口产品在国外的吸引力。事实上,美国公司的国际竞争对手从中国进口的产品不征收关税,或其产品进入中国不征收关税。只要关税仍然存在,这些组织就会要求政府通过恢复对特定商品的关税豁免程序来"减轻对美国工人和其他利益相关者的损害"。

尽管看起来,按照信中提出的思路与中国接触确实可能是对中产阶级友好的贸易政策,但很明显,两国之间存在许多未解决的分歧。例如,商业组织提到的补贴、政府采购、数字贸易、数据治理、美国制造商品的市场准入壁垒以及许多其他长期存在且未解决的问题。鉴于美国和中国的全球重要性,这些问题需要得到解决,最好是以透明和公平的方式,在适当的情况下通过多边协商解决。

以补贴为例。各主要经济体似乎都曾不时地进行某种形式的补贴。直到最近,美国人和欧洲人宣布休战,结束了长达 17 年的空客-波音补贴战,这是很有启发性的。一些补贴可能是有益的。例如,补贴太阳能电池板的生产可能会纠正与燃烧化石燃料相关的负外部性问题,并刺激向低碳经济的过渡。一些补贴可能会促进具有巨大社会效益的研发活动。

解决补贴问题,需要按照查德·布朗和詹妮弗·希尔曼的建议进行创造性思考。他们的想法是将补贴分为三类。允许的或"绿灯"补贴将是那些用于促进公共利益的补贴,如应对气候变化。各国将承诺限制其对"琥珀色灯"补贴的支出,这些补贴可能会扭曲生产和贸易。被禁止的或"红灯"补贴将是那些直接促进出口或偏护国内产品超过进口产品的补贴。就这样的框架达成国际协议需要时间——可能会长达 17 年!然而,34 个美国商业组织提议的深化接触似乎是解决此类长期分歧的正确起点。

Part IV

The Pandemic and the Chinese Government's Response

第四部分

新冠肺炎疫情和中国政府的应对之策

Advice From VoxEu: Act Fast and Do Whatever It Takes

April 10, 2020

VoxEu recently released an e-book of recommendations on how to think through the medical and economic policies that will be needed to mitigate the effects of COVID – 19. The e-book consists of 24 thought-provoking essays by renowned economists and a very informative introduction by its editors, Richard Baldwin and Beatrice Weder di Mauro, which sets the context for the collection.

The e-book, which I recommend highly, can be found here: https://voxeu. org/content/mitigating-covid-economic-crisis-act-fast-and-do-whatever-it-takes. What I want to do in the next few paragraphs is summarize the key points of the three China-related pieces.

In his essay ***Ten keys to beating back COVID – 19 and the associated economic pandemic***, Shang-Jin Wei takes stock of country-experiences and offers early lessons. His recommendations are sensible. Some, like ♯5 — enforcing social distancing as soon as there are signs of an outbreak — and ♯6 — rapidly offering emergency assistance to workers and firms — have already been implemented by a number of governments. Others, like ♯3 — having a workable contingency plan to ensure an adequate number of hospital beds, especially ICU beds — seem to be a challenge for many countries, given how quickly the disease has spread.

Mr Wei's tenth recommendation is that reducing tariffs and trade barriers can be helpful in fighting a pandemic-induced recession. He notes that there is a limit to how much more central banks can do to stimulate their economies, given the rate cuts that have already taken place. He points out that many countries maintain trade barriers that effectively raise the costs of production and reduce household incomes and he calls for a coordinated international effort to liberalize trade, led by the WTO and the G20. He wonders if the Trump administration would join such an endeavour and holds out hope that the threat of a looming recession might alter the US's calculation, making it more receptive.

Recent events show how important it is to heed Mr Wei's advice. As part of the Defence Production Act, President Trump ordered 3M to stop exporting masks to Canada and Latin America. 3M subsequently warned that since it was a "critical supplier" of masks to healthcare workers in those regions, Mr Trump's order could have "significant humanitarian implications". Canadian Prime Minister Justin Trudeau emphasized how intertwined the US and Canadian health care supply chains are. Indeed, nurses from Windsor, Ontario travel to Detroit, Michigan each day to care for the sick and 3M uses paper from British Columbia to make its masks. Should Canada take retaliatory action against the US, it could precipitate a downward spiral in which both Americans and Canadians would suffer from even fewer health care resources. Thankfully, Mr Trudeau said Canada would not retaliate. Moreover, 3M recently announced a plan to expand its imports of masks from its Chinese plants in the next three months. This would allow the company to continue sending it's US-made mask to Canada and Latin America, where 3M is the primary source of supply.

One of the most interesting recommendations made by Yi Huang and coauthors in *Saving China from the coronavirus and economic meltdown: Experiences and lessons* is leveraging internet fintech platforms to provide support to small business. They cite research showing that small firms which are able to access credit through online trading platforms like Alibaba have lower sales volatility and are less likely to go bankrupt. Such access to credit would be particularly useful in the face of the dislocation caused by the virus. Huang et al want policymakers to provide incentives for small firms to improve their digitalization. This would allow them to take advantage of the services that fintech platforms could provide by using big data to enhance credit assessment. The research they cite explains that, given the right information set, Ant Financial is able to provide loans based on a 3-minute online application, a 1-second approval process and zero manual intervention.

Indeed, there are encouraging signs that such leverage has begun. On March 5, Alibaba subsidiaries Ant Financial and MYbank launched the "No-Contact Micro Loan Assistance Plan", which involves digital online applications and no direct human contact. More than 100 Chinese banks have signed on to the Plan, including the Big Six state-owned institutions, which hopes to provide financial support to 10 million micro and small enterprises.

In the face of the economic damage wrought by the virus, many countries rapidly implemented huge fiscal and monetary support packages. Jonathan Anderson's *China's changing economic priorities and the impact of COVID – 19* provides three reasons why we should not expect China's response to be as large as seen elsewhere.

First, a precipitous rise in debt since the Global Financial Crisis will make the authorities think twice before loosening credit policy in a significant way. Mr Anderson notes that between 2008 and 2016, domestic financial debt rose by 100 percent of GDP, leaving Chinese banks with an "enormous hidden pile of bad credit claims". Since 2017, deleveraging has become an overriding policy priority.

Second, a dramatic fall in China's basic balance of payments surplus means that significant credit loosening could lead to external deficits. After having exceeded 15 percent of GDP in 2008, the sum of China's current account surplus plus foreign direct investment net inflows is now only one-tenth that level. The authorities are worried that slipping into deficit could lead to destabilizing capital outflows, like we saw in 2015 – 16.

Third, demographic changes mean that the Chinese authorities no longer have to pursue aggressive growth targets. For many years, the need to absorb large numbers of new labour force entrants led to growth being a key policy priority. Now, with the working age population having peaked and beginning to shrink, fear of unemployment does not motivate policymakers to the same degree.

Mr Anderson cautions that since much of China's economic stimulus comes from government-sponsored infrastructure projects, it is not easy to gauge the amount of economic support in real time. Nevertheless, he cautions against assuming that China will return to the playbook it used during the Global Financial Crisis.

In my view, each of these essays is worth reading for the insights they provide into China's experience with the virus and the type of policy response we should expect.

来自 VoxEu 的建议:不惜一切代价迅速行动

2020 年 4 月 10 日

　　VoxEu 最近发布了一本电子书,介绍了如何全面、仔细地考虑减轻新冠肺炎疫情影响所需的医疗和经济政策。这本电子书包含 24 篇由著名经济学家撰写的发人深省的文章,以及一篇由该书编辑理查德·鲍德温(Richard Baldwin)和贝特丽丝·韦德尔·迪莫洛(Beatrice Weder di Mauro)撰写的内容丰富的介绍。该介绍还为这一系列文章提供了背景信息。

　　这本我强烈推荐的电子书可以在下面的链接中找到①。我想在下面几段中总结三篇与中国有关的文章的要点。

　　经济学家魏尚进在他撰写的《击退新冠肺炎疫情以及其造成的相关经济影响的十个关键》一文中,评估、总结了受新冠肺炎疫情影响的国家的经验以及疫情发生早期的教训。他的建议是十分明智的,一些政府已经实施了其中的一些建议,比如第五条:一旦出现疫情暴发的迹象,就立即实施保持社交距离这一举措,以及第六条:迅速向工人和企业提供紧急援助。但考虑到疾病传播的速度,其中另外的一些建议,如第三条:制定可行的应急预案以确保足够数量的医院病床位,尤其是重症加护病房的床位,对许多国家来说,似乎是个不小的挑战。

　　魏尚进先生的第十条建议是降低关税和贸易壁垒有助于对抗由新冠肺炎疫情引起的经济衰退。他指出,考虑到已经发生的降息,央行为了刺激经济所能做的事是有限的。他同时也指出,许多国家维持着贸易壁垒,这实际上增加了生产成本,降低了家庭收入。他呼吁国际社会协同努力,在世贸组织和 G20 国家的领导下实现贸易自由化(放宽对贸易的限制)。他想知道特朗普政府是否会加入这一努力,并希望迫在眉睫的经济衰退威胁可能会改变美国的想法,使其更愿意

---

① 如何缓解新冠肺炎经济危机(https://voxeu.org/content/mitigating-covid-economic-crisis-act-fast-and-do-whatever-it-takes)。

接受贸易自由化。

最近发生的事件表明了听取魏先生建议的重要性。作为《国防生产法》的一部分,美国总统特朗普下令 3M 公司(医疗、防护产品制造商)停止向加拿大和拉丁美洲出口口罩。3M 随后警告说,由于该公司是这些地区医疗工作者口罩的"关键供应商",特朗普总统的命令可能会产生"重大的人道主义影响"。加拿大总理贾斯廷·特鲁多(Justin Trudeau)强调美国和加拿大的医疗保健供应链相互交织。事实上,加拿大安大略省温莎市的护士每天会前往美国密歇根州的底特律市照顾病人,而 3M 公司则使用加拿大不列颠哥伦比亚省的纸张生产口罩。如果加拿大对美国采取报复性行动,可能会导致恶性循环,使美国人和加拿大人的医疗资源变得更加匮乏。值得庆幸的是,特鲁多总理说加拿大不会采取报复行为。此外,3M 公司近期宣布计划在接下来的 3 个月增加从其中国工厂进口的口罩数量。这一举措将使该公司能够继续将其产自美国的口罩运往加拿大和拉丁美洲,而在这些地区,3M 是口罩的主要供应来源。

经济学家黄毅与其合著者在《从冠状病毒和经济崩溃中拯救中国:经验和教训》一文中提出的最有趣的建议之一是,利用互联网金融科技平台为小企业提供支持。他们引用的研究表明,能够通过阿里巴巴等在线交易平台获得信贷的小公司在销售方面的不稳定性较低,破产的可能性也较小。面对病毒造成的混乱,这种获得信贷的途径将会特别有用。黄毅等人希望政策制定者们为小公司提供激励措施以提高它们的数字化水平。这将使它们(小公司)能利用金融科技平台,通过大数据增强信用评估,进而获得信贷服务。他们引用的研究解释,在提供正确信息集的情况下,蚂蚁金服能够在 3 分钟在线申请的基础上,1 秒钟走完审批流程,零人工干预提供贷款。

事实上,有令人鼓舞的迹象表明,这种杠杆作用已经开始。3 月 5 日,蚂蚁金服和网商银行推出了"无接触贷款助微计划",该计划涉及数字在线应用,无需与人直接接触。100 多家中国银行签署了该计划,其中包括六大国有银行,它们希望为 1,000 万家小微企业提供金融支持。[①]

面对病毒造成的经济损失,许多国家迅速实施了大量的财政、货币政策支持。经济学家乔纳森·安德森(Jonathan Anderson)在《中国不断变化的首要经济任务以及新冠肺炎的影响》一文中讲述了我们不应期待中国的反应像其他地

---

① 100 家中国银行参与网商银行"无接触贷款助微计划"以帮助缓解新冠病毒造成的影响(http://www.chinabankingnews.com/2020/03/08/100-chinese-banks-sign-up-for-mybanks-non-contact-micro-loan-plan-to-help-mitigate-coronavirus-impacts/)。

方一样大的三个原因。

首先,全球金融危机以来债务的急剧上升,将使当局在大幅放松信贷政策之前三思而后行。安德森先生指出,2008—2016 年,国内金融债务的增幅与 GDP 相当,给中国银行业留下了"大量隐性不良信用债权"。自 2017 年以来,去杠杆已经成为压倒一切的政策重点。

其次,中国基本国际收支盈余(顺差)的大幅下降,意味着信贷的大幅放松可能导致对外赤字。在 2008 年超过 GDP 的 15% 之后,中国经常项目顺差加上外国直接投资净流入的总和现在只有此前水平的十分之一。主管部门担心陷入赤字可能会导致破坏稳定的资本外流,正如我们在 2015—2016 年看到的那样。

最后,人口结构的变化意味着中国有关部门不再需要追求激进的增长目标。多年来,吸收大量新劳动力的需求导致增长成为政策实施的首要目标。如今,随着劳动年龄人口数量达到顶峰并开始减少,对失业的恐惧使政策制定者们并没有像以前那样将追求增长作为政策实施的目标。

安德森先生提醒,由于中国的大部分经济刺激措施来自政府资助的基础设施项目,因此实时衡量经济支持措施的数量并不容易。尽管如此,他也告诫不要假设中国会重拾其在全球金融危机期间使用过的剧本。

在我看来,这些文章每一篇都值得一读,因为它们提供了有关中国应对新冠病毒的经验以及我们所期待的那类政策响应的见解。

How Will China Manage Massive Layoffs?

April 16, 2020

Unemployment in China is rising. While the economy is slowly recovering from having been shut down by COVID‑19, foreign demand has begun to evaporate, as the virus spreads among China's trading partners. The National Bureau of Statistics' (NBS) survey for February showed a jump in the unemployment rate to 6.2 percent from 5.2 percent in December. This implies that close to 5 million workers lost their jobs in early 2020.

As Figure 1 shows, the worst may not be over. Internet searches, through mid-April, for the term "失业" (unemployment) have spiked. At a minimum, this suggests widespread fear of unemployment, if not an actual sharp increase in joblessness, which has yet to be reflected in the official data.

How many workers might lose their jobs and what will become of the unemployed are questions on everyone's mind.

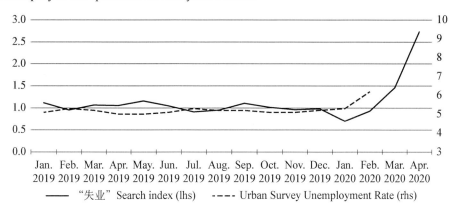

Figure 1　Unemployment Indicators

Source: CEIC, Baidu, Yicai

There is considerable uncertainty surrounding the evolution of the virus, the response of public health authorities and the effectiveness of supportive economic policies — both in China and abroad. This makes it extremely difficult to forecast the extent to which Chinese labour markets will come under pressure and how many workers will be laid off.

One of the more careful estimates I have seen comes from Plenum China, a research firm out of Washington DC, with offices in Beijing, Hong Kong, and Shanghai. Their analysts did a granular, sector-by-sector, estimate of job losses based on projected revenue declines.

Plenum sees employment in services falling by 15 million this year, with layoffs in accommodation and catering accounting for just over half the sector's total.

They expect the manufacturing sector to shed 9 million jobs, as employers continue to upgrade and use the virus as an opportunity to reduce their unskilled staff.

Construction is suffering now as a result of declining infrastructure and real estate investment. However, it should gradually pick up, as policies are eased. Plenum expects the construction sector to retain its employees.

Some industries could increase their employment this year. Plenum expects the IT sector to add 2. 2 million jobs, while public health and administration could hire an additional 1. 5 million.

On net, Plenum expects urban employment to fall by close to 21 million, or by about 4 percent.

Plenum's estimate is in the same ballpark as the Asian Development Bank's (ADB) forecast. The ADB recently projected job losses for the Chinese mainland and many other economies. It sees China's employment declining by between 4. 74 and 5. 25 percent, depending on the length of time it takes to contain the virus. This would translate into 25 - 28 million urban jobs lost, given Plenum's estimate of urban employment at 530 million.

While the loss of millions of jobs is clearly a setback for the economy and the cause of much human suffering, China has two advantages, compared to many other countries, in digesting such a large increase in unemployment.

The first of these is favourable demographics. Largely as a result of the one-child policy, China's working age population peaked in 2013 and has been declining ever since. Figure 2 shows that in both 2018 and 2019, the working age population fell by close to 5 million people.

While a shrinking working age population represents a long-run challenge for producing goods and services, in the short term it creates space to absorb a portion of the laid off workers.

The second advantage that China has, is the way in which the rural labour force can buffer fluctuations in the urban economy. Figure 3 shows the annual change in employment in both urban and rural areas as well as in the whole

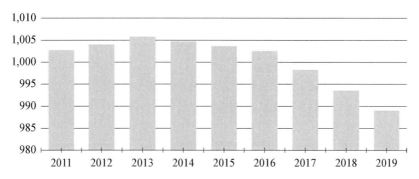

Figure 2   Population 15 – 64 Years Old (millions)

Source: NBS, Yicai

economy. On average, over the last five years, the urban economy created about 10 million net new jobs. With an essentially stagnant labour force, the only way these positions could be staffed was by inducing workers from the countryside to migrate to the city. Given that urban workers are, on average, much more productive than their rural counterparts, higher wages provide the incentive to move.

When the urban economy slows, as it did in 2008 – 09, fewer urban workspaces are created, the demand for rural labour falls and there is less migration. This year, urban jobs will disappear. The 10 million rural workers who had be planning to move to the cities will stay at home. Perhaps the same amount again will leave the cities and return to their villages, where they will be re-absorbed by their families, which form their social safety net.

Of course, many urban workers will lose their jobs as well. They will not have the option of moving to rural areas and living off of the land. However, China's favourable demographics and the flexibility provided by the migrants will make it somewhat easier for them to find new employment in these difficult circumstances.

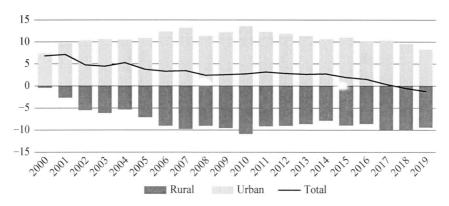

Figure 3   Annual Change in Employment (millions)

Source: CEIC, Yicai

中国将如何应对大规模裁员？

2020 年 4 月 16 日

中国的失业率正在上升。虽然经济正在从新冠肺炎疫情造成的停顿中逐渐恢复,但随着新冠病毒在中国的贸易伙伴间传播,国外需求已开始逐渐消失。中国国家统计局(NBS)2020 年 2 月的调查显示:失业率从 2019 年 12 月的 5.2%跃升至 6.2%。这意味着 2020 年初有近 500 万人失业。

如图 1 所示,最坏的情况可能还没有结束。到 4 月中旬,互联网上"失业"一词的搜索量激增。搜索量激增这一现象即使不能表明尚未在官方数据中反映出来的实际失业率的急剧上升,也至少表明人们普遍担心失业。

有多少人可能会失去工作,而失业者又会怎样,是大家关心的问题。

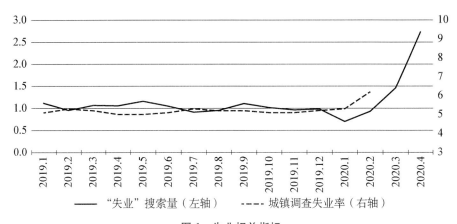

图 1 失业相关指标

数据来源:环亚经济数据、百度、第一财经

围绕病毒的演变,公共卫生部门的反应和支持性经济政策的有效性,无论在中国还是国外都存在相当大的不确定性。这使得预测中国劳动力市场将面临多大压力以及将有多少人失业变得极其困难。

我看到的一个较为细致的估算来自 Plenum China①，这是一家位于华盛顿特区的研究机构，在北京、中国香港和上海设有办事处。该公司的分析师根据预期的收入下降对每个行业的失业人数进行了细致地估算。

Plenum 预计 2020 年服务业就业人数将减少 1,500 万，其中，住宿和餐饮行业的裁员数仅占整个行业裁员总数的一半多一点。

由于雇主们在不断改进并将新冠肺炎疫情作为减少非熟练工人的一个机会，Plenum 预计制造业将裁减 900 万个工作岗位。

由于基础设施和房地产投资的减少，建筑业现在正遭受着损失。不过，随着政策的放松，该行业应该会逐渐好转。Plenum 预测，建筑业从业人员的数量不会有太大变化。

一些行业 2020 年可能会创造新的就业机会。Plenum 预计，信息技术行业将增加 220 万个工作岗位，而公共卫生和行政部门可能会再招聘 150 万名员工。

Plenum 预计城镇就业人数将净减少近 2,100 万，即大约 4%。

Plenum 的估算与亚洲开发银行（ABD）的预测大致相同。亚行最近预测了中国和许多其他经济体的失业情况②。它认为中国就业人数的下降幅度在 4.74% 到 5.25% 之间，具体幅度取决于控制住病毒传播所需的时间。鉴于 Plenum 估计的城镇就业人数为 5.3 亿，这个下降幅度意味着会有 2,500 万—2,800 万的城镇人口失业。

虽然数以百万计的工作岗位流失对经济发展来说是一个明显的阻碍，也是人们痛苦的根源所在，但与很多其他国家相比，中国在消化如此大幅增加的失业率方面拥有两个优势。

首先是有利的人口统计数据。中国的劳动年龄人口在 2013 年达到顶峰，此后一直下降，这在很大程度上是由于计划生育政策的实施。图 2 显示，2018 和 2019 年，劳动年龄人口均下降近 500 万人。

虽然劳动年龄人口的减少对于商品生产和服务业来说是一个长期的挑战，但短期来看，这种现象为吸收部分下岗人员创造了空间。

中国拥有的第二个优势是农村劳动力缓冲城市经济波动的方式。图 3 显示了城市和农村地区以及整个中国经济中就业岗位数的年度变化。平均来说，在过去的 5 年中，城市经济创造了约 1,000 万个新的就业岗位。由于劳动力数量

① Plenum China 官网（https://plenum.ai/）。
② 新冠病毒经济影响评估模板（http://data.adb.org/dataset/covid-19-economic-impact-assessment-template）。

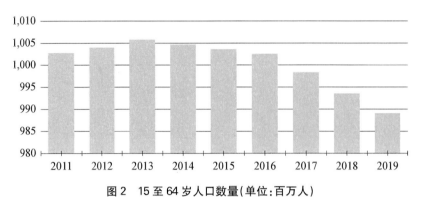

图2 15至64岁人口数量(单位:百万人)

数据来源:中国国家统计局、第一财经

基本上停滞不前,唯一能够使这些职位不至于空置的办法就是让来自农村的工作者迁移到城市。考虑到城市工作者的平均生产率比农村工作者高出许多,更高的工资给予他们移居的动力。

当城市经济发展放缓时,正如2008年至2009年那样,城市工作场所(机遇)的增量减少,对农村劳动力的需求也因此下降,从农村移居城市的人也会减少。2020年,城市的工作岗位将消失,原计划前往城市的1,000万农民工将留在家中。也许同样数量的工作者会再次离开城市回到他们在农村的家,重新被他们的家庭接纳,从而使他们获得社会保障。

当然,很多在城市中就业的人也会失去他们的工作。他们无法搬到农村地区并依靠土地过活。然而,中国有利的人口统计数据和由流动人口提供的灵活性将使他们即使在困难的情况下,也能更容易地找到新的工作。

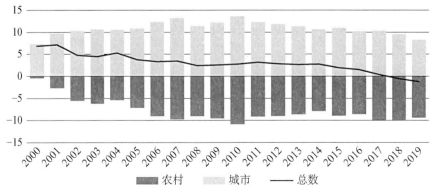

图3 就业岗位数年度变化情况(单位:百万)

数据来源:环亚经济数据、第一财经

Is China Decapitalizing Its Banks?

June 24, 2020

Last week, the State Council's executive meeting announced that it was encouraging banks to transfer up to CNY 1.5 trillion of their profits to the real economy. In particular, banks should lower interest rates, reduce fees and allow small- and medium-sized enterprises to defer their payments.

The China Banking and Insurance Regulatory Commission reported that the banks were already actively helping out in the first quarter. They rolled over CNY 577 billion in loans, mostly to small- and medium-sized enterprises. In addition, they allowed the deferral of principal and interest payments on CNY 880 billion worth of loans. This CNY 1.457 trillion represents 1.1 percent of the stock of outstanding commercial bank loans. Reported non-performing loans totalled CNY 2.6 trillion in the quarter, following the disposal of CNY 450 billion in bad credits. The commercial banks have loan-loss provisions of CNY 4.8 trillion, more than enough to cover both the stock of bad loans and the credits treated leniently in Q1.

In terms of economic stimulus, CNY 1.5 trillion ($214 billion) is large, representing 1.4 percent of GDP. Headline fiscal support, measured as the change of the National Deficit, is only about 1 percent of GDP and we estimate broader fiscal support at 3.7 percent of GDP. Thus, banks are being asked to make a significant contribution to the recovery.

There are two reasons for this. First, by encouraging forbearance, the government seeks to avoid a cascade of negative events precipitated by the calling of a loan. Second, the Chinese banking system generates a tremendous amount of profits.

The Chinese banking system is not only the biggest in the world, it is also among the world's most profitable. Figure 1 presents profitability data taken from the IMF's Financial Soundness Indicators. Compared to other countries with large banking systems, China ranks first in both return on assets and return on equity.

Chinese banks are profitable, in part, because they make very large loans. This significantly reduces their per unit overhead costs. According to the IMF data, Chinese banks' non-interest expenses were only 29 percent of gross income. Among the competitors shown in Figure 1, this ratio ranged between 60 percent for the US to 91 percent for South Korea. Moreover, according to the People's Bank of China, a considerable part of Chinese banks' loans is to large state-owned enterprises and local government financing vehicles. These exposures have hidden guarantees, which mitigate risk, lower management costs and inflate profits.

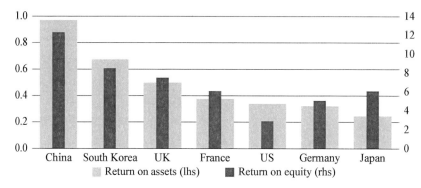

Figure 1　Commercial Bank Profitability Ratios (%)

Source: IMF, Yicai

In 2019, commercial bank profits were close to CNY 2 trillion. Thus, the State Council's plan to transfer CNY 1.5 trillion to the real economy represents a loss of three-quarters of last year's profits. Figure 2 shows that while commercial bank profits essentially doubled between 2011 and 2019, they have fallen, as a share of GDP, since 2014.

Notwithstanding the deep economic dislocation, commercial bank profits were CNY 600 billion, in the first quarter of 2020, up 5 percent year-over-year. Nominal GDP fell by 5 percent. As a result, commercial bank profits were close to 3 percent of GDP in Q1.

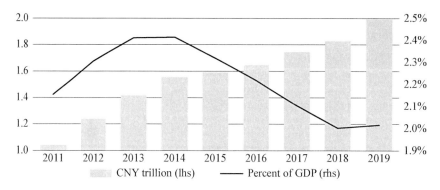

Figure 2　Commercial Bank Profits

Source: Wind, Yicai

It is understandable that, in these times of unprecedented uncertainty, the government wants to tap bank profits to support the economy. But, as economists are fond of saying, "there is no free lunch". In recent years, banks have used 60 percent of their profits to replenish their capital. So, the profit transfer policy will result in a slower buildup of the banks' capital buffers and will reduce their resilience to shocks.

Banks' resilience is typically measured by their capital to risk-weighted assets ratio. Figure 3 presents the IMF data for the Chinese banks and their major international competitors. It shows that, at 14. 5 percent, Chinese banks' capital to risk-weighted assets ratio is the lowest in the sample. Nevertheless, the Chinese aggregate ratio is well above regulatory minimums and not far from the US's 14. 7 percent.

The capitalization of Chinese banks appears more favourable when considered in terms of the capital to assets ratio: it is second highest after the US. In this metric, the assets are not risk-weighted but simply included at book value.

China's risk-weighted assets are relatively high compared to its book value assets. This is because its share of loans to non-financial corporations, which attract the highest risk weight, is double those of the other countries in the sample. Ironically, the loans to the large state-owned enterprises and local government financing vehicles, referred to above by the People's Bank, are included with high weights, even though their actual risk might be low.

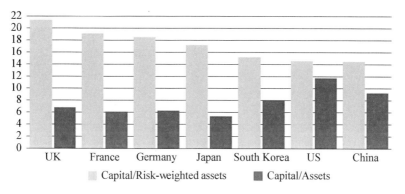

Figure 3 Commercial Bank Capital Ratios (%)

Source: IMF, Yicai

The analysis above suggests that, while Chinese banks are not poorly capitalized, they will need to find other sources of funding to replace the profits that will be transferred to the real economy.

Recently, the instrument of choice has been the perpetual bond. Perpetual bonds have lower seniority than regular bonds and pay a somewhat higher interest rate. They are cost-effective for the banks, compared to preferred shares, because the interest payment is deductible from their income. Chinese banks only began to issue perpetual bonds last year, using them to raise CNY 570 billion in capital. The media reports that issuance this year to date is five times as high, indicating that Chinese banks are diligently looking for ways to make up for transferred profits.

One of the features of the 2010 Basel III regulatory framework was a countercyclical capital buffer. This buffer is designed to dampen excess credit growth during good times and prevent the supply of credit being constrained by regulatory capital requirements during downturns. While China has not yet formally implemented such a buffer, last week's announcement by the State Council essentially puts the spirit of the Basel framework into practice.

中国欲削减银行资本？

2020 年 6 月 24 日

2020 年 6 月 17 日,国务院常务会议提出,鼓励银行向实体经济让利 1.5 万亿元。特别是银行要降低利率,减少收费并实施中小微企业贷款延期还本付息。①

根据中国银行保险监督管理委员会的报告,2020 年第一季度,银行积极采取措施,办理续贷超过 5,770 亿元,其中大部分资金流向了中小企业。此外,银行还对约 8,800 亿元的中小微企业贷款本息实施了延期。两项合计 1.457 万亿元,占商业银行未偿还贷款的 1.1%。数据显示,2020 年第一季度商业银行处置不良贷款 4,500 亿元,季末不良贷款余额为 2.6 万亿元,贷款损失准备余额为 4.8 万亿元,足以覆盖一季度的不良贷款和宽松处理的贷款。

作为经济刺激手段,1.5 万亿元(2,140 亿美元)的让利无疑是一笔不小的金额,占 GDP 的 1.4%。财政支持作为衡量财政赤字变化的指标,仅占 GDP 的 1% 左右,更广泛的财政支持估计②占 GDP 的 3.7%。因此,政府这次要求银行业为经济复苏做出重大贡献。

政府此举有两个原因,一是希望通过鼓励银行实施贷款延期避免催还贷款产生一系列负面事件,二是中国银行业拥有高额的利润。

中国的银行体系不仅是世界上最大的,其盈利能力也位居世界前列。图 1 为国际货币基金组织金融稳健指标下的盈利能力数据。与其他拥有大型银行体系的国家相比,中国的总资产收益率和净资产收益率都是最高的。

中国的银行盈利的部分原因在于发放了大量贷款,大大降低了银行的单位

---

① 快览:6 月 18 日国务院常务会议(http://english. www. gov. cn/policies/infographics/202006/18/content_WS5eeb082cc6d0a6946639c50a. html)。

② 2020 年预算:财政支持比看起来的更多(https://www. yicaiglobal. com/opinion/mark. kruger/budget-2020-more-fiscal-support-than-meets-the-eye)。

经营成本。国际货币基金组织的数据显示,中国银行业的非利息支出仅占总收入的29%,在图1所列的竞争对手中,这一占比从美国的60%高至韩国的91%。此外,根据中国人民银行的数据,中国银行业相当一部分贷款提供给了大型国企和地方政府融资平台①。这些风险敞口有隐性担保,可以降低风险,降低管理成本,提高利润。

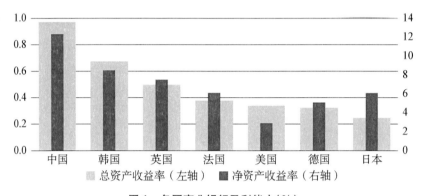

图1 各国商业银行盈利能力(%)

数据来源:国际货币基金组织、第一财经

2019 年商业银行利润接近 2 万亿元。因此,按照国务院的计划向实体经济让利 1.5 万亿元,意味着银行要拿出 2019 年利润的四分之三。图 2 显示,虽然2011—2019 年商业银行的利润基本翻了一番,但自 2014 年以来,其 GDP 占比有所下降。

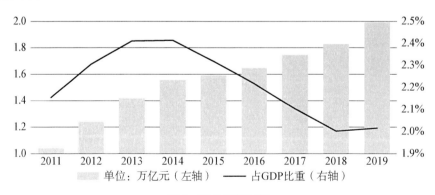

图2 商业银行利润

数据来源:万得资讯、第一财经

---

① 2019 年第四季度中国货币政策执行报告(http://www.pbc.gov.cn/zhengcehuobisi/125207/125227/125957/3830536/3974306/index.html)。

虽然经济有所起伏,但商业银行 2020 年第一季度仍实现利润 6,000 亿元,同比增长 5%,而同期名义 GDP 下降 5%,因此,第一季度商业银行利润占 GDP 的比重接近 3%。

这个时代充满了前所未有的不确定性,所以政府想用银行利润来支持经济是可以理解的。但是,正如经济学家开玩笑说的那样,"世上没有免费的午餐"。近年来,银行将 60% 的利润用于补充资本。因此,利润转移政策将减缓银行资本缓冲的积累,降低银行对抗冲击的韧性。

这种韧性一般通过银行的资本与风险加权资产比率来衡量。图 3 为国际货币基金组织提供的中国银行业及其主要国际竞争对手的数据。数据显示,中国银行业的资本与风险加权资产比率为 14.5%,是示例中最低的,但其整体比率远高于监管下限,与美国的 14.7% 相差不大。

中国银行业的资本资产比率排名第二,仅次于美国,由此来看,中国银行业的资本状况似乎更好一些。该指标中,资产未按风险权重进行计量,而是简单地按账面价值计入。

中国银行业的风险加权资产相对账面价值资产较高,原因是它向风险权重最高的非金融企业提供的贷款份额是示例中其他国家的两倍。具有讽刺意味的是,其中也包括人民银行统计的向大型国企和地方政府融资平台提供的高权重贷款,尽管这些贷款的实际风险可能很低。

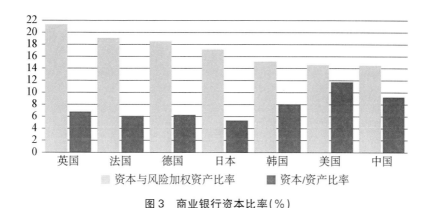

图 3　商业银行资本比率(%)

数据来源:国际货币基金组织、第一财经

上述分析表明,虽然中国银行业的资本状况并不差,但仍有必要寻找其他资金来代替利润转移到实体经济中。

永续债是近期选用的工具,其求偿权优先级比普通债券低,利率略高。对银行来说,永续债比优先股更具成本效益,因为利息支付可以从银行的收入中扣除。中国的银行 2019 年才开始发行永续债,筹集资金高达 5,700 亿元。据媒体报道,2020 年至今的发行规模是这个数字的 5 倍,表明中资银行正在努力寻找弥补让利的方法。

2010 年颁布的《巴塞尔协议 Ⅲ》监管框架的特点之一是逆周期资本缓冲。这一缓冲旨在抑制金融机构在经济扩张时期信贷过度增长,并防止信贷供给在经济衰退时期受到监管资本要求的限制。虽然中国还没有正式实施这样的缓冲机制,但国务院的声明实际上是在践行巴塞尔框架。

Are the Chinese Banks Really Supporting the Recovery?

August 31, 2020

Data from the China Banking and Insurance Regulatory Commission (CBIRC) show that the profits of Chinese banks fell 9 percent, to just over CNY 1 trillion, in the first half of the year (Figure 1). Their performance to-date seems to be extremely strong, given the State Council's encouragement that they transfer up to CNY 1.5 trillion in profits to the real economy and that full-year profits in 2019 were CNY 2 trillion.

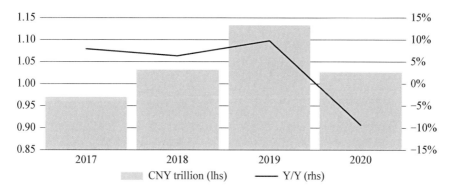

Figure 1   Chinese Bank Profits — First Half of the Year

Source: Wind, Yicai

Guo Shuqing, the CBIRC's Chairman, recently gave an interview in which he explained all the ways in which China's financial system is supporting the economy's recovery. He began by noting that the rate of credit growth is increasing, giving firms enhanced access to funds. Figure 2 depicts the growth of Total Social Financing (TSF), a broad credit indicator. It shows that TSF, which had been growing at close to 11 percent, began to accelerate in March and by July was nearing 13 percent.

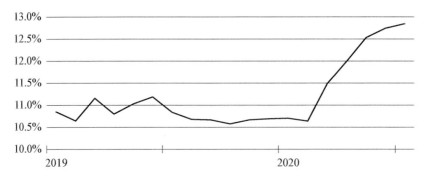

Figure 2　Growth of Total Social Financing（Y／Y）

Source: Wind, Yicai

Bank loans account for close to 60 percent of TSF and they have grown somewhat more rapidly since March. However, much of the acceleration in credit to firms has come from the issuance of corporate bonds（Figure 3）.

According to Chairman Guo, encouraging firms to raise funds directly — for example via the bond market instead of going through the banking system — is one aspect of "financial supply-side structural reform". Direct finance has two benefits. First, is typically cheaper for firms to borrow from markets than from banks. Second, it can also help spread the risks associated with corporate finance more widely, as the investor base for bonds grows.

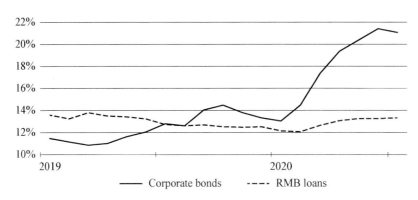

Figure 3　Financing Indicators（Y／Y）

Source: Wind, Yicai

Chairman Guo stated that lowering firms' cost of finance is a key way in which bank profits are transferred to non-financial firms. He posits the following example. The outstanding stock of local currency loans is about CNY 165 trillion. If the average lending rate was to fall by a percentage point, that would represent a saving to firms of CNY 1. 65 trillion.

Interest rates are, indeed, falling. Figure 4 shows that the average interest rate on general loans fell by 70 basis points between June 2019 and June 2020. This should provide firms with a sizable reduction in borrowing costs.

Note, however, that banks' net interest margins only fell by 10 basis points over the same period. This suggests that most of the firms' savings came from reduced payments on deposits. Thus, the lower lending rates appear to be more of a shift of funds from savers to borrowers than a transfer of bank profits to firms.

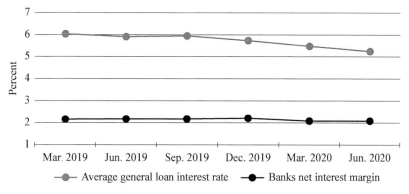

Figure 4   Loan Rates and Interest Margin

Source: Wind, Yicai

Part of the government's recovery program involves improving access to credit for smaller firms. However, the Chinese financial system has long had a proclivity to lend to large state-owned enterprises, because such exposures have hidden guarantees, which mitigate risk, lower management costs and boost profits. Moreover, banks often have a hard time assessing the credit quality of smaller firms.

Chairman Guo notes that banks have begun to leverage big data, cloud computing and artificial intelligence to better assess the risks involved with lending to smaller firms. These new technologies have allowed banks to improve smaller firms' access to financial services. Indeed, small- and medium-sized firms, obtained 23 and 19 percent, respectively, of all of the new non-mortgage bank loans issued so far this year. Nevertheless, as Figure 5 shows, the banks will have to continue working hard to bring small- and medium-sized enterprises' (SMEs) share of outstanding non-mortgage loans back to its December 2017 peak.

This year, as the economic situation deteriorated, the banks' non-performing loans (NPLs) rose by CNY 0. 32 trillion to CNY 2. 74 trillion (Figure 6). The banks took provisions of CNY 0. 50 trillion against these new bad loans, but, even so, the

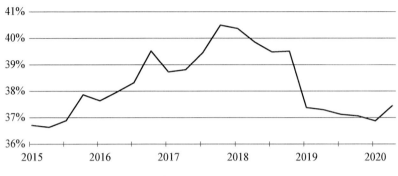

Figure 5　SME Share of Non-Mortgage Lending

Source: Wind, Yicai

NPL coverage ratio fell slightly.

Chairman Guo warned that the true magnitude of the NPLs has not yet emerged, as the banks are exercising forbearance and a number of firms are postponing interest and principal payments. He notes that a number of measures are being undertaken to prepare for the anticipated deterioration in credit quality: reinforcing supervision, raising capital, increasing provisions and selling bad loans. At last week's press conference, CBIRC officials suggested that sales of NPLs could reach CNY 3.4 trillion this year, up from CNY 2.3 trillion in 2019. Chairman Guo said that the CBIRC is looking at supporting the increased disposal of bad loans by creating an NPL trading platform.

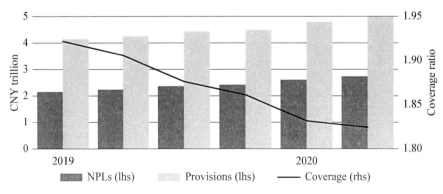

Figure 6　NPLs and Provisions

Source: Wind, Yicai

The modest decline in the banks' profits, combined with faster asset growth, resulted in a fall in return on equity to 10.4 percent in the second quarter. This is a pretty low rate of profitability for Chinese banks. However, as we have noted earlier, the Chinese banking system is not only the biggest in the world, it is also among the most profitable. Internationally, other banks would dearly like to attain such a high return on equity, especially during such trying economic circumstances. Indeed, Chinese banks' return on equity in the second quarter was well above what US and European banks achieved, on average, over the last decade. Thus, it seems that the Chinese banks have struck a good balance between supporting the recovery and reinforcing their own financial stability.

银行真在支持中国经济复苏吗？

2020 年 8 月 31 日

中国银行保险监督管理委员会（以下简称"银保监会"）的数据显示,2020 年上半年银行业实现利润 1 万亿元(图 1),同比下降 9%。考虑到国务院鼓励[①]银行向实体经济让利 1.5 万亿元,以及 2019 年银行业的利润高达 2 万亿元,中资银行迄今为止的表现似乎极为强劲。

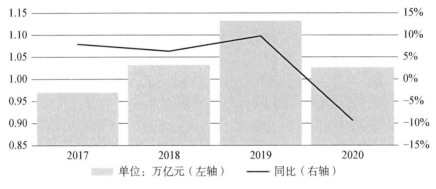

图 1　中资银行利润(2020 年上半年)

数据来源：万得资讯、第一财经

近日,银保监会主席郭树清在接受采访[②]时阐述了中国金融体系是如何支持经济复苏的。他首先指出,信贷增速攀升,为企业提供了更多资金。图 2 为广泛信贷指标社会融资规模的增长曲线。可以看到,社会融资规模增速一直为 11% 左右,但 2020 年 3 月开始加速,到 7 月份增速接近 13%。

---

① 快览:6 月 17 日国务院常务会议（http://english. www. gov. cn/policies/infographics/202006/18/content_WS5eeb082cc6d0a6946639c50a. html）。

② 金融助力经济行稳致远（权威访谈）——访中国人民银行党委书记、中国银保监会主席郭树清（http://www. cbirc. gov. cn/cn/view/pages/ItemDetail. html？ docId = 922894&itemId = 915）。

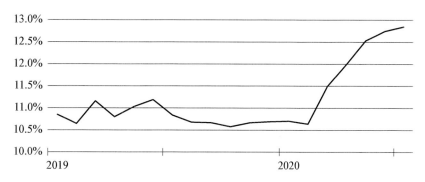

图 2　社会融资规模同比增速

数据来源：万得资讯、第一财经

银行贷款占社会融资规模近 60%，3 月份以来其增速有所加快，但企业信贷的加速大部分来自发行公司债券（图 3）。

郭树清表示，鼓励企业直接筹集资金是"金融供给侧结构性改革"的一个方面。例如，企业可以通过债券市场而不是通过银行系统来筹集资金。直接融资有两个好处，一是企业从市场借款通常比从银行借款更便宜，二是随着债券投资者基数的增加，有助于更广泛地分散与企业融资相关的风险。

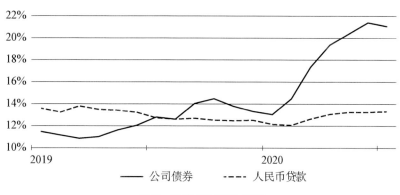

—— 公司债券　　---- 人民币贷款

图 3　融资指标同比增速

数据来源：万得资讯、第一财经

郭树清表示，降低企业融资成本是银行将利润向非金融企业转移的一个重要途径。他举了一个例子。目前人民币贷款余额是 165 万亿元，贷款利率平均下降 1 个百分点就意味着企业可以节省 1.65 万亿元。

而利率也确实在下降。图 4 显示，2019 年 6 月至 2020 年 6 月，一般贷款平均利率下降了 70 个基点，大幅降低了企业的借贷成本。

但需要注意的是,同期银行业的净利息收益率仅下降了 10 个基点。这说明企业节省的钱大部分是来自存款支付的减少。因此,降低贷款利率似乎更多的是让资金从储蓄者转移到借款者,而不是银行让利给企业。

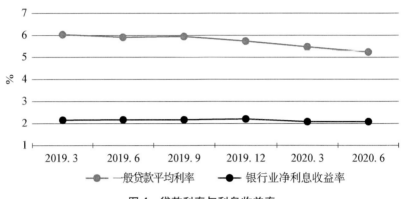

图 4 贷款利率与利息收益率

数据来源:万得资讯、第一财经

中国政府的经济复苏计划提到要改善小微企业获得信贷资金的途径。然而,中国金融体系长期以来都有向大型国有企业放贷的倾向,因为此类敞口具有隐性担保,可以降低风险,降低管理成本并提高利润。此外,银行通常很难评估小公司的信用水平。

郭树清指出,银行已经开始利用大数据、云计算和人工智能来更好地评估向小微企业贷款的风险。这些新技术使银行能够着力改善小微企业金融服务。事实上,在 2020 年已发放的所有新无抵押银行贷款中,小型和中型企业贷款分别占比 23% 和 19%。然而,如图 5 所示,银行必须继续努力,争取将未偿还的无抵押银行贷款中小企业占比恢复到 2017 年 12 月的峰值。

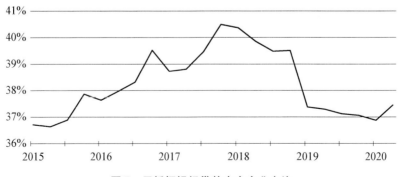

图 5 无抵押银行贷款中小企业占比

数据来源:万得资讯、第一财经

随着经济形势恶化,2020 年银行的不良贷款高达 2.74 万亿元,增加了3,200 亿元(图 6)。银行为这些新增不良贷款计提了万亿元拨备,但即便如此,不良贷款覆盖率仍小幅下降。

郭树清警告说,不良贷款的真实规模尚未显现,因为银行正在实行贷款延期,许多公司在推迟支付利息和本金。他指出,银行正在采取多项措施为预期的信贷质量恶化做准备:加强监管、筹集资金、增加拨备和出售不良贷款。在上周的新闻发布会上,银保监会新闻发言人表示[①],2020 年不良贷款的销售规模可能达到 3.4 万亿元,高于 2019 年的 2.3 万亿元。郭树清表示,银保监会正在考虑通过创建不良贷款交易平台来支持越来越多的不良贷款处置。

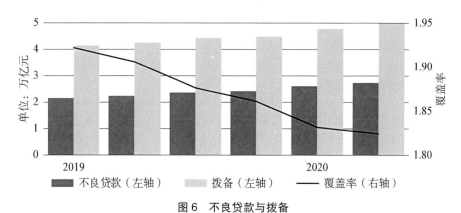

图 6　不良贷款与拨备

数据来源:万得资讯、第一财经

银行利润小幅下降,加上资产增长加快,导致第二季度净资产收益率下降至10.4%。对于中资银行来说,这是一个相当低的盈利水平。然而,正如我们之前指出[②]的,中国的银行体系不仅是世界上最大的,也是最赚钱的。在国际上,其他银行非常希望获得如此高的净资产收益率,尤其是在如此艰难的经济环境下。事实上,中资银行第二季度的净资产收益率远高于欧美银行过去 10 年的平均水平[③]。因此,中资银行似乎在支持复苏和加强自身金融稳定之间取得了良好的平衡。

---

① 中国银保监会新闻发言人答记者问(http://www.cbirc.gov.cn/cn/view/pages/ItemDetail.html?docId=924441&itemId=915&generaltype=0)。

② 中国正在削减银行资本(https://www.yicaiglobal.com/opinion/mark.kruger/is-china-decapitalizing-its-banks)?

③ 面临盈利危机,欧洲银行争相重组(https://www.wsj.com/articles/facing-a-profitability-crisis-europes-banks-rush-to-restructure-11598184000)。

COVID – 19 Is Accelerating China-US Convergence

July 2, 2020

Last week, the IMF released an update of its World Economic Outlook. The Fund was downbeat. Already in April, it had forecast an "unprecedented decline" in global economic activity due to COVID – 19. However, the pandemic has proven to be worse than expected, resulting in more widespread virus-prevention measures and a more severe downturn.

After taking the most recent economic data into consideration, IMF further reduced its growth forecasts for 2020 and 2021. It now expects the global economy to decline by 4. 9 percent this year and expand by 5. 4 percent next year. The level of the world's GDP in 2021 will essentially be the same as it was in 2019, implying two years of lost growth.

The IMF projects that China's economy will grow by 1. 0 percent in 2020 before rebounding by 8. 2 percent in 2021. Average growth of just over 4. 5 percent, over two years, is rather slow compared to the 6 – 7 percent China has recently recorded. Nevertheless, China's forecast performance is actually quite strong, when compared to those of other countries.

Figure 1 presents GDP indices, with 2019 = 100, based on the IMF's latest projections. The IMF expects the level of China's real GDP to be more than 9 percent higher in 2021 than it was in 2019. In comparison, GDP for Emerging Market and Developing Countries, excluding China, in 2021 is slightly below its 2019 level. The forecast outturn for Advanced Countries is even worse, with GDP in 2021 about 4 percent below 2019's level.

The IMF does not explain why it expects China to out-perform the rest of the world over the next two years, but the answer does not appear to lie in China's higher rate of trend growth. The Fund forecasts China's growth to slow by 5 percentage points between 2019 and 2020. But it forecasts even sharper slowdowns for the Euro Area (12 percentage points), the US (10 percentage points) and Japan (7 percentage points).

Some of the credit has to go to China's pandemic management efforts. After

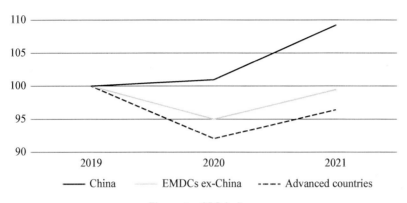

Figure 1   GDP Indices

Source: IMF, Yicai

all, China accounts for close to one-fifth of the world's population but only 1 percent of the COVID – 19 cases and only 1 percent of the virus-related deaths.

Should the IMF's forecast come to pass, it will serve to accelerate a two-decade old trend. The thick solid line in Figure 2 plots the size of China's economy, relative to the US's, at market exchange rates. For 2020 and 2021, I take the IMF's forecasts for real GDP growth, assume 2 percent inflation in each country and an exchange rate of 7 CNY per US dollar. Under these assumptions, the Chinese economy will be three-quarters the size of the US's in 2021, up from only two-thirds as large in 2019.

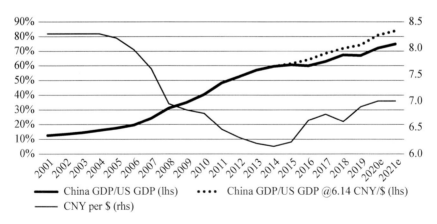

Figure 2   China-US Relative GDP and Exchange Rate

Source: Wind, Yicai

This economic convergence has proceeded a bit more slowly since 2014, as the renminbi (the thin line) has depreciated against the US dollar by close to 15 percent. The dotted line shows my estimate of the relative size of the Chinese economy, if the exchange rate had remained at its 2014 level (I also make an adjustment for the depressive effect that this appreciation would have had on China's exports and GDP). This counter-factual suggests that China's economy would rise to close to 85 percent the size of the US's in 2021.

When will China's economy surpass the US's?

The dramatic revision of the IMF's World Economic Outlook, in just six months time, shows how difficult it is to predict the future. Nevertheless, estimating when China will become the world's biggest economy only depends on five parameters: real growth and inflation in both China and the US and the exchange rate. For the purposes of this exercise, I assume 2 percent for real GDP growth in the US and for inflation in both countries.

Table 1 presents the year in which China's GDP exceeds the US's, based on naïve extrapolations from 2021, using various GDP growth and exchange rate combinations. If China grows at 6 percent from 2022 on and the exchange rate appreciates to 6 CNY per US dollar, it could occur as soon as 2025. Should China's growth slow to 4 percent per year from 2022 and the exchange rate remain at 7 CNY per US dollar, it will occur 12 years later, in 2037.

Table 1　Year in Which China's GDP Exceeds the US's

		CNY per $	
		6	7
China's Rate of GDP Growth	4%	2029	2037
	5%	2026	2032
	6%	2025	2029

Source: Yicai

China is already the world's largest economy in purchasing power parity (PPP) terms. What this means is that there are more goods and services produced in China than in any other country. Whereas PPP GDP measures the *volume* of activity, GDP at current exchange rates measures its *value* in the marketplace. Market-value measures of GDP are important because they indicate a country's economic gravity. The greater a country's economic gravity, the more it will attract international trade and investment and the more pull it will have over global markets.

We cannot be certain when China will become the world's largest economy at market exchange rates. However, over the next couple of years, it appears that China's economic gravity is set to increase.

新冠肺炎疫情加速缩小中美经济规模的差距

2020 年 7 月 2 日

国际货币基金组织于 2020 年 6 月 24 日发布了《世界经济展望报告》的更新版[①]，报告对全球经济前景颇为悲观。早在 4 月，国际货币基金组织就预测全球经济活动在新冠肺炎疫情的冲击下将出现"前所未有的下滑"。但事实证明，疫情带来的负面影响比预期更严重，引发了更广泛的疫情防控措施和更严重的经济衰退。

根据最新经济数据，国际货币基金组织进一步下调了全球经济增长预测，预计 2020 年全球经济收缩 4.9%，2021 年增长 5.4%。这将使 2021 年的全球 GDP 与 2019 年基本持平，意味着两年的增长滞缓。

国际货币基金组织预计，2020 年中国经济将增长 1.0%，并在 2021 年持续增长，增幅达 8.2%。两年平均增速预测略高于 4.5%，与中国近期 6% 到 7% 的经济增速相比较慢，但与其他国家相比，中国经济的预期表现实际上相当强劲。

图 1 为国际货币基金组织最新预测的 GDP 指数（2019 年 = 100）。国际货币基金组织预计，2021 年中国实际 GDP 水平会比 2019 年高出 9% 以上，而除中国外的新兴市场和发展中国家 GDP 会略低于 2019 年的水平。发达国家的预测数据更差，预计 2021 年 GDP 比 2019 年收缩约 4%。

至于为何预计中国未来两年的情况会好于其他国家，国际货币基金组织未作解释，但答案似乎并不在于中国更高的趋势增长率。国际货币基金组织预测，中国经济增速在 2019 年和 2020 年将放缓 5 个百分点，但欧元区、美国和日本的经济放缓幅度会更大，分别为 12 个百分点、10 个百分点和 7 个百分点。

这在一定程度上要归功于中国的疫情控制工作[②]。毕竟，中国人口占世界

[①] 《世界经济展望报告》更新：前所未有的危机，不确定的复苏（https://www.imf.org/zh/Publications/WEO/Issues/2020/06/24/WEOUpdateJune2020）。

[②] 揭秘中国疫情防控经验（https://www.yicaiglobal.com/opinion/mark.kruger/covid-19-unmasking-china-experience）。

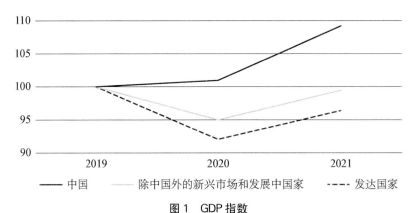

图 1　GDP 指数

数据来源：国际货币基金组织、第一财经

总人口的近五分之一，但其新冠肺炎病例只占全球的 1%，与病毒相关的死亡人数也只占全球的 1%。

　　如果国际货币基金组织的预测成真，中美两国经济规模在过去 20 年逐步接近的趋势将加速。图 2 中的粗实线为按市场汇率计算的中国相对美国的经济规模。对于 2020 年和 2021 年，这里采用了国际货币基金组织对实际 GDP 增长的预测，假设每个国家的通货膨胀率为 2%，汇率为 1 美元兑 7 元人民币。根据这些假设，到 2021 年，中国经济规模将达到美国的四分之三，而 2019 年其经济规模仅为美国的三分之二。

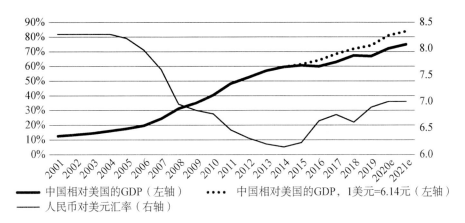

图 2　中美 GDP 之比与汇率

数据来源：万得资讯、第一财经

自 2014 年以来,随着人民币对美元汇率(图 2 中的细线)贬值近 15%,两国经济规模差距缩小的速度略有下降。虚线为笔者按 2014 年汇率对中国经济相对规模的估计(这里还根据人民币升值对中国出口和 GDP 的抑制效应做了调整)。这一反事实表明,到 2021 年,中国经济规模将接近美国的 85%。

中国经济何时能超越美国?

国际货币基金组织在短短六个月内对《世界经济展望报告》的大幅度更新表明未来很难预测。尽管如此,预测中国何时会成为世界上最大的经济体只取决于 5 个参数:中美两国的实际经济增速和通胀,以及汇率。作为演练,假设美国的实际 GDP 增长率和两国的通货膨胀率均为 2%。

基于以 2021 年为起点的朴素推断,运用各种 GDP 增速和汇率的组合,可以得出中国 GDP 超过美国的年份(表 1)。如果中国经济从 2022 年开始以 6% 的速度增长,汇率升值到 1 美元兑 6 元人民币,那么中国最快可能在 2025 年超越美国成为世界第一大经济体。而如果中国的经济增速从 2022 年开始放缓至每年 4%,汇率保持在 1 美元兑 7 元人民币,这一超越将发生在 12 年后的 2037 年。

表 1　中国 GDP 超过美国的年份

中国 GDP 增速		人民币兑美元汇率	
		6	7
	4%	2029	2037
	5%	2026	2032
	6%	2025	2029

数据来源:第一财经

根据购买力平价,中国已经是世界上最大的经济体。这意味着中国生产的商品和服务比其他任何国家都多。按购买力平价法计算的 GDP 衡量的是经济活动的数量,而按当前汇率计算的 GDP 衡量的是其在市场上的价值。GDP 的市场价值大小很重要,因为它们表明了一个国家的经济引力。一个国家的经济引力越大,它吸引的国际贸易和投资就越多,对全球市场的吸引力就越大。

我们无法确定汇率算法下中国何时会成为世界最大经济体。然而,在接下来的几年里,中国的经济引力似乎注定会增加。

Trust in Chinese Government Defies Global Trend

September 2, 2020

In recent days, we have seen disturbing images from Kenosha, Wisconsin, where armed vigilantes have taken to the streets to protect themselves and their property from rioters. These vigilantes believe that the US government is no longer capable of protecting good people from bad and that they are justified in taking the law into their own hands.

Kenosha is the most acute example of a global loss of trust in governments. The OECD found that trust in public institutions had been eroding for many years, among its membership, and that the 2008 global financial crisis and ensuing recession heightened these tensions. It points to three factors that have caused the public to lose faith in their governments: low income growth and rising inequality, persistent corruption and ineffectiveness in managing global pressures, such as climate change.

Global surveys conducted by the Pew Research Center show just how broad and deep the loss of trust in governments has been. Since 2002, it has asked respondents to agree or disagree with the statement "Generally, the state is run for the benefit of all people". In 2002, 60 percent of the respondents from 24 countries, on average, agreed with the question. By 2019, only 50 percent did, indicating increased frustration with leaders and political systems.

Figure 1 looks at this change in attitudes on a country-by-country basis. It presents the percentage of respondents who agreed with the statement in 2019 minus the percentage who agreed with it in 2002. It shows a deterioration in citizens' views of their governments in two-thirds of the countries surveyed. For the 16 countries in which faith in governments deteriorated, the median decline was 13 percentage points.

While China is not covered by the Pew survey data, there is evidence to suggest that it is among the minority of countries in which confidence in government is increasing. In July, researchers from the Ash Center for Democratic Governance and Innovation at Harvard's Kennedy School of Government published their survey of Chinese citizen satisfaction with government performance. The Ash Center has tracked the attitudes of Chinese citizens toward their government in eight separate

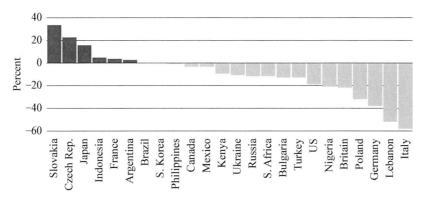

Figure 1   State is Run for the Benefit of All People (change in share agreeing 2019−2002)

Source: Pew Research Center, Yicai

surveys between 2002 and 2016. It designs the surveys, which are implemented by a domestic Chinese polling firm. The survey responses draw on more than 31,000 face-to-face interviews with individuals in both urban and rural settings.

Figure 2 shows the percentage of respondents that were satisfied with the performance of each of the four levels of their government over time. At any point in time, Chinese citizens' satisfaction with government performance increases with distance: they are happiest with the officials in Beijing and least happy with those closest to home. Nevertheless, over the thirteen years covered, there is a broad increase in satisfaction with government at all levels, and the perceptions of local officials made the biggest gains.

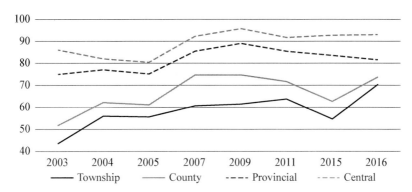

Figure 2   Percentage of Respondents Satisfied With Government Performance by Level

Source: Ash Center, Yicai

Differences in methodologies mean that the Ash Center surveys cannot be directly compared to the ones carried out by the Pew Research Center. Still, the

Ash Center's broad trend of increased confidence in China's government stands in sharp contrast to the rising dissatisfaction in the Pew Research Center's data.

Given that the Ash Center's surveys are conducted face-to-face, can we really believe their results?

The study's authors note that the variation in the survey's responses are meaningfully related to objective changes in the respondents' well-being. This suggests that the responses are truthful. For example, low income respondents reported much greater increases in satisfaction, over time, than high-income respondents. The authors attribute this to increasing access to social welfare programs. Similarly, they find that much of the variation in satisfaction comes from measurable flows of government-provided goods and services. Larger increases in satisfaction are observed in areas where a higher fraction of local spending is on education, health and welfare. The same is true for improvements in road infrastructure.

As the OECD explains, citizens will lose faith in public officials, if they are perceived as being corrupt. The Ash Center notes that through 2011, little progress was made in addressing corruption, " there was a general sense that, despite spurring economic development and raising living standards, efforts to promote good governance had stalled, or even regressed. "

The anti-corruption campaign, which began in 2013, appears to have had a meaningful effect on the perception of local government officials' integrity. Figure 3 shows that by 2016, the percentage of respondents that saw their local officials as "very clean" or "relatively clean" had risen to 65 percent from just 35 percent five years earlier.

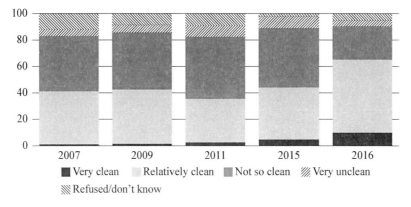

Figure 3　Perception of Local Government Officials' Integrity

Source: Ash Center, Yicai

The Ash Center's data end in 2016. To get a more recent picture of how Chinese citizens see their government, we turn to continuous sentiment data compiled by RIWI. RIWI is an innovative, Canadian trend-tracking and prediction firm. It captures the views of respondents representative of the global Web-using population. The company uses a technology that ensures that anyone online has an equal chance of random exposure to questions. The result of this approach is access to sentiment beyond typical survey respondents: more than 60 percent of RIWI China respondents report they have never answered a survey before. Respondents remain anonymous and RIWI does not collect, process, store or transfer personally identifiable data. This allows respondents to provide their views freely and securely. Respondents are not, in any way, incentivized to participate in RIWI's surveys.

As the OECD explains, citizens' trust depends, in part, on their government's effectiveness in responding to global pressures. The outbreak of COVID－19 is one such pressure. RIWI has been tracking public opinion, in both China and the US, on a continuous 24/7 basis since early 2020 with respect to confidence in health officials' ability to educate the public on treating or avoiding COVID－19.

Figure 4 presents public opinion in China and the US between June 1 and August 27. It shows that nearly three-quarters of the Chinese respondents have faith in their health officials' ability to manage COVID－19, compared to only 46 percent in the US.

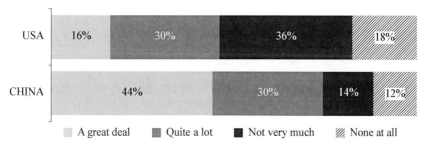

Figure 4   Confidence in Health Officials' Ability to Educate the Public on Avoiding or Treating COVID－19

Source: Riwi, Yicai

The OECD says that governments cannot function effectively without the trust of its citizens. Governments have a strong incentive to build trust, since a trusting public is more likely to be cooperative, while skeptical citizens may even resist policies that are in their own best interest. Indeed, the building of trust is not simply an indicator of successful policy, it is an ingredient that helps make success possible. China's experience suggests that policies which increase citizens' well-being are a good place to begin this virtuous circle.

全球信任度下滑之际，中国政府信任度逆势上升

2020 年 9 月 2 日

最近，美国威斯康星州基诺沙的情况令人不安，已经有武装的义务警员走上街头，保护民众的人身和财产安全。这些义务警员认为美国政府已经无法保护好人不受坏人伤害，他们要将法律掌握在自己手中。①

基诺沙事件是全球政府信任丧失的最为严重的案例。经合组织发现其成员国的公共机构信任度多年来一直在下降，2008 年全球金融危机和随之而来的经济衰退加剧了这种情况。② 经合组织指出，民众对政府失去信心有三个原因：收入增长缓慢和不平等加剧、持续腐败，以及政府在气候变化等全球压力管控方面的无能。

皮尤研究中心的全球调查显示，民众对政府的信任丧失是广泛而深入的。③ 自 2002 年以来，该中心一直在调查和询问受访者是否同意"政府总体上是为了大多数人的利益"这一说法。2002 年，在接受调查的 24 个国家中，平均有 60% 的受访者表示同意这一说法，但到 2019 年，认可该说法的只有 50%，这说明民众对领导人和政治制度的不满在持续上升。

图 1 着眼于国家层面上的民众态度变化，显示了 2019 年和 2002 年同意上述说法的受访者比例之差。可以看出，三分之二的被调查国家出现公民对政府的看法恶化。政府信任度下降的 16 个国家的降幅中位数为 13 个百分点。

虽然皮尤的调查数据不包括中国，但有证据表明，中国是少数几个民众对政

---

① 义务警员声称要维护法律和秩序，但真正意图是拯救白人（https://www.washingtonpost.com/outlook/2020/08/28/vigilantes-kenosha-white-grievance/）。

② 信任与公共政策——更好的治理如何帮助政府重建公众信任（https://www.oecd.org/corruption-integrity/reports/trust-and-public-policy-9789264268920-en.html）。

③ 全球广泛认同民主权利，但对其信心不足——大多数认为民选官员与民众脱节（https://www.pewresearch.org/global/2020/02/27/democratic-rights-popular-globally-but-commitment-to-them-not-always-strong/）。

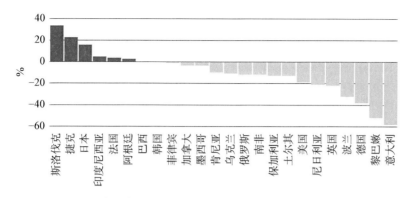

图1　同意政府是为了所有人的利益这一说法的受访者变化

数据来源：皮尤研究中心、第一财经

府信心增强的国家之一。哈佛大学肯尼迪政府学院艾什民主治理与创新中心
（以下简称"艾什中心"）的研究人员在 2020 年 7 月发布了他们关于中国民众对
政府绩效满意度的调查。[①] 艾什中心在 2002—2016 年进行了 8 次独立的调查，
追踪中国民众对政府的态度。艾什中心进行调查设计，交由一家中国国内的民
调公司实施。调查结果来自对城市和农村地区个人的 31,000 多次面对面访谈。

　　图 2 显示了对中国各级政府的绩效感到满意的受访者比例。图中的任何时
间点上，中国民众对政府绩效的满意度都是随着距离的增加而上升：他们对北京
的官员最满意，对离家最近的官员最不满意。尽管如此，在调查的 13 年中，人们
对各级政府的满意度普遍提高，对地方官员的满意度提高最大。

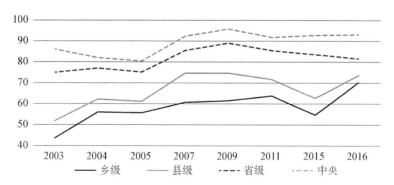

图2　对中国各级政府绩效感到满意的受访者比例

数据来源：艾什中心、第一财经

① 理解中国共产党的韧性：中国民意长期调查（https://ash. harvard. edu/files/ash/files/final_policy_
brief_7. 6. 2020. pdf）。

由于方法不同,我们不能直接比较艾什中心与皮尤研究中心的调查。但是,艾什中心呈现的中国民众对政府信心增强的广泛趋势与皮尤研究中心数据显示的持续上升的不满情绪形成了鲜明对比。

考虑到艾什中心的调查是面对面的方式,调查结果的可信度高吗?

这项研究的作者指出,对所调查问题的不同回答与受访者幸福感的客观变化之间存在显著的联系。这说明这些回答是真实的。例如,随着时间的推移,低收入受访者的满意度远高于高收入受访者。作者将此归因于越来越多的人可以享受到社会福利项目。同样,他们发现满意度的变化在很大程度上与政府不断提供大量的物品和服务有关。在地方教育、医疗和福利支出比例较高的地区,满意度的增长幅度更大。道路基础设施得到改善的地方也是如此。

正如经合组织所说,如果民众认为政府官员存在腐败,就会对他们失去信心。艾什中心指出,截至 2011 年,中国在解决腐败问题方面进展甚微,"人们普遍认为,虽然政府刺激了经济发展,提高了人民生活水平,但在推进善政和廉政方面却停滞不前,甚至有所倒退"。

2013 年开始的反腐倡廉似乎极大影响了中国民众对地方政府官员廉洁的看法。图 3 显示,到 2016 年,认为地方官员"十分廉洁"或"较为廉洁"的受访者比例从 5 年前的 35% 上升至 65%。

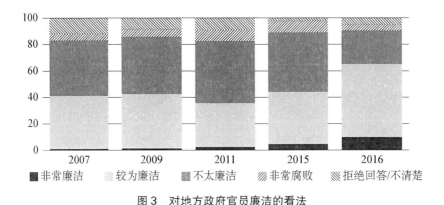

图 3　对地方政府官员廉洁的看法

数据来源:艾什中心、第一财经

艾什中心的数据只到 2016 年。为了了解近期中国民众对政府的态度,我们来看一下 RIWI 公司统计的持续情绪数据。RIWI 是一家致力于趋势跟踪和预测的加拿大创新公司,主要收集以全球互联网用户为代表的受访者的观点。该公司采用技术手段确保调查问题随机、均等地呈现给所有线上受访者。采用这种方法的结果是获得了典型调查受访者群体之外的情绪数据：超过 60％ 的 RIWI 中国受访者表示，他们以前从未接受过调查。受访者匿名参与，RIWI 不收集、处理、存储或传输个人身份数据。这使得受访者可以自由、安全地表达自己的观点。受访者没有以任何方式被激励参与 RIWI 的调查。

正如经合组织所说，民众对政府的信任在一定程度上取决于政府能否有效应对全球压力。新冠肺炎的爆发就是一个例子。自 2020 年初以来，RIWI 一直在全天候跟踪中美两国民意，关注卫生官员是否有能力向公众普及如何治疗或预防新冠肺炎。

图 4 显示了 2020 年 6 月 1 日至 8 月 27 日中美两国的民意。调查显示，近四分之三的中国受访者认为他们的卫生官员有能力控制新冠肺炎，而在美国这一比例仅为 46％。

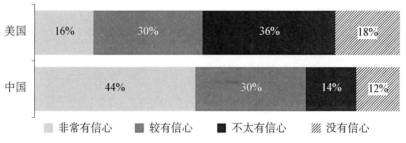

图 4　对卫生官员普及如何预防或治疗新冠肺炎能力的信心

数据来源：RIWI、第一财经

经合组织认为，失去民众的信任，政府将无法有效运作。政府希望建立信任，因为信任政府的民众会更加配合政府的工作，而对政府持怀疑态度的公民甚至可能会抵制符合他们最大利益的政策。事实上，建立信任不仅是成功政策的指标，也是促进成功的因素。中国的经验表明，为公民谋取更多福利的政策可以很好地开启这种良性循环。